SPREADSHEETS MADE SIMPLE FOR ADMINISTRATORS, TEACHERS, AND SCHOOL BOARD MEMBERS

Harvey Singer

ScarecrowEducation
Lanham, Maryland • Toronto • Oxford
2004

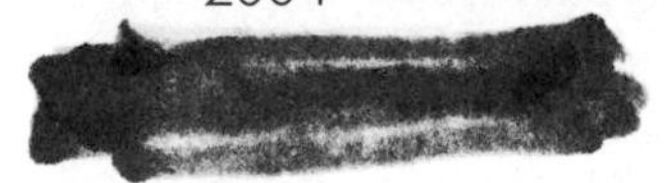

Published in the United States of America
by Scarecrow Press, Inc.
An imprint of The Rowman & Littlefield Publishing Group, Inc.
4501 Forbes Boulevard, Suite 200, Lanham, Maryland 20706
www.scarecroweducation.com

PO Box 317
Oxford
OX2 9RU, UK

British Library Cataloguing in Publication Information Available

Library of Congress Cataloging-in-Publication Data

Singer, Harvey, 1940–
Spreadsheets made simple for administrators, teachers, and school board members / Harvey Singer.
p. cm.
ISBN 1-57886-121-7 (pbk. : alk. paper)
1. Education—Data processing. 2. School management and organization—Data processing. 3. Electronic spreadsheets. I. Title.
LB1028.43.S59 2004
370'.285—dc22

2004005896

∞™ The paper used in this publication meets the minimum requirements of American National Standard for Information Sciences—Permanence of Paper for Printed Library Materials, ANSI/NISO Z39.48-1992.
Manufactured in the United States of America.

CONTENTS

ACKNOWLEDGMENTS

This book is an outgrowth of the many traditional and online courses that I have taught at Suffolk Community College, Dowling College, and Broward Community College. As such, I owe a very real debt of gratitude to the students in my classes who have spurred me on to seek better, and still better, ways of presenting this material.

I would also like to thank my family and close friends, who have always been supportive of my efforts and who in a very real sense have made this book possible. I would also like to express my appreciation to the many great teachers I have been fortunate to have learned from and known, and from whom I have learned both the art and craft of teaching.

Finally, I would like to specifically thank Dr. Stephen Schneider who hired me to teach my first computer science class at Suffolk Community College many years ago, whose skill as an administrator I have long admired, and whose friendship I continue to value.

DISCLAIMER

Microsoft® and Windows® are registered trademarks of Microsoft Corporation in the United States and/or other countries. *Spreadsheets Made Simple for Administrators, Teachers, and School Board Members* is an independent publication and is not affiliated with, nor has it been authorized, sponsored, or otherwise approved by Microsoft® Corporation.

INTRODUCTION

Microsoft Excel is an incredibly useful program. Businesses have used Excel for years to keep track of all kinds of business activities. And now, school administrators, teachers, and school board members are finding that Excel can be just as useful in the school environment. Excel can be an extremely useful tool for anyone who has school-related responsibilities.

Certainly most school districts have already computerized, and many data and analysis capabilities are already available to administrators and teachers. While school district computerization has been, and continues to be, extremely useful to the school administrator, teacher, and school board member, it does present a few significant shortcomings.

1. The organization of the data collected and the data themselves have been determined by someone else. Consequently, it does not necessarily meet the specific needs of an individual administrator or teacher.
2. Much school and school district information, particularly when it is related to individual school issues (say a school fund-raising drive, the use of athletic facilities, or an individual teacher's record of students' quiz scores), has not been computerized—and because of its unique nature, it is unlikely that it ever will be.

3. The integrity of confidential data often cannot be guaranteed when data are stored on district computers.

You may have heard that Excel is difficult to learn. Actually, nothing could be further from the truth. Excel is very straightforward, and the basic concepts are very easy to learn. Even most of the advanced concepts are not particularly difficult.

This book is based on the experiences of literally thousands of students in Excel classes, students in business training programs, students in traditional college classes, and students in online classes. When one of my students asked a question it caused me to rethink how I had presented the course material so that I could, hopefully, present it more clearly the next time.

Based on the success of many, many students, I am confident that this book will enable you to learn Excel quickly and easily, and that in a very short time you will be using Excel on a daily basis to enable you to perform your responsibilities more efficiently and effectively. Once you have become proficient with Excel, you may wonder how you ever got along without it.

Notice that as you work on these chapters, you will create a considerable number of worksheets. Please save all the worksheets because you will frequently be asked to return to a worksheet that you had completed in an earlier chapter.

I wish you much success in this endeavor—and in all your endeavors.

1

BASIC CONCEPTS

This chapter introduces a number of spreadsheet terms. You will probably be familiar with some, but don't try to remember all the terms. The most important terms in this chapter are *columns, rows, cells, text entries*, and *number entries*. Any other terms that are important will be repeated so many times that you will become very familiar with them.

There is a mystique that Excel is difficult to learn. Excel is extremely powerful and useful in addition to being fairly easy to learn. However, you might want to perpetuate the mystique. After all, if you know how to do something that people perceive as being difficult, it is much more impressive than if you know how to do something that is easy!

THE HISTORY OF THE ELECTRONIC SPREADSHEET

In 1979, two young students at Harvard University created the first computer spreadsheet for their own use. But as news of the program spread, more and more people wanted copies. The two young men started a company and called their program *VisiCalc*, and a new era in personal computing had begun.

Those were the days when very few businesses had personal computers. But VisiCalc had so much potential for businesses that many organizations bought computers so they could use VisiCalc. Think about it. This program was in large part responsible for the initial growth of the personal computer!

VisiCalc was a runaway success. And as with any successful idea, there are always people who try to copy a successful product, perhaps improve it, and market it themselves. Of the many companies that created programs similar to VisiCalc, one would become extremely successful. The success of this new spreadsheet program, called *Lotus 1-2-3*, was a result of some improvements the new company made to the concept of the electronic spreadsheet, and also to a very successful and aggressive marketing campaign. Lotus 1-2-3 became the most popular spreadsheet program in the world and, in fact, for a time the most popular program of any kind.

Of course technology refuses to stand still. After developing the Windows operating system, the Microsoft Corporation developed a spreadsheet that took full advantage of their new graphical operating environment. They called their spreadsheet program *Excel*, and it was not long before Excel became the most popular computer spreadsheet program in the world.

Why has Excel become so popular? It is because it is so incredibly powerful and not particularly difficult to learn. You will also see that Excel has many uses in schools as well as for your personal record keeping and accounting.

STARTING EXCEL

Start Excel as you would any other Windows program. There may be an Excel icon on your computer desktop, in which case simply double click on the Excel icon. Otherwise, click on the Start button, select Programs, Microsoft Office, and finally, select Microsoft Excel.

THE EXCEL WINDOW

The Excel window will now appear on your screen. You will notice many similarities between it and other programs you are already familiar with. There are, however, several differences.

- **Task Pane** The task pane is a new feature that made its appearance in the XP version of Microsoft Excel. It is a vertical "pane" that covers a part of the right side of the Excel work area. It enables you to start a new worksheet, or to open one you worked on before, and also, to perform a few other tasks simultaneously.

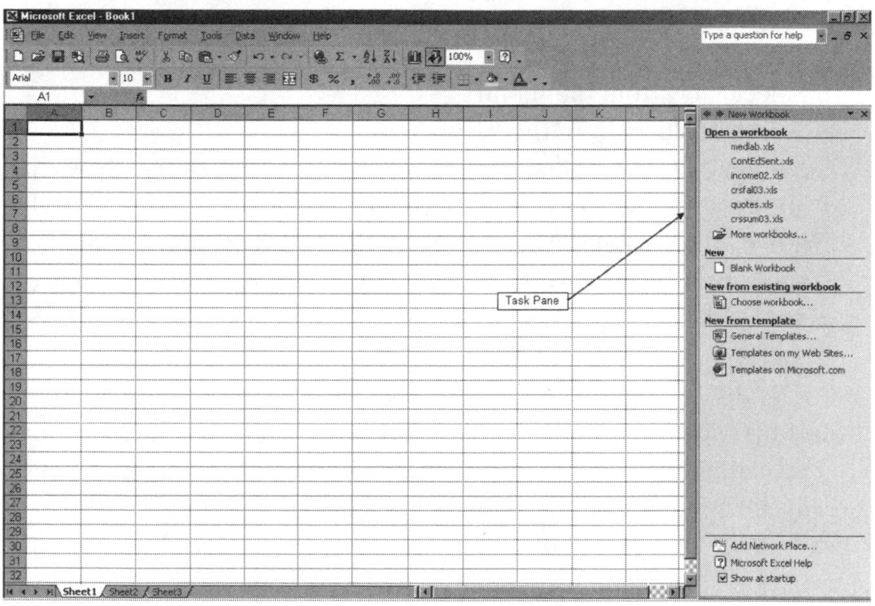

Figure 1.1.

- **Title Bar** The title bar tells you that you are working in Microsoft Excel, and also that you are working on a document that is tentatively called *Book 1*. After you create a worksheet, you will change the file name from Book 1 to a name of your choice.

Figure 1.2.

- **Menu** As in all Windows programs, the menu allows you to issue commands to Excel.

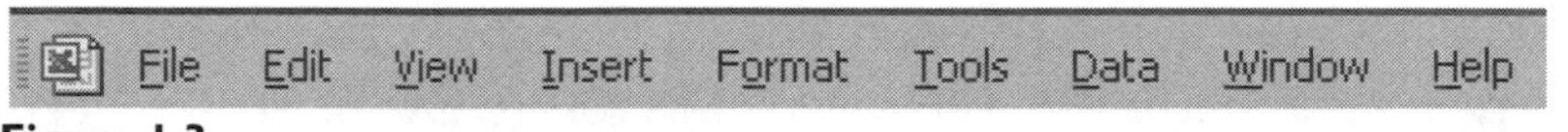

Figure 1.3.

- **Toolbar** The toolbar appears below the menu. You may see one, two, or even more than two rows of toolbar buttons (Fig. 1.4).

If the toolbar is not visible on your screen, display it by following these steps:

1. Select View from the menu.
2. Select Toolbars from the View menu.
3. Depending on the version of Excel you are using, the toolbars that are displayed will have either a checkmark or an X displayed to the left of their names. You will want the Standard and Formatting toolbars to be displayed. If they are not selected (that is, if they do not have a checkmark or an X to their left), click on them to select them.

Starting with Microsoft Excel version 2000, both the Standard and the Formatting toolbars are displayed on one line. Unfortunately, there is really not enough room for both toolbars on one line, so Excel displays most, but not all, of the toolbar buttons. Specifically, Excel displays the buttons you have used most recently (Fig. 1.5).

How does Excel do this? Notice that a downward or right-facing arrow is at about the middle of the toolbar and a rightward-facing double arrow is at the right edge of the toolbar. When you click on one of these arrows, Excel will display the buttons that are not currently visible. Click on one of these buttons to use it, and from that point on, that button will appear on the toolbar. Of course, because of space limitations, one of the buttons you have not used recently will no longer appear on the toolbar (Fig. 1.6).

Many people do not like this feature. That is, they would prefer to have the Standard and Formatting toolbars appear on two separate lines so that all the buttons are visible at one time. You can easily modify Excel to do this.

1. Select View from the menu.
2. Select Customize from the View menu.

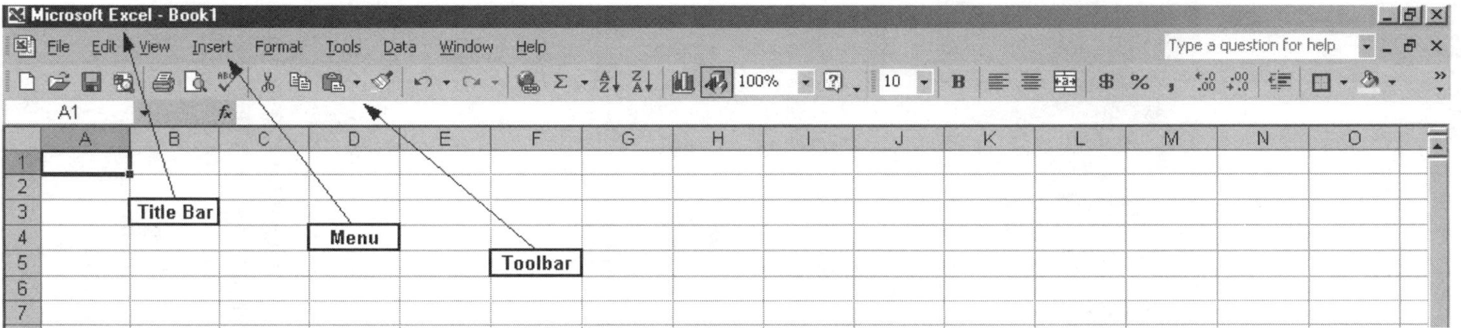

Figure 1.4.

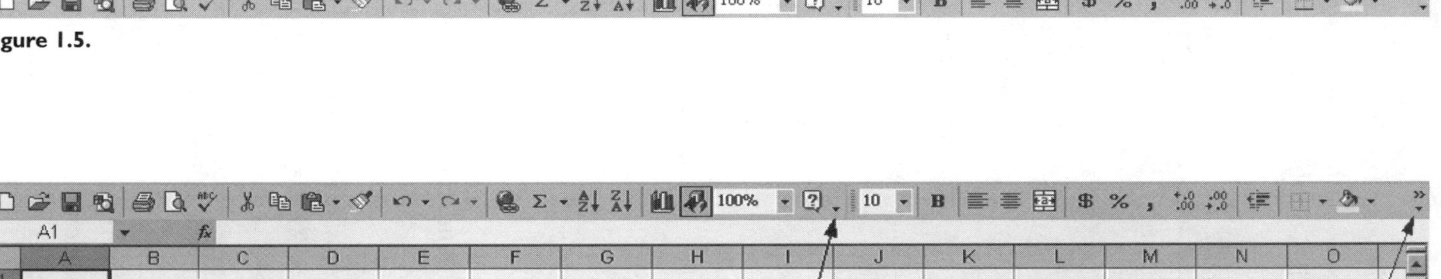

Figure 1.5.

Figure 1.6.

3. Click on the box to the left of "Show Standard and Formatting toolbars on two rows."
4. Click on the Close button.

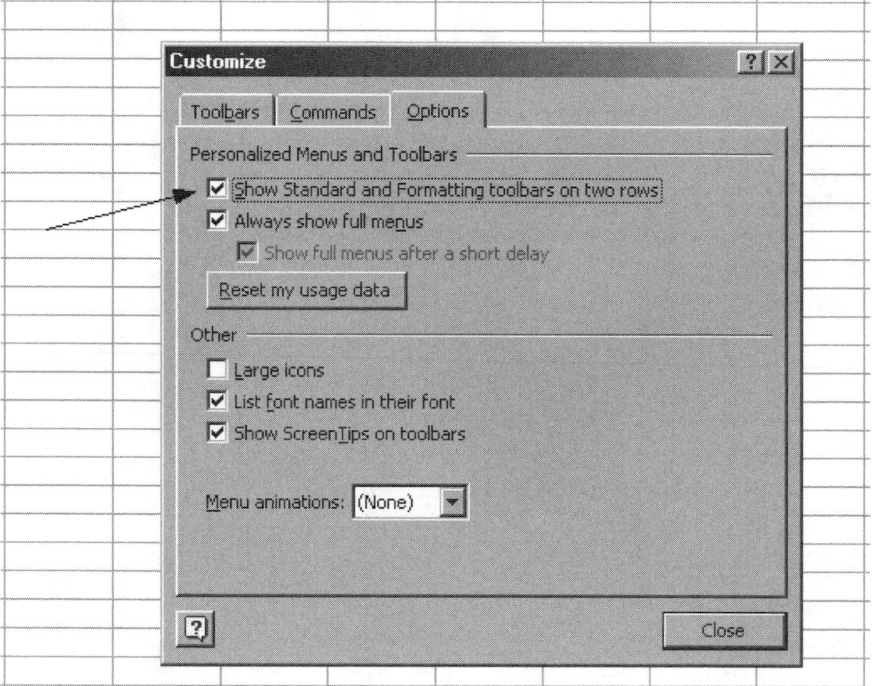

Figure 1.7.

The Standard and Formatting toolbars will now be displayed in their entirety on two separate rows (Fig. 1.8).

- **Formula Bar** The formula bar (Fig. 1.9) appears just below the toolbars. At the moment, it probably displays A1. Soon you will see that when you enter something into a worksheet cell, your entry will also appear on the formula bar, just to the right of the equals sign (=).
- **Status Bar** The status bar is located just below the worksheet. At the moment, it probably indicates READY (Fig. 1.10). That is, Excel is ready to accept input from you. The status bar may provide additional information to you, such as whether the Num Lock and Caps Lock features are turned on.

Figure 1.8.

Figure 1.9.

Ready NUM

Figure 1.10.

- **Work Area** The work area is the place where you will create your Excel worksheets. It is really nothing more than a big grid. You will become very familiar with the work area as you complete these chapters (Fig. 1.11).

WORKBOOKS

Notice that the title bar indicates that you are using Microsoft Excel, and also that you are using Book 1. Think of a book or a workbook as a binder that can contain many related worksheets and charts.

Worksheets

The bottom of the Microsoft Excel window displays several tabs. The tabs are labeled *Sheet 1*, *Sheet 2*, and so on. Currently, Sheet 1, or worksheet 1, is displayed. You can display the other worksheets in the workbook by clicking on the appropriate tabs.

Sheet1 Sheet2 Sheet3

Figure 1.11.

Your workbook probably has three tabs, for three worksheets. Actually, a workbook may contain many more than three worksheets. In fact, a workbook can contain as many as 255 worksheets. For now, you will be concerned with only one worksheet, Sheet 1.

At the moment, your worksheet is empty. Soon you will see how easy it is to enter data into it.

Columns

The vertical lines in the Excel worksheet define *columns*. Each column is designated by a letter of the alphabet (A, B, C . . .). At the moment, you can probably see only about eight or nine columns on your screen.

You might think that because there are twenty-six letters in the alphabet, that at most an Excel worksheet can contain only twenty-six columns. Actually, there are many more than twenty-six columns available to you in

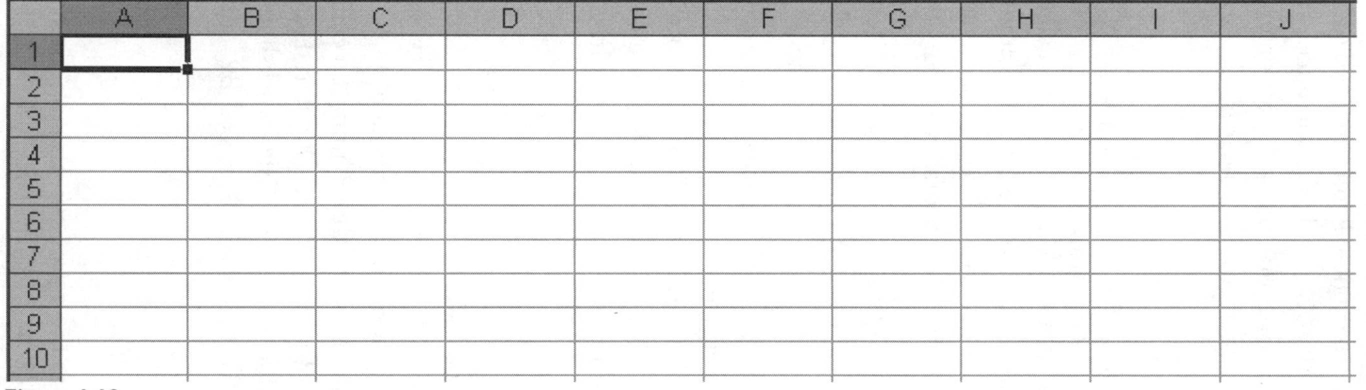

Figure 1.12.

an Excel worksheet because double letters are used to designate columns beyond column Z (AA, AB, AC . . .). In fact, an Excel worksheet can have as many as 256 columns. But you don't need to remember this number. You will probably never use anywhere near all the columns that Excel makes available.

Rows

The horizontal divisions within a worksheet are called *rows*. Each row is designated by a number (1, 2, 3 . . .). If 256 columns sounded like a lot of columns, recent versions of Excel provide more than 65,000 rows—65,536 rows to be exact. Of course, you will never use anywhere near all of those rows.

Cells

Cells are the individual boxes that appear on the worksheet at the intersection of a column and a row.

If you multiply 256 columns by 65,536 rows, you will see that an Excel worksheet has potentially 16,777,216 individual cells. As you can imagine, very few will ever use more than a small fraction of these cells.

Cell Addresses

Wherever you live, you have an address. Your address enables people to locate you. Similarly, each cell in an Excel worksheet has an address, which indicates exactly where on the worksheet the cell is located.

The *cell address* is the letter of the column the cell is located in, followed by the number of its row. When you start Excel, the address of the cell at the upper left corner of the Excel worksheet is cell A1. To the right of cell A1 is cell B1, below cell B1 is cell B2, and so on.

THE ACTIVE CELL

One cell is referred to as the *active cell*. You can always tell which cell is active—it is the cell that has a dark border surrounding it. At the moment, the active cell is cell A1.

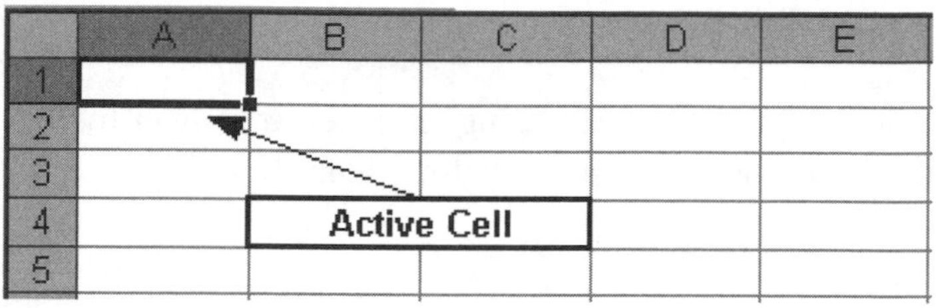

	A	B	C	D	E
1					
2					
3					
4		Active Cell			
5					

Figure 1.13.

Many people refer to the active cell by saying that it is the *selected cell*. Or they say that the *cursor* is in that cell. They find it easier than referring to the cell as the *active cell*. So you can say that A1 is currently the active cell, or that it is the selected cell, or simply that the cursor is in cell A1.

The most common ways of moving from one cell to another (to put it another way, of changing the active or selected cell) are:

1. By pressing the arrow (cursor movement) keys on your keyboard.
2. By positioning the mouse pointer, which appears as a plus sign, on a cell and clicking the left mouse button.

Note that the address of the active cell is displayed in the formula bar that is located at the top left of the Excel window, just below the menu and toolbar.

ADDITIONAL WAYS OF CHANGING THE ACTIVE CELL

In addition to changing the active cell with the arrow keys and the cursor, there are a few other ways to move from one cell to another.

1. Press the [Home] key on your keyboard to return the cursor to Column A of the row it is currently in.
2. Press [Ctrl] [Home] to return the cursor to cell A1, the cell at the upper left-hand corner of the worksheet.

CELL ENTRIES

You are now ready to begin creating an Excel worksheet by typing data into individual cells. You can enter three kinds of data into cells:

- Text
- Numbers
- Formulas (some people consider formulas to be a special kind of number entry)

Text Entries

Text refers to words you enter into Excel cells. Position the cursor in the cell you want your entry to appear in, type the word, and press [Enter]. By default, Excel left aligns text entries. That is, the first letter of a text entry practically touches the left edge of the cell.

Note that as you type an entry your keystrokes are displayed in the cell and also on the formula bar, just above the worksheet. However, your entry is not actually entered into the cell until you press [Enter].

Note also that after you have entered data into a cell, if you return the cursor to that cell the data in the cell will be displayed on the formula bar.

Remember, text entries are:

1. Words.
2. They are left aligned in their cells.

Remember also that cell entries:

1. Are not actually entered until you press the [Enter] key.
2. When the cursor is in a cell, the entry in that cell also appears on the formula bar.

Number Entries

You enter numbers into an Excel worksheet exactly the same way you enter text. However, unlike text entries that Excel left aligns, Excel *right aligns* numbers. You may type numbers in any of the following ways, and Excel will still recognize them as numbers:

123, $123, $123.00, 12.3%.

In most cases, Excel will not display unnecessary zeros after a decimal point. For example, if you type 16.10 in a cell, Excel will display 16.1. However, if the zeros are important, as in $16.10, Excel will display them.

Remember:

1. When you enter a number into a cell, Excel simply refers to it as a number.
2. Numbers are right aligned in their cells.
3. Excel does not display unnecessary zeros after a decimal point.

TEXT ENTRIES THAT LOOK LIKE NUMBERS

Some entries that we normally think of as numbers are not really numbers, like your telephone number. The problem is that although we call it a *telephone number*, your telephone number is not really a number in the sense that $25 is a number.

Think of it this way. A number is a mathematical concept. So a number is something that you can perform mathematical calculations on. If you can add 3 to something, for example, or multiply it by 2, and it makes sense, then it is a number. You can add the 9 boys in a class to the 11 girls, to arrive at 20 students. So 9 and 11 in this case are numbers. But you cannot add 3 to your telephone number. It would not make any sense. So your telephone number is not a number in the mathematical sense. Neither is your social security number or your ZIP code.

If your telephone number is not a number, then what is it? The answer is that your telephone number is text. In the "old days," we used to call things like telephone numbers *alphanumerics*. That is, whether they contained text or numbers, they functioned like words rather than numbers. Today, in the interest of simplicity, we just call them *text entries*.

In most cases, when you enter something like a telephone number or a social security number into a cell in an Excel worksheet, Excel determines that although it might look like a number, it is really text. But in some cases, such as when you enter a ZIP code in a cell, Excel cannot distinguish it as text. In these cases, you must tell Excel that your entry is text. You do this by typing an apostrophe (') in front of the entry. For example, if your ZIP code is 10010, and you want to enter it into a cell in an Excel worksheet, you would enter it by typing '10010. Because the apostrophe is there only to indicate that the entry is text, Excel will not display the apostrophe in the cell.

Formulas

Excel formulas always begin with an equals sign (=). For example, if you want to add 2 and 3, you would type =2+3. Note that the result of the calculation, in this case 5, is displayed in the cell. But if you look at the formula bar just above your worksheet, you will see exactly what you typed, in this case =2+3.

CELL CONTENT AND CELL DISPLAY

The reference to formulas brings up a very important distinction between a cell's content and its display.

- **Cell Content** What the cell actually contains. That is, exactly what you typed.
- **Cell Display** What you see displayed in the cell.

Most often, a cell's content and its display will be the same. For example, if you type BOY into a cell, BOY appears in the cell. In this case, the cell content and the cell display are the same. But if you type =2+3 into a cell, the cell content, what you typed, is =2+3. But the cell display, what you see in the cell, is 5.

Of course you can always tell what the cell display is by simply looking at the cell. How can you tell what the cell content is? You can always tell what the cell content is by selecting the cell and looking at the entry in the formula bar (which is located just above your worksheet).

	A	B	C	D	E	F
1						
2	5					
3				Cell Content		
4						
5	Cell Display					
6						

Figure 1.14.

Although the distinction between cell content and cell display might seem insignificant, it will become very important as you learn more about Excel worksheets.

Remember:

1. Cell display is what you *see* in the cell.
2. Cell content is what you actually *typed* into the cell.
3. Cell content and cell display are often the same, but sometimes they are different.

Remember also:

1. If you want to know what a cell's display is, look at the cell.
2. If you want to know what a cell's content is, move the cursor to that cell and look at the formula bar.

THE STATUS BAR

The status bar appears on the bottom of the screen. It generally displays the message READY, which means that Excel is ready for you to make an entry in a cell. The status bar will often display messages other than READY, such as the status of the Caps Lock and Num Lock functions.

FUNCTION KEYS

Excel makes use of the function keys at the top of your keyboard (F1, F2, F3 . . . F12). You will learn about those later in the book.

MENUS

The Excel menu appears at the top of the Excel window, just below the title bar. The menu options are shown in figure 1.15.

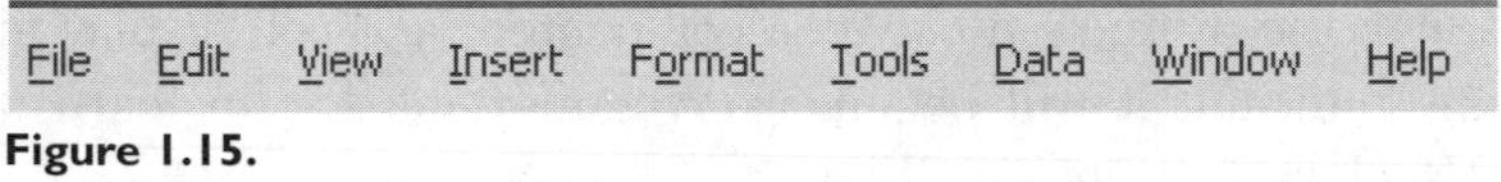

Figure 1.15.

You issue commands to Excel by using its powerful menu system. You can access menu items in either of two ways:

1. Point to a menu item with the mouse, and click the left mouse button.
2. Press [Alt] and the underlined letter of your choice (for example, [Alt] [F] for File, or [Alt] [E] for Edit).

When you select a menu option, a *submenu* will appear below the menu item.

3. Select your submenu choice from within the menu by clicking on it with your mouse, or by typing its underlined letter on the keyboard.

Note that some submenu options are black, while others are gray. Only the black submenu options are available to you. Note also that some menu options are followed by three dots, which is called an *ellipsis* (. . .). When you choose one of these items, a dialog box will appear on your screen. The dialog box will ask you for additional information regarding your choice.

EXITING FROM EXCEL

When you have finished working with Excel, exit from the program by selecting File, then selecting Exit from the menu.

EXERCISE 1

1. Describe the major components of the Excel window.
2. Explain the following terms:

   Column
   Row
   Cell
   Cell Address
   The Active Cell
3. Explain how to move the cursor from one cell to another (that is, how to change the *active* or *selected* cell).
4. What is a text entry?
5. What is the default alignment of text entries?
6. What is a number entry?
7. What is the default alignment of number entries?
8. Explain why a telephone number is a text entry.
9. Explain how you would enter a ZIP code to ensure that it is entered as text.
10. Define the term *cell display*.
11. Define the term *cell content*.
12. How can you tell what a cell's content is?
13. How can you tell what a cell's display is?
14. Describe the two ways to select a menu item.
15. What does a gray submenu item mean?
16. Explain how to exit from Excel.

2

CELL ENTRIES AND MENU COMMANDS

You have learned about columns, rows, cells, and cell addresses. And you have also learned about the kinds of entries you can make in cells:

1. Text
2. Numbers
3. Formulas

MAKING CELL ENTRIES

You are now ready to begin making entries into cells, which is the first step in creating a worksheet. So start Excel and make the following cell entries:

1. Type the word BOY in cell A1, and press [Enter]. BOY is a word, so it is a text entry. Note that, as is the case with all text entries, BOY is left aligned in its cell.
2. Note that when you pressed the [Enter] key, the word BOY was entered into cell A1, and the cursor jumped to cell A2. Since you will most often be making entries downward in a column, Excel

facilitates the process by automatically moving down one cell each time you press [Enter].

3. Type the word GIRL in cell A2, and press [Enter]. Note that GIRL is also a text entry, and consequently is also left aligned.
4. Type the word DOG in cell A3, and press the [Down Arrow] key on your keyboard. Pressing any of the arrow keys is like pressing [Enter]. The difference is that when you press [Enter] the cursor moves down one cell, but when you press an arrow key, the cursor moves in the direction of the arrow key you pressed.
5. Type 123 in cell A4, and press [Down Arrow]. This is a number entry. Note that because 123 is a number entry, it is right aligned in its cell.
6. Type 12.3 in cell A5, and press [Down Arrow].
7. Type 1.23 in cell A6, and press [Down Arrow]. Note that although number entries are right aligned in their cells, Excel does not align numbers according to their decimal points.
8. Type 16.00 in cell A7, and press [Down Arrow]. Note that Excel displays only 16 in the cell. Remember, Excel does not display unnecessary zeros after a decimal point.
9. Type NOW IS THE TIME FOR ALL GOOD MEN in cell A8, and press the [Right Arrow] key. Note that if you type a long text entry in a cell, the entry will spill over into adjacent cells. This happens only if: (a) the entry is a text entry, and (b) the cells to the right of the entry are empty.
10. Type the number 1 in cell B8, and press [Enter]. Note that the long text entry in cell A8 no longer spills over into the adjacent cells because cell B8 is no longer empty.

It is really important to understand that the entry in cell A8 has *not changed*. It is still NOW IS THE TIME FOR ALL GOOD MEN. However, because there is an entry in cell B8, you cannot see the entire entry in cell A8.

Remember the discussion of cell display and cell content in the previous chapter:

- Cell display refers to what you see in the cell.
- Cell content refers to what you actually typed.

If you look at cell A8, you see only part of what you typed. But if you move the cursor to cell A8 and look at the formula bar, you will see the cell content, exactly as you typed it.

The cell display in cell A8 is: NOW IS T. But the cell content in cell A8 is exactly what you typed: NOW IS THE TIME FOR ALL GOOD MEN.

A8 | NOW IS THE TIME FOR ALL GOOD MEN

	A	B	C	D	E	F	G
1	BOY						
2	GIRL						
3	DOG						
4	123				Cell Content		
5	12.3						
6	1.23		Cell Display				
7	16						
8	NOW IS T	1					
9							

Figure 2.1.

11. Now type 123456789012345 in cell A9. Note that only long text entries spill over into adjacent empty cells. Long number entries are converted into what is called *scientific format*. However, if you move the cursor back to cell A9 and look at the formula bar, you will see that the formula bar displays the number exactly as you typed it.

A9 | 123456789012345

	A	B	C	D	E	F	G
1	BOY						
2	GIRL						
3	DOG						
4	123				Cell Content		
5	12.3						
6	1.23		Cell Display				
7	16						
8	NOW IS THE	1					
9	1.23457E+14						
10							

Figure 2.2.

All you need to remember about scientific format is that if you type a really big number into a cell it may appear differently from the way you typed it. You will learn how to deal with this in a later chapter.

12. Type IGLOO in cell A10, but do not press [Enter] or an arrow key. Press the [Esc] key at the upper left-hand corner of your keyboard. If you make a typing mistake and you have not yet pressed [Enter] or an arrow key, pressing [Esc] will cancel what you have typed.
13. Type HOUSE in cell A10 and press [Enter].
14. Now go back to cell A10. Type TENT in cell A11 and press [Enter]. Note that if you want to change the entry in a cell, simply type the new entry over the old one. The new entry will overwrite or replace the old entry.
15. Press [Ctrl] [Home] to move the cursor to cell A1.

	A	B	C	D	E	F
1	BOY					
2	GIRL					
3	DOG					
4	123					
5	12.3					
6	1.23					
7	16					
8	NOW IS THE	1				
9	1.23457E+14					
10	TENT					
11						

Figure 2.3.

A FEW IMPORTANT MENU COMMANDS

The Excel menu offers a number of very useful commands to Excel. These are the ones you will find most useful.

Clear a Cell

Use this command to clear or erase an entry in a cell.

1. Move the cursor to the cell you want to clear.
2. Select Edit, Clear, All from the menu.

Now use this technique to clear the entry in cell A1.

Clear a Range of Cells

A range of cells is a group of cells that meets two conditions:

1. The cells are attached to one another.
2. They form a rectangle or square on the screen.

If you want to clear a range of cells:

1. Point to the first cell in the range you want to clear. Be sure you are pointing to the center of the cell and that your cursor looks like a big plus sign.
2. Hold down the left mouse button.
3. Drag the mouse downward and to the right to select or highlight all the cells you want to clear (you will notice that the first cell in the range is lighter than the rest—this has no significance).
4. Select Edit, Clear, All from the menu.

Now use this technique to clear the range of cells A3 through A6.

	A	B	C
1	BOY		
2	GIRL		
3	DOG		
4	123		
5	12.3		
6	1.23		
7	16		
8	NOW IS THE	1	
9	1.23457E+14		
10	TENT		
11			

Figure 2.4.

	A	B	C
1	BOY		
2	GIRL		
3			
4			
5			
6			
7	16		
8	NOW IS THE ⁻	1	
9	1.23457E+14		
10	TENT		
11			

Figure 2.5.

Undo

The Undo command is very helpful any time you have made a mistake and want to reverse or undo the last thing, or the last of several things you have done.

1. Select Edit, Undo from the menu.

When you select Edit, Undo from the menu, the entries will be returned to the range of cells you had previously cleared.

Close a Worksheet

When you have finished working with a worksheet, you will want to close it.

1. Select File, Close from the menu.

Since you have not saved your worksheet, Excel will ask if you want to save your changes. Since you will not be working with this worksheet again, in this case select No.

Start a New Worksheet

When you want to create a new worksheet, ask Excel to display a blank grid for you.

1. Select File, New from the menu.

Exit from Excel

You have already learned how to exit from Excel, but as a reminder:

1. Select File, Exit from the menu.

KEYBOARD AND TOOLBAR SHORTCUTS

There are a number of keyboard and toolbar shortcuts that will accomplish the same operations as the menu commands you have just learned.

Clear a Cell or Range of Cells

- Menu—Select Edit, Clear, All.
- Keyboard—Press the [Delete] key.

Undo an Action

- Menu—Select Edit, Undo.
- Keyboard—Press [Ctrl] [Z].
- Toolbar—Click on the toolbar button that has a picture of a counterclockwise facing arrow.

Figure 2.6

Start a New Worksheet

- Menu—Select File, New.
- Keyboard—Press [Ctrl] [N].

- Toolbar—Click on the button with a picture of a blank sheet of paper—it is probably the leftmost button on your toolbar.

Figure 2.7.

Exit from Excel

- Menu—Select File, Exit.

REMEMBERING MENU COMMANDS

It is *not* necessary to memorize the menu commands, keyboard shortcuts, and toolbar buttons. Rather, refer to the tables in Appendix A at the end of this book, or copy the commands onto an index card. After you have used a command several times, you will begin to remember it.

EXERCISE 2

1. How are text entries aligned in their cells?
2. How are number entries aligned in their cells?
3. If you type 123.50 in a cell, Excel will display 123.5. Explain why Excel does not display the last zero.
4. Explain what will happen if you type a long text entry into a cell when the cell to the right is empty.
5. Explain what will happen if you type a long text entry into a cell when the cell to the right contains an entry.
6. Explain what will happen if you type a long number entry into a cell.
7. If you begin typing an entry into a cell but have not yet pressed [Enter], explain how to cancel the entry.
8. Explain how to clear an entry from a single cell.
9. What two conditions must a group of cells meet in order to be considered a range?

10. How do you clear the entries from a range of cells?
11. Explain how the Undo command works.
12. How do you close a worksheet?
13. How do you start a new worksheet?
14. Listed are the Excel operations you have already learned. For each operation, indicate how to perform the operation using the Excel menu, and if available, using the keyboard shortcut and the toolbar.
    - Clear a cell
    - Clear a range of cells
    - Undo an action
    - Close a worksheet
    - Start a new worksheet
    - Exit from Excel
15. Create the Excel worksheet shown in figure 2.8.

	A	B	C	D
1	Teacher Contact List			
2				
3				
4	First	Last	Telephone	
5	John	Smith	987-6543	
6	Mary	Jones	333-4444	
7				
8				

Figure 2.8.

16. Enter several additional names and telephone numbers into your worksheet.
17. Close the worksheet. When you are prompted, indicate that you do not want to save your changes.
18. Exit from Excel.

3

CREATING A WORKSHEET

You have learned how to enter data into cells and how to issue the most common commands by using the Excel menu, keyboard shortcuts, and toolbar buttons. You are now ready to take an exciting step—in this chapter you will create your first Excel worksheet. Creating an Excel worksheet is really quite simple—all you need to do is enter text and numbers into specific cells. In later chapters, you will learn how to write formulas and improve and fine-tune your worksheets.

ENTERING TEXT

Before you start entering data into your worksheet, here are two tips that will save you time and effort:

1. If you are entering data downward through a column, type an entry into a cell and then press either [Enter] or the [Down Arrow] key. As you have seen, when you press either of these keys Excel will enter your data into the cell and move the cursor to the cell below so you are ready to make your next entry.

2. If you are entering data across a row, press the [Right Arrow] key after you type each cell entry. This is much easier than pressing [Enter] and then moving the cursor to the next cell to the right by pressing the [Right Arrow] and then the [Up Arrow] keys.

Begin by creating the worksheet as shown in figure 3.1.

	A	B	C	D	E	F
1	Student Population					
2						
3						
4	Grade	1999	2000	2001	2002	Total
5	One					
6	Two					
7	Three					
8	Four					
9	Five					
10	Six					
11						
12	Total					
13						
14	Free Milk					
15						
16	Free Lunch					
17						
18	Free Transportation					
19						

Figure 3.1.

Now enter the numerical data shown in figure 3.2 into your worksheet.

SAVING YOUR WORKSHEET

You will want to save worksheets that you will use again in the future. But saving your worksheets will also protect your data while you are working. Imagine that you have been working on a new worksheet for an hour or two when there is an unexpected power interruption. Even if the interruption

	A	B	C	D	E	F
1	Student Population					
2						
3						
4	Grade	1999	2000	2001	2002	Total
5	One	325	375	425		
6	Two	300	350	400		
7	Three	275	325	375		
8	Four	250	300	350		
9	Five	225	275	325		
10	Six	200	250	300		
11						
12	Total					
13						
14	Free Milk					
15						
16	Free Lunch					
17						
18	Free Transportation					
19						

Figure 3.2.

is momentary, there is a very real likelihood that all your work will be lost. But if you had been saving your work every ten minutes or so, the most you would lose would be the work since your last saved your worksheet.

Saving a paper document in an office involves the following steps:

1. You put your document in a folder.
2. You label the folder.
3. And finally, you put the folder into your file cabinet.

The process of saving an Excel worksheet is very similar to saving a paper document except you will use Excel's menu commands to perform the operation.

1. From the menu, select File, and then from the File menu, select Save As . . .

2. Type STUDPOP, the name you will assign to this worksheet.
3. Click the Save button on the toolbar (the button with a picture of a diskette on it, which is probably the third button from the left end of the toolbar).

How do you know that your worksheet has been saved? Simply look at the title bar. Previously, it displayed Book 1 next to the words Microsoft Excel.

Microsoft Excel - Book1

Figure 3.3.

But now that you have saved your worksheet, Book 1 has been replaced with the name you assigned to your worksheet, in this case, STUDPOP.

Microsoft Excel - StudPop.xls

Figure 3.4.

Although it is not immediately obvious, when you save a worksheet, Excel automatically adds the *file extension* .XLS to the end of the name you assign to the worksheet. In this case, you named your worksheet STUDPOP, but Excel called it STUDPOP.XLS. There is nothing mysterious about the .XLS. Think of it as Excel's way of assigning a last name .XLS. This indicates to the computer that the file is an Excel worksheet. As you may have guessed .XLS stands for EXceL Spreadsheet. Note also that file names need not be typed in uppercase characters—we have done that here only for clarity.

FILES AND WORKSHEETS

When you create a worksheet, you see it on your screen. Technically, it exists in your computer's memory. When you save a worksheet, you save it on a disk—most commonly, your computer's hard disk. When you save a worksheet, it then becomes a *file*.

Remember:

- Worksheets exist in your computer's memory.
- Files exist on your computer's hard disk, a diskette, or other storage media.

A FEW WORDS ABOUT FILE NAMES

In the early days of computers there were very specific rules about creating file names. For example, you couldn't use spaces, most symbols, or more than eight characters in a file name.

Today, most names for your worksheets will be appropriate. However, you should not use punctuation marks or symbols within a file name, since these can cause problems. Some people still believe it is safer to assign relatively short file names—generally consisting of eight characters or fewer.

Remember:

When you save a worksheet, or when you are working with a worksheet you have previously saved, the name you assigned to it will appear in the title bar at the top of the screen.

Figure 3.5.

RESAVING A WORKSHEET

Let's say that you have created a worksheet and saved it. Then you make some changes to that worksheet. You will want to resave your worksheet, so that the changes you have made are also saved.

1. Select File, Save from the menu, or click on the Save button on the toolbar.

Figure 3.6.

Your worksheet has now been resaved, and the new file includes all the changes you have made. Note that when you resave a worksheet, the old version is replaced by the new version of your worksheet.

If you want to have access to both the old and new versions of your worksheet, use the File, Save As . . . command rather than File, Save, and assign a different file name to it, say, STUDPOP2. That way, you will have two different files with two different file names.

CLOSE THE WORKSHEET

Now close your worksheet.

1. Select File, Close from the menu.

REOPEN THE WORKSHEET

Opening a previously saved worksheet is much easier than creating it.

1. Select File, Open from the menu.
2. If you have saved more than one worksheet, you will see all your filenames displayed in alphabetical order. Find the file you want to open, in this case, STUDPOP.
3. Click on STUDPOP to select it.
4. Click on the Open button.

Shortcut

You can accelerate the process slightly.

1. Select File, Open from the menu.
2. Find the file you want to open, in this case, STUDPOP. Left double click on STUDPOP to open the worksheet.

EXIT FROM EXCEL

Now that you have created and saved your first worksheet, you are ready to exit from Excel.

1. Select File, Exit from the Excel menu.

EXERCISE 3

1. Explain why it is important to save your worksheets.
2. Which menu option do you use to save your worksheets?
3. Explain how to save a worksheet you have not previously saved.
4. How can you tell if the worksheet you are working on has been saved?
5. What does .XLS at the end of a file name indicate?
6. Where do worksheets exist?
7. Where do files exist?
8. Explain which characters should not be used in file names.
9. Explain how to resave a worksheet you have previously saved.
10. Create a worksheet with the data as shown in figure 3.7.

	A	B	C	D	E	F
1	Daily Attendance					
2	Week of January 1					
3						
4		Mon	Tue	Wed	Thu	Fri
5	Grade 1	100	114			
6	Grade 2	109	107			
7	Grade 3	140	146			

Figure 3.7.

11. Save the worksheet as ATTJAN01 (use File, Save As . . .).
12. Close the worksheet.
13. Open ATTJAN01.XLS.
14. Add data for Wednesday—make up your own data.
15. Resave the worksheet (select File, Save from the menu).
16. Close the worksheet.
17. Exit from Excel.

4

COPYING AND MOVING: BASIC CONCEPTS

This chapter explains how to copy and move the contents of one cell to another cell or cells. Although it will not be immediately apparent, learning these extremely important concepts will make it possible to create worksheets in minutes rather than many hours.

COPYING AND MOVING CELL ENTRIES—A FEW DEFINITIONS

There is a subtle difference between copying and moving the contents of one cell to another.

- **Copy** When you copy a cell entry, the original entry remains in the original cell, but a copy of that entry will also appear in the cell you choose.
- **Move** When you move a cell entry, you take the original entry from the original cell and place it in a new cell. It no longer exists in the original cell.

In other words, when you copy something, it appears in your worksheet twice—once in the original cell and again in another cell. When you move something, it appears in your worksheet only once—in the cell you have moved it to.

For the purposes of our discussion, it will be helpful to know two additional terms:

- **Source Cell** The cell that contains the entry you are going to copy or move.
- **Destination Cell** The cell you are copying or moving the entry to.

CREATE A SIMPLE WORKSHEET

Begin by making the cell entries that are indicated in figure 4.1.

	A	B	C	D	E	F
1	1					
2	2					
3	3					
4	4					
5	5					
6	6					
7	7					
8	8					

Figure 4.1.

Copying from One Cell to One Cell—Standard Method

The copying process involves the following steps:

1. Click on the cell you want to copy, the source cell. In this case, click on cell A1.
2. Select Edit, Copy from the Excel menu. You will see moving dotted lines around the source cell. These dotted lines are referred to as a *marquee*. They indicate that you have selected the cell for copying and that you have started the copy process.

3. Click on, or move the cursor to the cell you want to copy the entry to, the destination cell. In this case, click on cell C1.
4. Select Edit, Paste from the menu.

Note that the entry in cell A1 has been copied to cell C1.

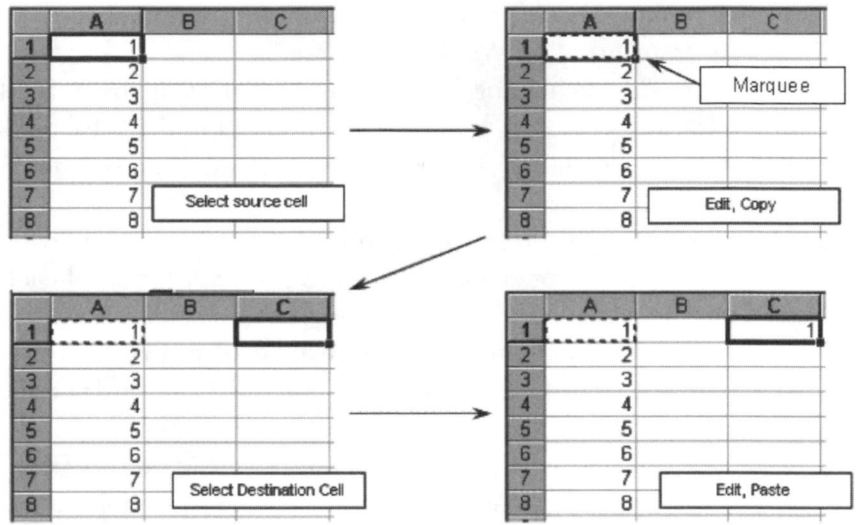

Figure 4.2.

THE THEORY

Before you practice what you have learned, it will be useful to understand what is actually happening when you copy an entry from one cell to another. The Windows *Clipboard* is a reserved section of your computer's memory.

When you select Edit, Copy from the menu, the marquee indicates that you have copied the contents of the source cell to the Windows Clipboard. That is, the contents of the cell now exist in two places. It is still in the cell, but it is *also* in the Windows Clipboard. When you select Edit, Paste from the menu, Excel copies the contents of the Clipboard to the destination cell. In other words, you copy *to* the Clipboard, and you paste *from* the Clipboard.

Clipboard Characteristics

In order to copy and paste successfully, it is important to understand the basic characteristics of the Clipboard.

1. The Clipboard is available to all Windows programs. That is, you can copy something to the Clipboard from a Microsoft Excel worksheet, or a Microsoft Word document, or a Microsoft Access database, or from any other Windows program.
2. If you can select something, you can copy it to the Clipboard. Most often, you will copy text, numbers, or formulas to the Clipboard. But as you will learn later, you can also copy graphics and other objects to the Clipboard.
3. Virtually nothing is too small or too large to fit in the Clipboard. The Clipboard can contain as little as a single character, say the letter X, or the contents of your entire worksheet.
4. With many computer programs, the Clipboard can contain only one thing at a time. Copy a second object to the Clipboard and the first will be lost.
5. In recent versions of Microsoft Excel and other Microsoft Office applications, the Clipboard can contain several separate items at one time. If you have copied more than one selection to the clipboard, all the saved selections will be displayed in the Task Pane. You can select any one to be pasted into your worksheet.
6. The contents of the Clipboard will be automatically discarded when you exit Windows

COPYING FROM ONE CELL TO ONE CELL—PRACTICE

Now, let's try it again. Copy the entry in cell A1 to cell E1.

1. Click on cell A1, which will be the source cell.
2. Select Edit, Copy from the Excel menu. Note the marquee around cell A1. Remember that this indicates you have started the copy process by sending a copy of the data in cell A1 to the Windows Clipboard. The contents of cell A1 now exists in two places. It is still in cell A1, and it is also in the Windows Clipboard.

3. Click on cell E1, the destination cell.
4. Select Edit, Paste from the menu. The Edit, Paste command has copied the contents of cell A1, from the Windows Clipboard, into cell E1.

For more practice of this function:

1. Copy the entry in cell A1 to cell F1.
2. Copy the entry in cell A1 to cell G1.
3. Copy the entry in cell A1 to cell H1.

RANGES

Before you learn to copy from one cell to several cells, you will need to know more about a concept that was briefly mentioned in a previous chapter—*ranges*. Look at the worksheet in figure 4.3. The shaded cells represent cells that contain data.

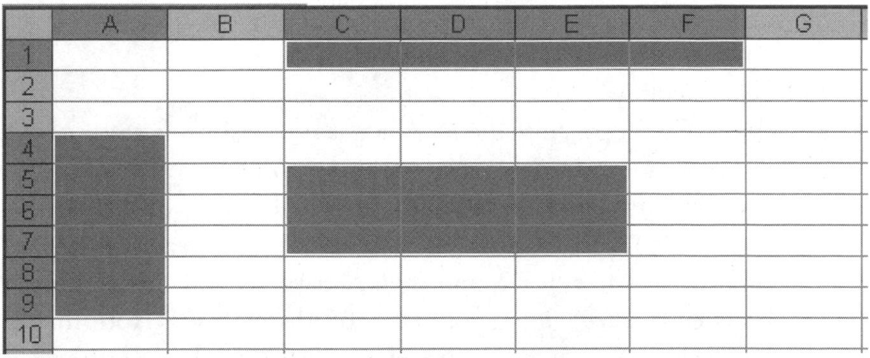

Figure 4.3.

You will recall that the definition of a range is a group of cells that meet two criteria: (1) the cells are *attached*, and (2) they form a *rectangle* or a *square* on the screen. Remember, for a group of cells to be considered a range, the cells must be attached to each other, *and* they must form a rectangle or a square on the screen.

Your sample worksheet contains three ranges of cells:

1. Cells A4 through A9.
2. Cells C1 through F1.
3. Cells C5 through E7.

Ranges are defined by noting the first and last cells in the range, and separating them with a period (.) or a colon (:). Using this method of notation, the ranges in the above example are:

A4.A9 or A4:A9
C1.F1 or C1:F1
C5.E7 or C5:E7

We usually define a range by moving from left to right, or top to bottom, but the other ways are also acceptable. For example, the first range indicated above could be either A4.A9, or A9.A4.

COPYING FROM ONE CELL TO A RANGE OF CELLS

You are now ready to copy from cell A2 to the range of cells B2:E2.

1. Click on cell A2.
2. Select Edit, Copy. Note the marquee is now visible around cell A2.
3. Use your mouse to move the cursor to point at cell B2. Be sure that your cursor is in the middle of the cell and that it looks like a big plus sign. Hold down the left mouse button and move the pointer across to cell E2, and then release the left mouse button. This is called *dragging* across cells B2 through E2. Note that all the cells in the range you selected are surrounded by a border and highlighted (although the first cell is lighter than the rest).
4. Select Edit, Paste from the menu.

You have copied the entry in cell A2 to the range of cells B2.E2.

As practice, perform the following copy operations:

1. Copy from cell A3 to the range of cells B3:H3.
2. Copy from cell A4 to the range of cells B4:G4.

COPYING AND PASTING FROM THE KEYBOARD

You have learned how to issue the Copy and Paste commands from the menu:

1. Edit, Copy
2. Edit, Paste

You can also issue the Copy and Paste commands from the keyboard.

1. Press [Ctrl] [C] to copy.
2. Press [Ctrl] [V] to paste.

Here is how it works. Suppose you want to copy the entry in cell A5 to the range of cells C5:F5.

1. Click on cell A5 to select it as the source cell.
2. Press [Ctrl] [C] to copy the contents of the source cell to the Clipboard. Note the marquee, just as if you had selected Edit, Copy from the menu.
3. Now drag across the range of cells C5:F5 to select them as the destination range.
4. Press [Ctrl] [V] to paste the contents of the Clipboard to the destination range.

COPYING AND PASTING FROM THE TOOLBAR

You can also issue the Copy and Paste commands from the toolbar. The Copy button is a picture of two documents on it. It is most likely located on the left side of the toolbar.

Figure 4.4.

The Paste button is a picture of a clipboard and a document on it. It should be located just to the right of the Copy button.

Figure 4.5.

Suppose that you want to use the toolbar buttons to copy the entry in cell A6 to the range of cells E6:G6:

1. Click on cell A6 to select it.
2. Click on the Copy button on the toolbar.

Figure 4.6.

3. Drag across cells E6:G6 to select them.
4. Click on the Paste button on the toolbar.

Figure 4.7.

EXERCISE 4

1. Describe the difference between copying and moving.
2. Describe the four steps involved in copying an entry from one cell to another.
3. Describe how to copy an entry from cell A1 to cell C1. From cell A1 to cell A5.
4. What is the Windows Clipboard?
5. How is the Clipboard involved in the copying process?
6. What characteristics apply to the Clipboard?
7. What two conditions must exist for a group of cells to be considered a range of cells?
8. Describe how to define a range of cells.
9. Explain how you would copy an entry from cell A2 to the range of cells D2.G2.
10. Explain how to issue the Copy and Paste commands from the keyboard.

11. Explain how to issue the Copy and Paste commands from the toolbar.
12. Create the worksheet shown in figure 4.8.

	A	B	C	D
1	Monthly Average Attendance			
2				
3	Class	January	February	
4	101	22		
5	102	24		
6	103	26		
7	104	21		
8	105	23		
9	106	25		
10				

Figure 4.8.

13. The average monthly attendance for all classes in February except Class 103 is the same as it was for January. Copy all the entries in B4:B5 to C4:C5, and all the entries in B7:B9 to C7:C9.
14. The average monthly attendance for February for Class 103 is 24. Enter 24 in cell C6.
15. Save the worksheet with the file name MonAtt.

5

COPYING AND MOVING: ADVANCED CONCEPTS

You have learned how to copy and move the contents of one cell to another or to a range of cells. You are probably wondering what the big deal is about. It might seem as if you could have typed the cell entries more quickly than you copied them. And to this point, that is probably true. But in this chapter you will see how important it is to be able to copy an entry from one cell to another and how copying a cell entry is often much faster than retyping it. This chapter explains a number of advanced concepts, which are actually easier to learn than the basic concepts.

A BRIEF REVIEW OF COPYING

First, let's review the basic steps in copying:

1. Begin by selecting (moving the cursor to, or clicking on) the source cell.
2. Select Edit, Copy from the menu. Notice the marquee around the source cell, which indicates that the contents of the source cell have been copied to the Windows Clipboard.

3. Now select the destination cell, or if you will be copying to more than one cell the destination range of cells.
4. Select Edit, Paste from the menu.

Remember:

1. When you copy the contents of the source cell, you are really copying it to the Windows Clipboard.
2. When you paste something to a destination cell (or to a range of cells), you are really pasting it from the Windows Clipboard.

Remember too:

1. You can issue the Copy command from the keyboard by pressing [Ctrl] [C].
2. You can issue the Paste command from the keyboard by pressing [Crtl] [V].
3. You can issue the Copy command from the toolbar by clicking on the Copy button.

Figure 5.1.

4. You can issue the Paste command from the toolbar by clicking on the Paste button.

Figure 5.2.

Finally, remember:

1. You can copy anything that you can select to the Windows Clipboard.

FILL COPYING—AN EASIER WAY TO COPY

The most common copying process involves copying an entry from one cell to one or more cells adjacent to it. In these cases, there is an even easier way to copy that is called *filling*.

1. Use the mouse to point the cursor to the cell you want to copy. Be certain your pointer is in the middle of the cell and that it looks like a big plus sign.
2. Press and hold down the left mouse button. Starting with the cell you want to copy, drag across the range that starts at the cell you want to copy, and continues across the range of cells that you want to copy it to. Release the mouse button. The cell you want to copy will be highlighted in white. The cells you want to copy to will be highlighted in a darker color, most likely blue.
3. From the menu, select Edit, Fill.
4. Indicate whether you are filling *right, down, left,* or *up* (Fig. 5.3).

DRAG COPYING—PROBABLY THE EASIEST WAY TO COPY

Drag copying is an even easier way to copy, but as with fill copying, it is only appropriate in cases in which you want to copy an entry in one cell to one or more cells that are adjacent to it.

1. Select the cell you want to copy by clicking on it. Look carefully at the cell. Notice that there is a dark border around the cell. Notice also that there is a very small box in the lower right corner of the cell (Fig. 5.4).
2. Point the mouse cursor to the *small box* at the lower right corner of the cell you want to copy. Your cursor will now appear as a crosshair (Fig. 5.5).
3. Hold down the left mouse button, and drag across the range you want to copy to (Fig. 5.6).
4. When you release the mouse button, your entry will be copied to the range of cells you indicated (Fig. 5.7).

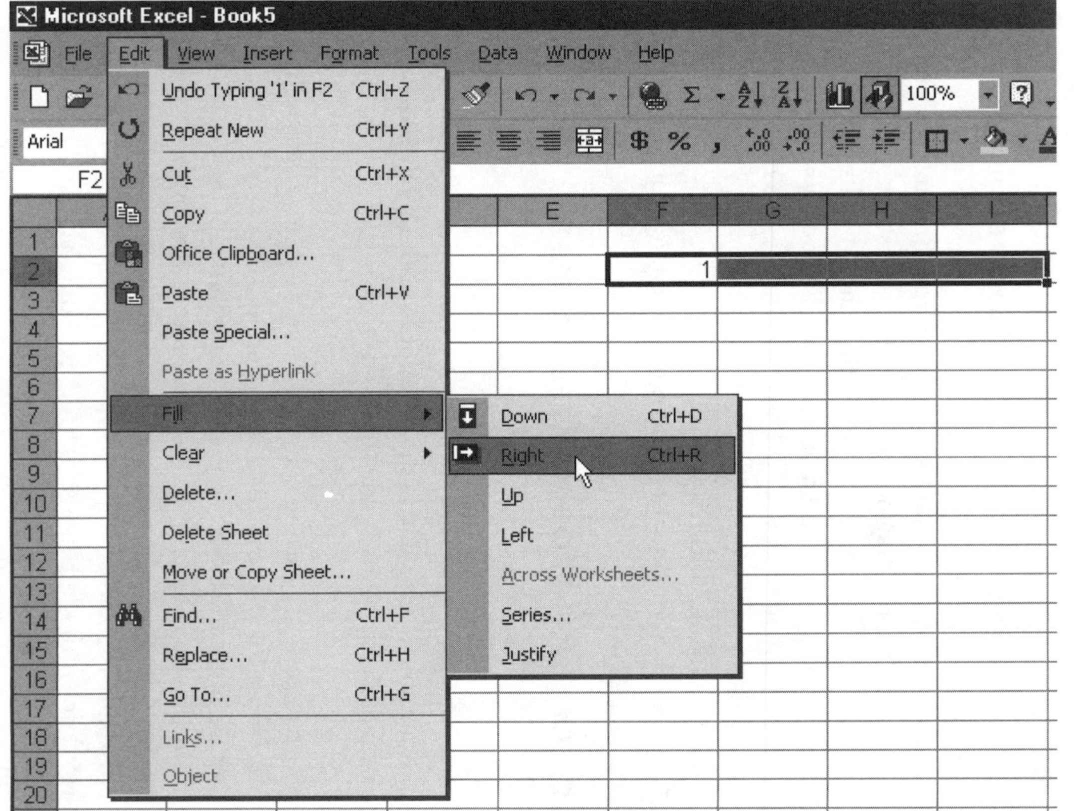
Microsoft Excel - Book5
File
Edit
View
Insert
Format
Tools
Data
Window
Help
100%
Arial
F2
Undo Typing '1' in F2 Ctrl+Z
Repeat New Ctrl+Y
Cut Ctrl+X
Copy Ctrl+C
Office Clipboard...
Paste Ctrl+V
Paste Special...
Paste as Hyperlink
Fill
Clear
Delete...
Delete Sheet
Move or Copy Sheet...
Find... Ctrl+F
Replace... Ctrl+H
Go To... Ctrl+G
Links...
Object
Down Ctrl+D
Right Ctrl+R
Up
Left
Across Worksheets...
Series...
Justify
E
F
G
H
I
1

Figure 5.3.

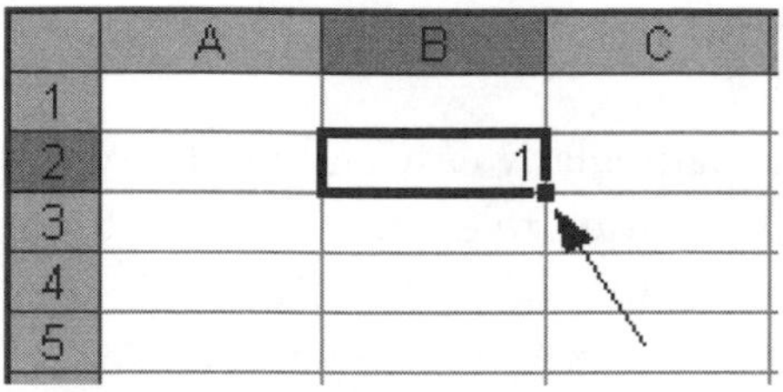

Figure 5.4.

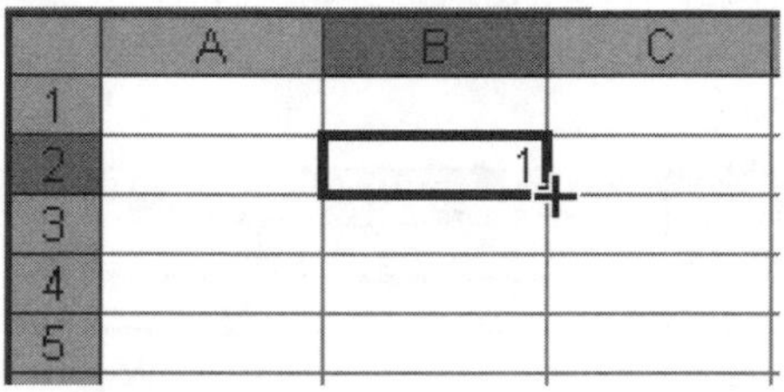

Figure 5.5.

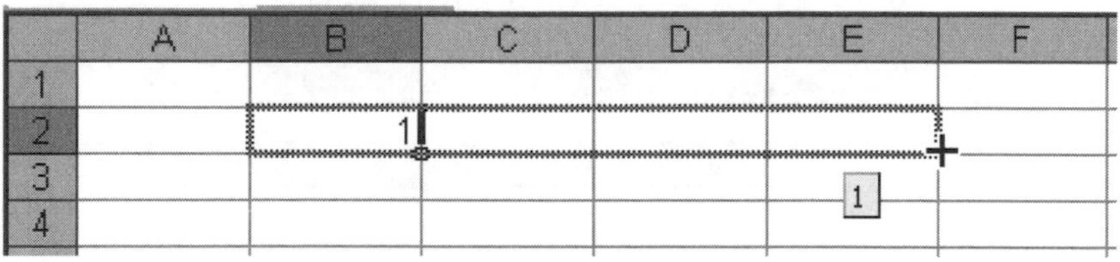

Figure 5.6.

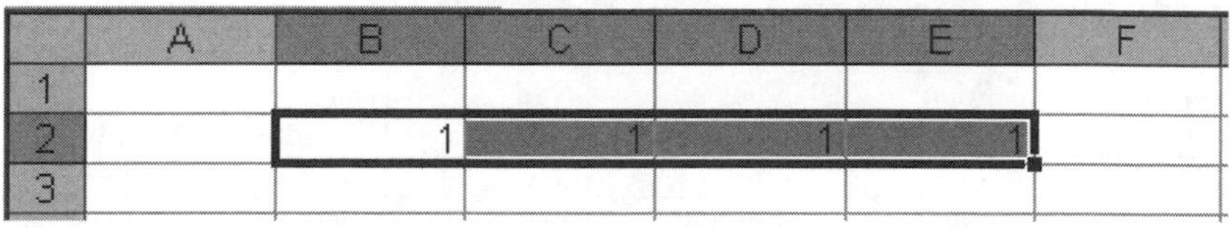

Figure 5.7.

COPYING A SERIES

This last method is particularly easy and most often used. But it has an added advantage if you want to enter a series of items, such as the days of the week or months, to a range of cells.

1. Enter Mon in cell B2, and press [Enter].
2. Now click on cell B2 to select it.
3. Point the cursor to the small box at the bottom right corner of cell B2. Your mouse pointer will appear as a crosshairs.
4. Hold down the left mouse button and drag all the way across to cell F2.

	A	B	C	D	E	F	G
1							
2		Mon					
3					Fri		
4							

Figure 5.8.

Notice that when you release the mouse button the series Mon, Tue, Wed, Thu, Fri has been entered into the range of cells you selected.

	A	B	C	D	E	F	G
1							
2		Mon	Tue	Wed	Thu	Fri	
3							

Figure 5.9.

Try the same thing by entering Monday, Jan, January, Qtr 1, and Exam 1 into other cells.

	A	B	C	D	E	F
1						
2		Mon	Tue	Wed	Thu	Fri
3		Monday	Tuesday	Wednesday	Thursday	Friday
4		Jan	Feb	Mar	Apr	May
5		January	February	March	April	May
6		Qtr 1	Qtr 2	Qtr 3	Qtr 4	
7		Exam 1	Exam 2	Exam 3	Exam 4	Exam 5
8						

Figure 5.10.

Copying a series in this way works in most cases, but it does not work with all cell entries. For example, if you entered the current year into a cell and used this technique to copy it to several other cells, you would not get successive years. When it does work, this technique can be a real time-saver. But, of course, when it does not, you will have to enter your series in a more conventional way.

MOVING CELL ENTRIES

Remember that moving is similar to copying, but that there is a significant difference between the two:

1. When you copy something from one cell to another, the original entry remains in the source cell, and a copy of the entry appears in the destination cell.
2. When you move something from one cell to another, the original entry is moved from the source cell to the destination cell.

Although moving the contents of one cell to another is useful, you will probably find you use the Copy command much more frequently than you use the move function.

STANDARD METHOD OF MOVING

1. Click on the source cell, the cell that contains the entry you want to move.
2. Select Edit, Cut from the menu. This tells Excel you want to remove the entry from the source cell and place it in the Windows Clipboard.
3. Click on the destination cell, the cell you want to move the entry to.
4. Select Edit, Paste from the menu.

Note that you can only move an entry from one cell to one other cell. You cannot move an entry from one cell to a range of cells.

MOVING FROM THE KEYBOARD

You can also move an entry from one cell to another by issuing the Cut and Paste commands from the keyboard.

1. Click on the cell that contains the entry you want to move.
2. Press [Ctrl] [X] to cut the entry from the source cell to the Clipboard.
3. Click on the cell you want to move the entry to.
4. Press [Ctrl] [V] to paste the entry to the destination cell.

MOVING FROM THE TOOLBAR

You can also move an entry from one cell to another by issuing the Cut and Paste commands from the toolbar.

1. Click on the cell that contains the entry you want to move.
2. Click on the Cut button, which has a picture of a scissors on it, to cut the entry from the source cell and place it in the Windows Clipboard.

Figure 5.11.

3. Click on the cell you want to move the entry to.
4. Click on the Paste button, which you will remember has a picture of a clipboard, to paste the entry to the destination cell.

Figure 5.12.

DRAG AND DROP MOVING

There is one final technique to move an entry from one cell to another.

1. Click on the cell that contains the entry you want to move.
2. Move the mouse to point to any *edge* of the cell, but *not* the small box at the lower right corner of the cell. The cursor will appear as an arrow.
3. Hold down the left mouse button and drag the entry to another cell.
4. Release the mouse button to "drop" the entry into the new cell.

	A	B	C
1			
2		Mon	
3			
4			
5			
6			

	A	B	C
1			
2			
3			
4		Mon	
5			
6			

Figure 5.13.

EXERCISE 5

1. Review the standard method of copying an entry from one cell to another cell.
2. Review the standard method of copying an entry from one cell to a range of cells.
3. Explain the role of the Clipboard in the copying process.
4. Describe how to issue the Copy and Paste commands from the keyboard.
5. Describe how to issue the Copy and Paste commands from the toolbar.
6. Explain how fill copying works.
7. Explain how drag copying works.
8. Describe the easiest way to enter Jan, Feb, Mar, Apr, May, Jun, Jul, Aug, Sep, Oct, Nov, Dec into a range of cells.
9. Describe the difference between copying and moving.
10. Describe the standard method of moving an entry from one cell to another.
11. Explain how to move a cell entry from one cell to another using keyboard commands.

12. Explain how to move a cell entry from one cell to another using the toolbar.
13. Explain how to use drag and drop moving.
14. Create the following worksheet.

	A	B	C	D	E
1	Textbook Inventory				
2	English Department				
3					
4			2001	2002	2003
5	English 9 Grammar		200	223	
6	English 10 Grammar		250	248	
7	English 11 Grammar		250	246	
8	English 12 Grammar		250	247	
9	Catcher in the Rye		60	58	
10	Silas Marner		60	55	
11	Hamlet		75	75	
12	Macbeth		75	71	
13					

Figure 5.14.

15. Save the worksheet with the file name TxtInv.
16. Close the worksheet.
17. Open TxtInv.XLS.
18. Enter some additional data.
19. Resave the worksheet.
20. Close the worksheet.
21. Exit from Excel.

FORMULAS: PART I

You have already accomplished a lot. You have learned the basic concepts of using Microsoft Excel, and you have created several worksheets. One of the things that makes Excel an incredibly powerful program is its ability to manipulate numbers—to perform mathematical calculations. This chapter shows how to write formulas that will enable Excel to perform calculations in your worksheets.

Do not be concerned if you are not very good in math. Excel makes writing formulas easy. There is no question about it—you will be able to do it! Writing formulas in Excel is not much harder than using a pocket calculator. Or perhaps, it's even easier. You simply tell Excel what you want it to do, and Excel will do the hard work for you.

DISTINGUISHING FORMULAS

Humans are smarter than Excel. Certainly Excel is fast, and certainly Excel is accurate. And Excel never gets tired. But when it comes to intelligence, you win hands down—Excel isn't even close. Not sure that you believe that? Suppose you had a sheet of paper with the following written on it:

2+3.

You would most certainly recognize that 2+3 is a formula. And you would understand that you were expected to add 2 and 3. Now suppose on another sheet of paper you saw:

987-1234.

You would probably expect that 987-1234 was a telephone number—that you were not expected to subtract 1234 from 987. You were able to make these conclusions because of your superior intelligence. Based on your intelligence and your past experience you know that 2+3 is most likely a formula. And you also know that 987-1234 is most likely a telephone number, not a formula. This might not appear to be very impressive to you. But Excel, not having your intelligence, cannot do it. To Excel, 2+3 and 987-1234 look very much alike.

For this reason, if you want Excel to perform a calculation you must tell Excel that you are writing a formula even *before* you write the formula. You do this by typing an equals sign (=) at the beginning. In other words, every formula in Excel must begin with an equals sign.

WRITING A SIMPLE FORMULA

Create a worksheet as shown in figure 6.1.

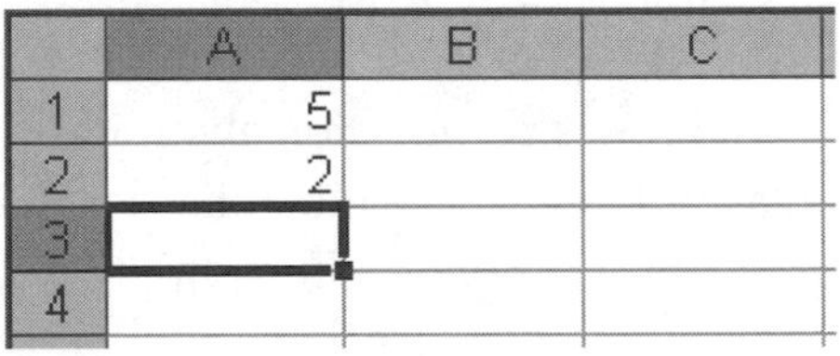

	A	B	C
1	5		
2	2		
3			
4			

Figure 6.1.

Now type the following formula in cell A3:

=5+2

Notice that because you began your cell entry with an equals sign, Excel understood that the entry was a formula. Notice also that Excel performed the calculation the formula called for.

Now, think back to our discussion of cell content and cell display. Remember that:

1. Cell content is what you type into a cell.
2. Cell display is what you actually see in the cell.
3. To determine what the cell display is, look at the cell.
4. To determine what the cell content is, select the cell and then look at the formula bar.

The content of cell A3 is your formula, =5+2. But cell A3's display is the result of performing the calculation the formula called for, in this case, 7.

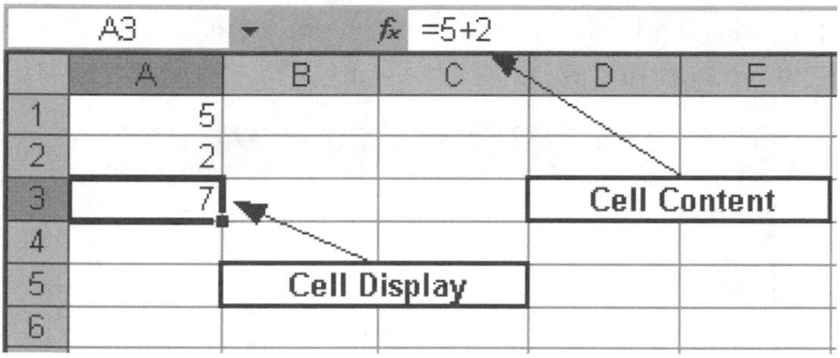

Figure 6.2.

BETTER FORMULAS

The formula you have typed, =5+2, certainly works. But it is not an ideal formula. Suppose you change the numbers in cells A1 and A2. Your formula will no longer produce the correct result. In order for the formula to work, it is necessary for you to rewrite it. But it is possible to write a better formula, one that will produce the correct results even if you change the numbers in cells A1 and A2.

Fortunately, it is easy to write formulas that always produce the correct results. The trick is not to use the numbers you want to add in your formulas. Rather, you will use the *addresses* of the cells that contain the numbers you want to add. It may sound complicated, but it is really very easy. Think about it. Whenever possible, you are going to write formulas using the addresses of the cells that contain your numbers, rather than the numbers themselves.

In cell A4, type the following formula:

=A1+A2

Notice that the formula in cell A4 produces the same result as the formula in cell A3. But now, change the entry in cell A1 from 5 to 7. Notice that the formula in cell A3 no longer produces the correct result. But the formula in cell A4 does!

This has incredible implications for your worksheets. You can create a worksheet, for example, which will add all your student attendance for this week. Next week, you can use the same worksheet by simply entering next week's student attendance figures. The formulas that you write this week will still work next week—and every week! Of course you can write a formula to add the numbers in several cells.

Make the cell entries as shown in figure 6.3.

	A	B	C	D
1			2	
2			4	
3			6	
4			8	
5				
6				

Figure 6.3.

Now type a formula in cell C5 to add all these numbers. The formula is:

=C1+C2+C3+C4

	A	B	C	D
1			2	
2			4	
3			6	
4			8	
5			20	
6				

Figure 6.4.

A BRIEF REVIEW

Remember, the basic rules for writing formulas:

1. To distinguish formulas from other cell entries, Excel requires that all formulas begin with an equals sign (=).

2. Whenever possible, use cell addresses rather than numbers in your formulas.

Subtraction

Writing a subtraction formula is almost identical to writing an addition formula. The only difference, as you probably imagined, is that you use a minus sign (or a hyphen) (−) rather than a plus sign (+).

In cell A5, type the following formula:

=A1-A2

Multiplication

Multiplication is a little more complicated than addition and subtraction. And the complication, again, is a result of the fact that you are more intelligent than Excel.

Look at the following word:

EXTRA

If you were asked what follows E, you would indicate, without hesitation, "*The letter X.*" Now look at the following formula:

=3X4

What follows the 3? *The multiplication sign*, of course. But your computer does not have the ability to differentiate the letter X from the multiplication sign X. It has been taught that X is the letter X. Whenever it sees an X, it sees it as a letter, never as anything else.

So what we need is another symbol to represent multiplication. The symbol that has been chosen to represent multiplication in computer formulas is the asterisk or star (*). Note that if you are using a full-size keyboard (as opposed to a laptop computer keyboard), your computer keyboard probably has two asterisks:

1. The shifted number 8 key at the top of your keyboard.
2. There is another asterisk key on the numeric keyboard at the right side of your keyboard.

They both produce an asterisk. Use whichever you find most convenient.

Now type a formula in cell A6 to multiply the numbers in cells A1 and A2.

=A1*A2

Note that the asterisk or star is used to represent multiplication, not only in Excel, but in all computer programs.

Division

Once you know how to add, subtract, and multiply in Excel, division is easy. The only problem is finding the division sign on the keyboard. Don't spend too much time looking—it isn't there. In Excel, and in all other computer programs, division is represented by the slash (/). Note that there are two slash keys on your keyboard—[/] and [\]. The slash that goes from upper right to lower left [/] is the one that represents division.

In cell A7 type:

=A1/A2

Why the slash? Recall that the slash is used in mathematics to represent division. When you write a fraction, say 1/2, the slash indicates that 1/2 really means 1 divided by 2.

	A	B	C	D
1	7		2	
2	2		4	
3	=5+2		6	
4	=A1+A2		8	
5	=A1-A2		=C1+C2+C3+C4	
6	=A1*A2			
7	=A1/A2			
8				

Figure 6.5.

Percentages

Percentages are calculated as they are in ordinary mathematics. Suppose that you wanted to find 25 percent of the number in cell A1. You would multiply the number in cell A1 by 25 percent.

Type the following formula in cell A8 to perform that calculation:

=A1*25%

Be sure to include the percent sign (%) in your formula. On most keyboards, the percent sign (%) is the shifted number 5 key.

SO WHAT!

Not impressed? You say you could have done the same thing with a pencil and piece of paper or most certainly with an inexpensive pocket calculator? Well, here's something that your pocket calculator cannot do:

1. Change the number in cell A1 to something complicated, say 1234.567.

	A	B	C	D
1	1234.567		2	
2	2		4	
3	=5+2		6	
4	1236.567		8	
5	1232.567		20	
6	2469.134			
7	617.2835			
8				

Figure 6.6.

Notice that as soon as you press [Enter] all your formulas automatically recalculate—instantly!

Wait! The formula in cell A3 did not recalculate. But remember, you wrote that formula before you really knew how to write formulas in Excel—by using cell addresses rather than numbers.

Still not impressed.

2. Now change the entry in cell A2 to 7.00045 and press [Enter]. Again, all your formulas will recalculate the instant you press [Enter].

	A	B	C	D
1	1234.567		2	
2	7.00045		4	
3	=5+2		6	
4	1241.567		8	
5	1227.567		20	
6	8642.525			
7	176.3554			
8				

Figure 6.7.

WRITING FORMULAS BY POINTING

You can also write formulas without typing the actual cell addresses. The steps below will show you how it works. If the idea of doing this appeals to you, you will have to practice. It seems complicated at first, but after you have written several formulas by pointing, it becomes easy.

1. In cell E1, enter the number 5.
2. In cell E2, enter the number 6.
3. Click on cell E3, the cell that will contain the formula, to select it.
4. Type an equals sign [=].
6. Click on cell E1. Notice that the formula bar, at the top of your worksheet, displays =*E1*.
6. Type a plus [+]. The status bar now displays =*E1*+.
7. Now click on cell E2. The completed formula, =*E1*+*E2*, appears on the status bar.
8. Press [Enter] to enter the formula you have created in cell E3.

Try using the pointing method to write subtraction, multiplication, and division formulas in cells E4, E5, and E6.

Remember that writing formulas by pointing seems complicated. But after you have done it several times you will begin to feel really comfortable doing it.

EXERCISE 6

1. How do you indicate to Excel that you are writing a formula? Why is this necessary?
2. Which of the following formulas is better? Explain why?
   =5+2
   =A1+A2
3. Explain how to write an addition formula in Excel.
4. Explain how to write a subtraction formula in Excel.
5. Explain how to write a multiplication formula in Excel.
6. Explain how to write a division formula in Excel.
7. Why is the asterisk (*) used to represent multiplication, rather than the letter X?
8. Why is the slash (/) used to represent division?
9. Explain how to write a formula that calculates 18 percent of a number that appears in cell B6.
10. Describe how to write a formula by pointing.
11. Create a worksheet from the data in figure 6-8.

	A	B	C	D
1	Basic Calculations			
2				
3		5	9	
4		2	3	
5	Add			
6	Subtract			
7	Multiply			
8	Divide			
9	12% of Row 3			
10				

Figure 6.8.

12. Write appropriate formulas in cells B5, B6, B7, B8, and B9 and in cells C5, C6, C7, C8, and C9.
13. Save the worksheet with the file name Basic.

7

FORMULAS: PART 2

In chapter 6 you learned how to write Excel formulas, and this chapter continues that study by explaining some advanced concepts and adding formulas to the STUDPOP file you created and saved in chapter 3.

OPEN THE STUDPOP FILE

Begin by opening STUDPOP.XLS.

1. From the menu, select File, Open.
2. If necessary, select the directory and/or the drive on which you saved STUDPOP.XLS.
3. Click on STUDPOP.XLS to select it.
4. Click on Open.

WRITING ADDITION FORMULAS

You will want to begin by writing a formula in cell F5 to total the Grade 1 figures for each of the four quarters.

1. Click on cell F5 to select it.
2. Type: =B5+C5+D5+E5 and press [Enter].

Note that you want to include cell E5 in the formula, even though it does not currently contain any data. That way, when you do enter data into cell E5, it will not be necessary for you to rewrite the formula. Also do not write formulas in cells F6, F7, F8, F9, or F10 at this time.

You will also want to know the total number of students in Grades 1 through 6 for 1999.

1. Click on cell B11 to select it.
2. Type: =B5+B6+B7+B8+B9+B10 and press [Enter].

Do not write formulas in cells C11, D11, or E11 at this time.

WRITING MULTIPLICATION FORMULAS

You do not know, at this point, how many students will be receiving free milk. But from prior experience, you know it has usually been 20 percent of your total student population. In cell B13, write a formula to calculate 20 percent of the total student population for the school year that began in September 1999:

=B11*20%

Be sure to include the percent sign in your formula.

Similarly, you know that approximately 10 percent of your students receive free lunch. In cell B15, write a formula to calculate 10 percent of the total student population for the school year that began in September 1999:

=B11*10%

Finally, you know that approximately 65 percent of your students receive free transportation. In cell B17, write a formula to calculate 65 percent of the total student population for the school year that began in September 1999.

=B11*65%

	A	B	C	D	E	F	G
1	Student Popluation						
2							
3							
4	Grade	1999	2000	2001	2002	Total	
5	One	325	375	425		=B5+C5+D5+E5	
6	Two	300	350	400			
7	Three	275	325	375			
8	Four	250	300	350			
9	Five	225	275	325			
10	Six	200	250	300			
11							
12	Total	=B5+B6+B7+B8+B9+B10					
13							
14	Free Milk	=B12*20%					
15							
16	Free Lunc	=B12*10%					
17							
18	Free Tranp	=B12*65%					
19							
20							
21							
22							

Worksheet With Formulas Displayed

Figure 7.1.

	A	B	C	D	E	F	G
1	Student Popluation						
2							
3							
4	Grade	1999	2000	2001	2002	Total	
5	One	325	375	425		1125	
6	Two	300	350	400			
7	Three	275	325	375			
8	Four	250	300	350			
9	Five	225	275	325			
10	Six	200	250	300			
11							
12	Total	1575					
13							
14	Free Milk	315					
15							
16	Free Lunch	157.5					
17							
18	Free Tranp	1023.75					
19							
20				Worksheet With			
21				Calculations Displayed			
22							

Figure 7.2.

RESAVE THE WORKSHEET

Since you have made some significant changes to your worksheet, resave it now.

1. Select File, Save from the menu, or click on the Save button on the toolbar, or press [Ctrl] [S].

COPYING FORMULAS

One of the most impressive operations in Excel involves copying a formula from one cell to another or from one cell to a range of cells. When you copy a formula, Excel will automatically adjust the formula for its new location. You will see this by copying the formula in cell B13, to the range of cells C13:E13.

1. Click on cell B13.
2. Select Edit, Copy from the menu.
3. Position your mouse pointer over cell C13—remember, the pointer must appear as a big plus sign. Hold down the left mouse button and drag from cell C13 through cell E13.
4. Select Edit, Paste from the menu.

The formula now appears in each cell in the range B13:E13.

1. Click on cell B13. Look at the formula bar to see the cell content. It is exactly the formula you wrote, =B11*20%.
2. Now click on cell C13 and look at the formula bar. The cell content is =C11*20%.
3. The same thing is true of the entries in cells D13 and E13.

In each case, not only has the formula been copied, but it has also been adjusted or changed so that it is appropriate for its new location.

THIS IS INCREDIBLY IMPORTANT!

Suppose you want to create a worksheet to keep track of total student attendance for every school day of the year. There is no need to write 200 formulas (assuming that your school year is 200 days in length). Simply write one formula, and copy it to the remaining 199 cells! Excel will adjust your original formula 199 times. Automatically!

Now that you know how to copy formulas, copy the remaining formulas in the worksheet. Type the formula in cell:

B15 to the range of cells C15:E15
B17 to the range of cells C17:E17
F5 to the range of cells F6:F10
F5 to cell F13
F5 to cell F15
F5 to cell F17
Finally, resave the worksheet.

1. Select File, Save from the menu, or click on the save button on the toolbar, or press [Ctrl] [S].

	A	B	C	D	E	F	G
1	Student Popluation						
2							
3							
4	Grade	1999	2000	2001	2002	Total	
5	One	325	375	425		1125	
6	Two	300	350	400		1050	
7	Three	275	325	375		975	
8	Four	250	300	350		900	
9	Five	225	275	325		825	
10	Six	200	250	300		750	
11							
12	Total	1575	1875	2175	0	5625	
13							
14	Free Milk	315	375	435	0	1125	
15							
16	Free Lunch	157.5	187.5	217.5	0	562.5	
17							
18	Free Tranp	1023.75	1218.75	1413.75	0	3656.25	
19							

Figure 7.3.

ORDER OF PRECEDENCE

There is something else that you should know about formulas. It is a concept you might have learned in school. But since you probably have not used it in a long time, you may have forgotten it. First, perform the following calculation. Do not type it into a worksheet. Just perform the calculation in your head:

$$=2 + 3 * 4$$

If you are like most people, you answered 20. You added 2 + 3, to get 5. And you then multiplied the result, 5, by 4. Unfortunately, 20 is *not* the correct answer. The correct answer is 14.

There is a rule in mathematics called the *order of precedence*. According to the order of precedence, if a formula includes several different operations, a combination of addition, subtraction, multiplication, and division, the multiplication and division must be done before the addition and subtraction. According to the order of precedence, in this problem you must first multiply 3 * 4, and then add 2 to the result.

1. 3 * 4=12
2. 12 + 2 = 14

Now there are occasions in which you will want to perform the addition and subtraction first. For example, if you want to find the average of 2, 3, and 4, you will want to add 2 + 3 + 4 *before* you divide by 3. The formula =2 + 3 + 4/3 will produce the wrong answer, because it will require that you divide 4 by 3, and then add 2 and 3. For situations such as this one, there is another rule in mathematics, another part of the order of precedence, which says that any part of a formula that is enclosed in parentheses is to be done first, even before multiplication and division. So the order of precedence requires the following:

1. First, do anything that appears within parentheses.
2. Next do multiplication and division that are not enclosed within parentheses.
3. And finally, do addition and subtraction that are not enclosed within parentheses.

The formula to find the average of the numbers 2, 3, and 4 is:

=(2 + 3 + 4)/3

This formula requires that the operations will be carried out in the following order:

1. (2 + 3 + 4) = 9
2. 9/3 = 3

DIVISION BY ZERO

Finally, let's talk about one additional mathematical concept that is frequently misunderstood. Perform the following calculation:

=5/0

The answer: *there is no answer!*

There is a rule in mathematics that you can never divide a number by zero. *NEVER!* Because Excel knows this rule, if you write a formula that involves dividing a number by zero, Excel will display an error message in the cell that will read:

=DIV/0!

This message is an indication that you have asked Excel to perform a calculation that is not permitted.

EXERCISE 7

1. When you ask Excel to copy a cell that contains a formula, does Excel copy the cell content or the cell display?
2. Explain how to copy a formula from one cell to another. From one cell to a range of cells.
3. Describe one worksheet that would be very difficult to create if you did not have the ability to copy formulas.
4. Explain why 2 + 3 * 4 = 14.
5. Perform the following calculation: =9/0. Explain your answer.
6. Create a worksheet from the data in figure 7.4.

	A	B	C	D	E
1	School Bake Sale				
2					
3	Grade	Cookies	Pastries	Cakes	Total
4	1	37	12	15	
5	2	42	8	20	
6	3	22	9	25	
7	Total				
8					

Figure 7.4.

7. Save the worksheet with the file name BakeSale.
8. Write a formula in cell E4 to calculate the total sales for Grade 1.
9. Copy the formula in cell E4 to cells E5:E6.
10. Write a formula in cell B7 to calculate total cookies sold.
11. Copy the formula to cells C8:E8.
12. Resave the worksheet.

13. Close the worksheet.
14. Reopen the worksheet.
15. Change the number of cakes sold in Grade 1 to 17.
16. Resave the worksheet.
17. Close the worksheet.
18. Create a worksheet based on figure 7.5.

	A	B	C	D
1	Library Inventory			
2				
3		2002	2003	Increase
4	Fiction	8234	9214	
5	Non-Fictio	15826	16230	
6	Biography	1246	1246	
7	Reference	1423	1528	
8				

Figure 7.5.

19. Write a formula in cell D4 to calculate the increase in the number of fiction books.
20. Copy the formula to D5:D7.

8

FUNCTIONS

You now know how to create a worksheet and how to include formulas in your worksheet. The formulas you learned certainly do what you want them to. But writing some formulas can be awkward. Look at the worksheet illustrated in figure 8.1.

	A	B	C
1	1		
2	2		
3	3		
4	4		
5	5		
6	6		
7	7		
8	8		
9	9		
10	10		
11			
12			

Figure 8.1.

Assume, for example, that you need to write a formula in cell A11 to add the numbers in cells A1 through A10. The formula would be:

=A1+A2+A3+A4+A5+A6+A7+A8+A9+A10

Although this formula works, typing it is tedious. And if you accidentally press just one incorrect key while you are typing the formula, either your formula will not work or it will return an incorrect answer. Even worse, suppose you had to write a formula to add the numbers in cells A1 through A100. Or cells A1 through A1000! Excel *functions* provide a special way to simplify writing these kinds of formulas.

EXCEL FUNCTIONS

Begin by creating the worksheet as illustrated in figure 8.2.

	A	B	C
1		1	
2		2	
3		3	
4		4	
5		5	
6		6	
7		7	
8	Total		
9			

Figure 8.2.

You could type the following formula in cell B8 to add up all the numbers in cells B1 through B7:

=B1+B2+B3+B4+B5+B6+B7

But writing the formula this way would be inefficient: (1) It would take a relatively long time to type and (2) you might inadvertently type an incorrect character. Excel has many built-in functions that make writing certain kinds of formulas easier. One function allows you to add up the numbers in a range of cells. But before you learn how to use functions, take a minute to review the concept of ranges.

Remember:
A range of cells is a group of cells that meets two conditions:

1. The cells in a range form a continuous area (that is, they are all attached).
2. The cells must form a rectangle or square on the screen.

Remember also:
A range of cells is described by:

1. Indicating the address of the first cell in the range.
2. Then, typing a colon (:) or a period (.).
3. Indicating the address of the last cell in the range.

For example, cells B1, B2, B3, B4, B5, B6, and B7 constitute the range B1:B7, or if you prefer using a period, B1.B7.

For their part, all Excel functions have certain characteristics:

1. Because functions are special formulas, every function begins with an equals sign (=).
2. Every function has a name, which follows the equals sign.
3. All functions contain parentheses, which contain one or more *arguments,* and which follow the name of the function.

Note that spaces are not permitted in functions (there is one special exception, but more about that in a later chapter).

THE SUM FUNCTION

In theory, it sounds complicated. But in practice, you will see that functions are very easy. The SUM( ) function has the following format: =SUM(range). Obviously, range is the range of cells that contains the numbers you want to add.

Now, type a sum function in cell B8 to add all the values in the range of cells B1:B7.

=SUM(B1:B7)

The answer is exactly the same as if you had entered =B1+B2+B3+B4+B5+B6+B7 in cell B8. But, of course it was much easier to type.

Note:

1. Use only a colon (:) or a period (.) to describe a range of cells. If you use anything else, your results will be incorrect.
2. You can copy a function exactly the same way you copy a formula.
3. As with formulas, when you copy a function, it will be adjusted for its new location.

Now copy the function in cell B8 to the range C8:F8.

1. Click on cell B8 to select the function you have written.
2. Select Edit, Copy from the menu.
3. Highlight cells C8:F8.
4. Select Edit, Paste from the menu.

Or use any of the other methods for copying that you have learned.

OTHER FUNCTIONS

You have already learned how to use the =SUM( ) function to simplify writing formulas that add the numbers in a range of cells. Before learning some other commonly used functions, take a moment to review the general rules that apply to all Excel functions:

1. All functions begin with an equals sign (=).
2. All functions must have a name and a beginning and an ending parenthesis. Usually, but not always, there are one or more arguments within the parentheses.
3. Spaces are not permitted in function statements.

Excel has many functions available that have very specialized uses. There are functions for accountants, engineers, statisticians, and for a wide variety of other people who have very specialized needs. But most people use only a relatively small number of Excel's many functions.

The following are the Excel functions that most people find useful:

- **=SUM(range)** adds the values in a range of cells.
- **=MAX(range)** finds the highest number in a range of cells.
- **=MIN(range)** finds the lowest number in a range of cells.
- **=AVERAGE(range)** calculates the average of the numbers in a range of cells.
- **=COUNT(range)** counts the number of cells in a range that contain numbers.
- **=COUNTA(range)** counts the number of cells in a range that contain any entries (text, numbers, and formulas).

To see how they work, include the functions shown in figure 8.3 in your worksheet.

	A	B	C
1		1	
2		2	
3		3	
4		4	
5		5	
6		6	
7		7	
8	Total	=SUM(B1:B7)	
9	Average	=AVERAGE(B1:B7)	
10	Highest	=MAX(B1:B7)	
11	Lowest	=MIN(B1:B7)	
12	Number	=COUNT(B1:B7)	
13			

Figure 8.3.

Of course, your worksheet will display the numbers, rather than the functions.

	A	B	C
1		1	
2		2	
3		3	
4		4	
5		5	
6		6	
7		7	
8	Total	28	
9	Average	4	
10	Highest	7	
11	Lowest	1	
12	Number	7	
13			

Figure 8.4.

THE AUTO SUM BUTTON

Of the functions you have learned, which do you think you will use most often? For most people, the answer is the =SUM( ) function. For this reason, Excel has made it even easier to use the =SUM( ) function. There is an Autosum button on the toolbar. It is the button that looks like the Greek letter S, which is called Sigma. If you are not familiar with the Greek Sigma, it looks like a crude capital letter E (Σ). Find the Autosum button on your toolbar.

Figure 8.5.

Using the Autosum button will usually simplify writing formulas that calculate the sum of the numbers in a range of cells. Amazingly, the Autosum button will generally determine the range of cells you want to add without your having to enter it.

Clear all the functions that you have typed in your worksheet.

1. Use your mouse to drag across cells B8:B12.
2. Select Edit, Clear, All from the menu, or press [Delete].

You will now use the Autosum button to write a formula in cell B8 that will add the numbers in cells B1:B7.

1. Click on cell B8 to select it.
2. Press the Autosum button on the toolbar. Your formula will appear in cell B8, with the range to be summed faintly outlined.
3. Check to see that the formula is correct. If it is, press [Enter] to actually enter the formula into cell B8.

	A	B	C	D
1		1		
2		2		
3		3		
4		4		
5		5		
6		6		
7		7		
8	Total	=SUM(B1:B7)		
9		SUM(**number1**, [number2], ...)		
10				

Figure 8.6.

Important note:

Autosum usually works. But there are times when it will not correctly identify the range of cells you want to add. When you use the Autosum button, always check that the formula is correct before you press [Enter].

The following example shows a situation in which Autosum does not work. Erase the worksheet and create a new worksheet based on figure 8.7.

In this worksheet, you will write a formula in cell B7 that will add all the numbers in the range B1:B6.

	A	B	C
1		3	
2		6	
3			
4		9	
5		12	
6		15	
7	Total		
8			

Figure 8.7.

1. Click on cell B7 to select it.
2. Click on the Autosum button.
3. Look at the formula bar. Excel has written the formula =SUM(B4:B6).

	A	B	C	D
1		3		
2		6		
3				
4		9		
5		12		
6		15		
7	Total	=SUM(B4:B6)		
8		SUM(**number1**, [number2], ...)		
9				

Figure 8.8.

4. Since the range is not the range you had intended, it will be necessary to manually correct the range.
5. Use the mouse to point the cursor to the center of cell B1—your cursor should look like a big plus sign.
6. Hold down the left mouse button.
7. Drag the mouse down until you reach the center of cell B6.
8. Release the mouse button.
9. The formula bar now indicates the correct formula. Press [Enter] to enter the correct formula into cell B7.

	A	B	C	D
1		3		
2		6		
3				
4		9		
5		12		
6		15		
7	Total	=SUM(B1:B6)		
8		SUM(**number1**, [number2], ...)		
9				

Figure 8.9.

OTHER AUTOFUNCTIONS

Starting with version XP, Excel makes several other commonly used Autofunctions available from the toolbar. The process is very similar to using the Autosum button. For example, in the worksheet shown in figure 8.10, suppose you wanted to write a formula in cell B6 to calculate the average of the numbers in cells B1:B5.

	A	B	C	D	E	F
1		2				
2		4				
3		6				
4		8				
5		10				
6	Average					
7						

Figure 8.10.

1. Click on cell B6 to select it.
2. Click on the [Down Arrow] key just to the right of the Autosum button.
3. Click on Average (Fig 8.11).
4. Check to see that the formula is correct. Because it is, press [Enter] to enter the formula into cell B6 (Fig 8.12).

EXERCISE 8

1. What are the disadvantages of writing long formulas?
2. What two conditions must a group of cells meet for them to be considered a range?
3. Explain how to describe a range of cells.
4. Explain what the =SUM( ) function does, and how to use it.
5. What happens when you copy a function from one cell to another?
6. Describe the functions you have learned and how to use each.
7. Describe how to use the Autosum button.

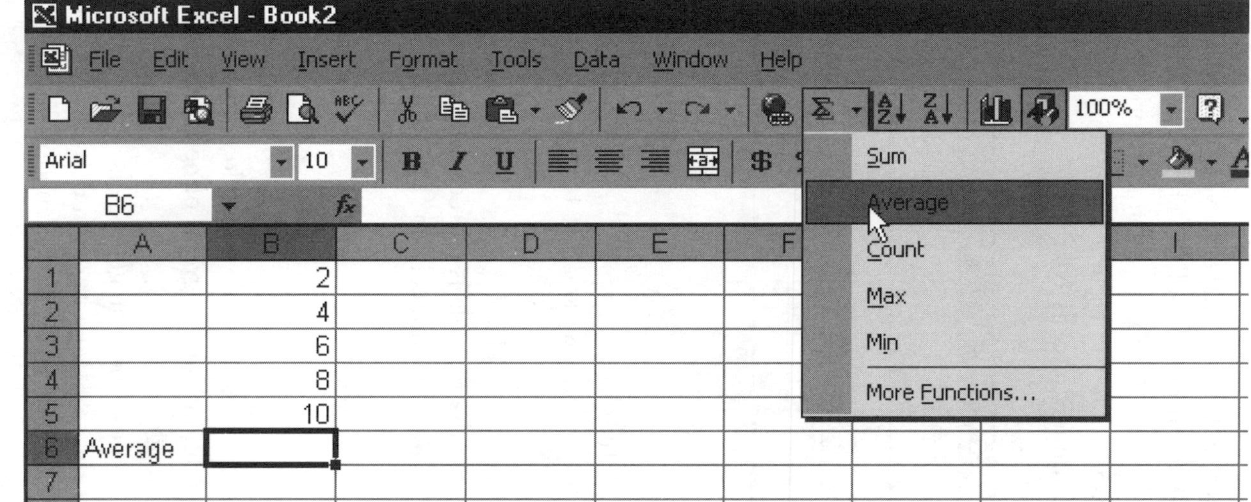
Microsoft Excel - Book2
File
Edit
View
Insert
Format
Tools
Data
Window
Help
100%
Arial
10
B6
A
B
C
D
E
F
I
1
2
3
4
5
6
7
2
4
6
8
10
Average
Sum
Average
Count
Max
Min
More Functions...

Figure 8.11.

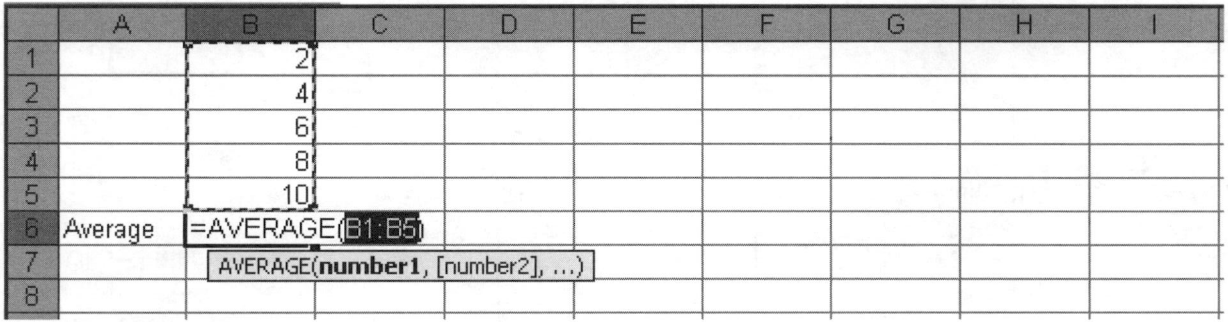

	A	B	C	D	E	F	G	H	I
1		2							
2		4							
3		6							
4		8							
5		10							
6	Average	=AVERAGE(B1:B5)							
7		AVERAGE(**number1**, [number2], ...)							
8									

Figure 8.12.

	A	B	C	D	E	F	G	H	I	J
1	Daily Attendance Analysis									
2	Students Absence By Day Of Week									
3										
4	Week Of:	3-Mar-03								
5										
6		Mon	Tue	Wed	Thu	Fri	Total	Average	Highest	Lowest
7	Grade 10	5	7	9						
8	Grade 11	4	5	2						
9	Grade 12	8	3	5						
10	Total									
11	Average									
12	Highest									
13	Lowest									
14										

Figure 8.13.

8. Why is it important to always check a function created with the Autosum button before you press [Enter]?
9. If Autosum produces a formula with the incorrect range, explain how to correct the formula.
10. Describe how to use the Autosum button to write a function to calculate the average of a range of numbers.
11. Create a worksheet from the data in figure 8.13.
12. Save the worksheet with the file name DailyAtt.
13. Write appropriate formulas in cells G7, H7, I7, J7, B10, B11, B12, and B13.
14. Copy the formulas as appropriate.
15. Resave the worksheet.

9

FORMATTING NUMBERS: PART I

You now know how to create worksheets, how to save and open worksheets, and how to include formulas and functions in your worksheets. Your worksheets do what they were designed to do. But your worksheets do not look very pretty. For example, numbers appear in their most basic form, rather than as currency or percentages.

Excel allows you to format individual cells and ranges of cells so that the numbers they contain will look more attractive and more professional. For example, if 1500.5 appeared in a cell in your worksheet and represented currency, you could direct Excel to display it as $1,500.50.

Something important to remember is that formatting changes only the *appearance* of your worksheet, rather than the actual entries in the cells. In other words, when you format a cell, you change only the *cell display*. The *cell content* remains unchanged. Using the example above, if you format a cell that contains the number 1500.5 for currency, the cell display will be $1,500.50. But the cell content remains 1500.5. This may not seem very important right now, but you will see later that it can be extremely important.

UNDERSTANDING HOW EXCEL FORMATS NUMBERS

When you format a number in an Excel worksheet, you must first select the cell (or the range of cells) that contains the number (or numbers) you want to format. Then, you select a format from a collection of predefined formats that Excel provides for you. Excel displays the predefined formats as pictures. The pictures are fairly easy to understand in the more recent versions of Excel. But the system for formatting numbers in older versions was much more difficult and cumbersome.

You probably have a version of Excel that uses the newer formatting system. However, if you are using an older version of Excel, you will find formatting instructions for your version at the end of this chapter.

CREATE A WORKSHEET

Begin by creating a worksheet like the one in figure 9.1.

	A	B	C	D	E
1	1.1				
2	1.4				
3	1.7				
4	123				
5	123.4				
6	123.45				
7	123.456				
8	1234				
9	1234.56				
10	-1234.56				
11					
12					
13					
14		Minus or Negative 1234.56			
15					

Figure 9.1.

You will now begin by formatting the number in cell A1.

1. Click on cell A1 to select it.
2. Select Format, Cells from the menu.
3. The formatting dialog box will open. The dialog box contains several tabs along the top. If the Number tab is not selected, click on the Number tab to select it.
4. On the left side of the Number dialog box you will see the types of formats that are available to you—Number, Currency, and so on. Select Number format.
5. On the right-hand side of the Number dialog box is a section labeled, *Sample*. Inside the Sample section, you should see 1.10. If you leave the settings the way they are, that is what your number will look like when formatted. That is, your number will be displayed with two decimal places.
6. Below the Sample box is the *Decimal Places* section. Currently, the number of decimal places is set at 2. You can select another number of decimal places by typing a new number over the number 2, or by clicking on the upward or downward facing arrows next to the number 2. Notice that as you change the number of decimal places, the number in the Sample box changes to reflect your selection.
7. Below the Decimal Places section is a check box with the title, *Use 1000 Separator*. Currently the box is not checked.
8. The Use 1000 Separator box only affects numbers that are greater than 999. If you were formatting a cell that contained the number 1234, and you did not place a checkmark in this box, the number 1234 would appear as 1234 (that is, without a comma to set off the thousands). But if you checked this option, the number 1234 would appear as 1,234.
9. Below the Use 1000 Separator section is the *Negative Numbers* section.

Notice that there are currently four choices in this section.

a. −1234.10—negative numbers will appear preceded by a minus sign (−).
b. 1234.10 [in red]—negative numbers will appear in red, but without a minus sign (−).

   c. (1234.10) [in black]—negative numbers will appear in parentheses and in black.
   d. (1234.10) [in red]—negative numbers will appear in parentheses and in red.
10. Select the negative number option you prefer.
11. Click on OK. Your format will be applied to the number in cell A1.

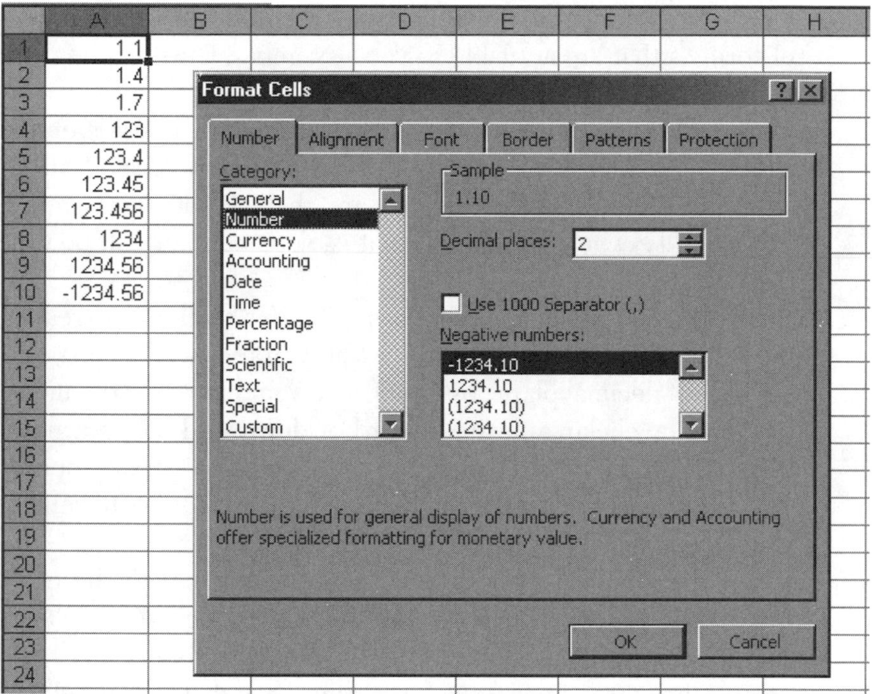

Figure 9.2.

CELL CONTENT VERSUS CELL DISPLAY

Remember the distinction between cell content and cell display:

1. Cell content is what you typed into a cell.
2. Cell display is what you see if you look at the cell.

Remember also that you can easily determine cell content and cell display:

1. To determine cell display, simply look at what appears in the cell.
2. To determine cell content, look at the formula bar at the top of your worksheet.

NOW THIS IS REALLY IMPORTANT

1. When you format a cell, you change the cell display—that is, what the number in the cell looks like.
2. When you format a cell you do *not* change the cell content—the number you have entered into the cell.

For example, assume that you entered the number 1.1 in cell A1. If you format the cell for 0 decimal places, the cell display will be 1 (that is, 1.1, rounded to the nearest whole number). But the cell content will still be 1.1.

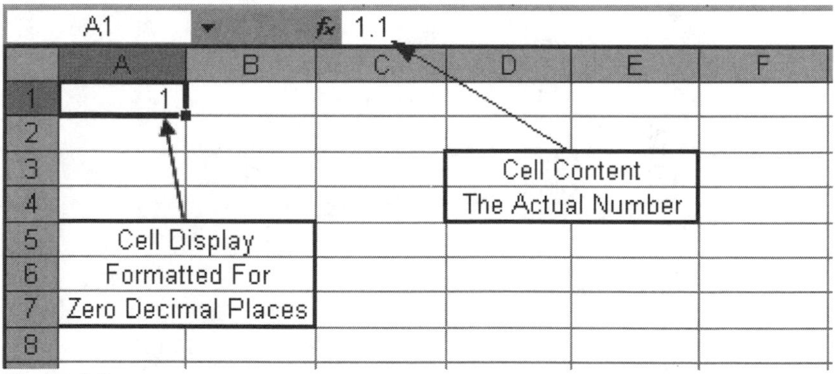

Figure 9.3.

And even more importantly, if you write a formula that references a number in a formatted cell, Excel will use the cell content, not the cell display, in the calculations that involve that cell.

FORMAT A RANGE OF CELLS

You are now ready to format all the numbers in Column A.

1. Use your mouse to point the cursor to the center of cell A1—the cursor will appear as a big plus sign. Hold down the left mouse

button as you drag your mouse downward, across the range of cells A1:A10 to select (highlight) them.
2. Select Format, Cells from the menu.
3. If the Number tab is not selected, click on it.
4. Select the following format:
   a. Two decimal places.
   b. Use 1000 separator.
   c. Negative numbers displayed in parentheses and in red.
5. Click OK.
6. Note that all your numbers are displayed in the format you have selected.

	A	B	C	D
1	1.10			
2	1.40			
3	1.70			
4	123.00			
5	123.40			
6	123.45			
7	123.46			
8	1,234.00			
9	1,234.56			
10	(1,234.56)			
11				

Figure 9.4.

Now, experiment by applying several different formats to the cells in A1:A10.

FORMATTING AND ENTIRE COLUMN OR ROW

You will often find it easiest to format an entire column or row at one time.

1. To select an entire column, click on the letter of the column just above your worksheet. You will select every cell in that column.

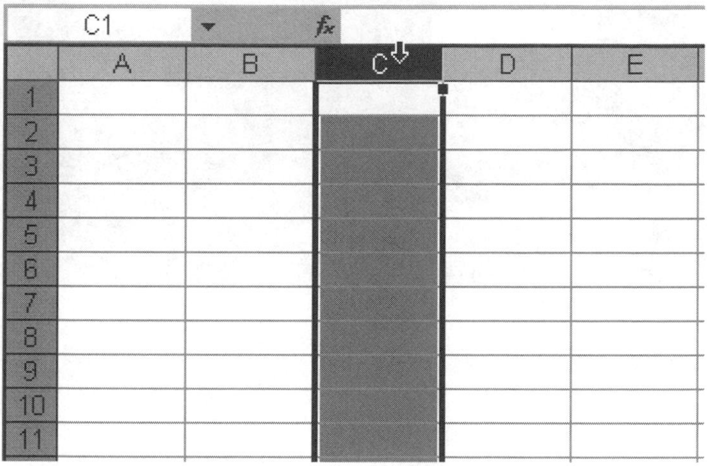

Figure 9.5.

2. To select an entire row, click on the number of the row, just to the left of your worksheet. You will select every cell in that row.

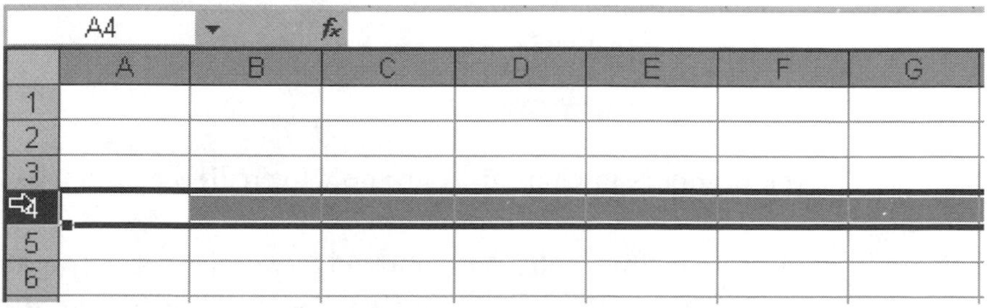

Figure 9.6.

3. You can also select all the cells in an entire worksheet. Notice that just to the left of the A that represents Column A, and just above the 1 that represents row 1, there is a small rectangle. Click on that rectangle to select every cell in your worksheet.

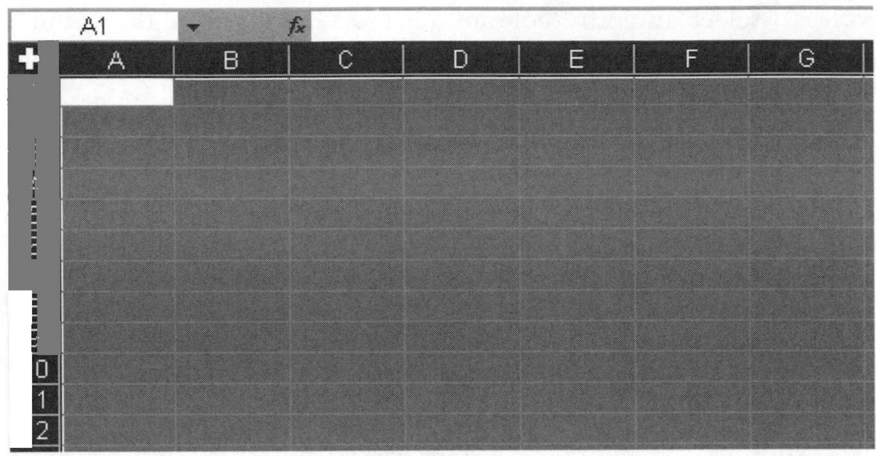

Figure 9.7.

Use the first technique to format all the cells in Column A.

1. Click on the letter A at the top of Column A to select all the cells in Column A.
2. Now select Format, Cells, from the menu, and click on the Number tab.
3. Select Number format.
4. Select a format you feel is appropriate.
5. Click OK.

Note that all the numbers in Column A are now formatted as you have chosen.

Next, type numbers into cells A11 and A12, which to this point have not contained any numbers. Note that they are formatted according to the format you selected. This points out a very important concept: *You do not format a number—you format a cell.* So, any number that you type into a formatted cell will take on that cell's format.

You formatted all the cells in Column A, even the cells that were empty. Then, when you typed something into one of those cells, it took on the format you had previously assigned to the cell.

FORMATTING AS YOU ENTER DATA

Excel allows you to format cells as you enter data into them.

1. Type $123 into a blank cell, and press [Enter].
2. You have entered the number 123 into the cell and formatted the cell for currency format in one step.
3. Now type 456 into the same cell (that is, replace 123 with 456) and press [Enter]. Since the cell is already formatted, any number you type into that cell will be displayed in the format that you previously assigned to the cell.

CLEARING A CELL

You have learned how to clear a cell by selecting Edit, Clear, All from the menu. Actually, the Edit, Clear command gives you several options.

- **Edit, Clear, All** Clears the cell's contents *and* the cell's formatting.
- **Edit, Clear, Formats** Clears the cell's formatting, but not its contents (that is, the number remains in the cell, but it is no longer formatted).
- **Edit, Clear, Contents** (Edit, Clear, Formulas in some earlier versions of Excel) Clears only a cell's contents (the number, text, or formula that is in the cell), but the cell's formatting remains.

SAVING CELL FORMATS

When you save a worksheet in which you have formatted cells, your formatting will be automatically saved with the worksheet.

GENERAL FORMAT

General format refers to a number in its natural state—without any formatting. That is, the number appears just as you have typed it into the cell, with only the required number of decimal places, and no formatting.

FORMATTING NUMBERS IN EARLIER VERSIONS OF EXCEL

Note: Unless you are using an older version of Excel, you can skip this section.

If you are using a version of Excel prior to version 7 or version 97, Excel uses the following formatting symbols to create formatting pictures. You use these formatting pictures to format the cells in your worksheets. This is a little complicated—but you can do it.

Formatting Symbol Zero (0)—Required Digit

The 0 symbol in an Excel formatting picture represents a required digit. That is, Excel format 0 requires at least one required digit, and since there are no decimal points in 0 format, no decimal places will be displayed.

In 0 format:

- The number 1 would be displayed as 1 (0 format calls for at least one required digit—in this case, there is only one digit).
- The number 12 would be displayed as 12 (0 format calls for at least one required digit—in this case, there are two).
- The number 12.3 would be displayed as 12 (since 0 format does not permit decimal places, the number is rounded to the nearest integer or whole number).
- The number 12.8 would be displayed as 13 (again the number is rounded to the nearest integer).
- The number 0.2 would be displayed as 0 (0 format requires at least one digit—when rounded to the nearest whole number, 0.2 becomes 0).

Formatting Symbol Period (.)—Decimal Point

The period represents a decimal point. Using both the 0 and the decimal point, you can create formatting picture 0.00. The format 0.00 would require at least one digit, a decimal point, and exactly two decimal places.

In 0.00 format:

- The number 1 would be displayed as 1.00.
- The number 1.2 would be displayed as 1.20.
- The number 1.234 would be displayed as 1.23 (rounded off to two decimal places).
- And the number 1.238 would be displayed as 1.24 (also rounded off to two decimal places).

Formatting Symbol Comma (,)—Thousands Separator

The comma is used to indicate thousands.

- In the 0,000 format, the number 1234.56 would be displayed as 1,235.
- And in 0,000.00 format, the number 1234.56 would be displayed as 1,234.56.

But this introduces a problem. Remember that the 0 formatting symbol indicates a required digit. So in format 0,000, the number 2 would be displayed as 0,002. Another formatting symbol, #, corrects this problem.

Formatting Symbol Number Sign (#)—Optional Digit, Display Only if Reasonable

The number sign (#) symbol directs Excel to display a number only if it makes sense to display it. That sounds complicated, but here is how it works.

- In format #,##0 the number 1234 is displayed as 1,234.
- And in format #,##0 the number 2 is displayed simply as 2.
- Similarly, in format #,##0.00 the number 1234 is displayed as 1,234.00.
- And in format #,##0.00 the number 2 is displayed as 2.00.

Formatting Symbol Dollar Sign ($)—Indicate Currency

The dollar sign ($) simply indicates that a dollar sign is to be displayed.

- In format $#,##0, the number 1234 is displayed as $1,234.

Formatting Symbol Percent Sign (%)—Indicate Percentage

The percent sign (%) simply indicates that a percent sign is to be displayed.

- In format 0.00%, the number .25 would be displayed as 25.00%.
- In format 0%, .25 would be displayed as 25%.

Formatting Symbol Semicolon (;)—Separates Positive and Negative Formats

The semicolon separates positive and negative formats. The format before the semicolon is the format if the number is positive, and the format after the semicolon is the format if the number is negative.

- In format $#,##0;($#,##0) the number 1234 would be displayed as $1,234.
- In the same format, the number −1234 would be displayed as ($1,234).
- In format $#,##0.00;[red]($#,##0.00) the number 1234 would be displayed as $1,234.00.
- And in the same format, −1234 would be displayed in red as ($1,234.00).

Review of Formatting Symbols

The following symbols are used in earlier versions of Excel to describe various number formats.

- zero (0)—required digit
- period (.)—decimal point
- comma (,)—thousands separator
- number sign (#)—optional digit
- dollar sign ($)—currency
- percent sign (%)—percentage
- semi-colon (;)—separates positive and negative formats

Once you know these symbols, formatting is accomplished very similar to the way it is done in later versions of Excel.

1. Select the cell or cells you want to format.
2. Select Format, Cells from the menu.
3. In the Format dialog box, if the Number tab is not selected, click on it.
4. Select the kind of formatting you want (e.g., Number, Currency, Percent).
5. Select an appropriate format from the formatting pictures that are displayed.
6. Click OK.

EXERCISE 9

1. Describe how to format a cell.
2. Explain the difference between cell content and cell display.
3. How can you determine a cell's display? A cell's content?
4. When you format a cell, are you changing the cell's content or its display? How can you tell?
5. Describe how to format a range of cells.
6. Describe how to format an entire column or row.
7. Explain how to format cells as you enter data.
8. Why is it important to save a worksheet after you have formatted it?
9. Create a simple worksheet from figure 9.8.

	A	B
1	1.4	
2	1.4	
3	=SUM(A1:A2)	
4		

Figure 9.8.

10. Format the range of cells A1:A3 for number format with 0 decimal places.
11. Your worksheet indicates that 1 + 1 = 3. How can that be?
12. Also format the numbers in two of the worksheets you have previously created.

10

FORMATTING NUMBERS: PART 2

You should now feel reasonably comfortable formatting numbers. In this chapter you will learn some advanced formatting techniques. You will also format the numbers in some of the worksheets you have previously created, and you will learn what to do when your formatted numbers are too big to fit in cells. Finally, you will learn some easier ways to format numbers.

Easier ways! You must be wondering if there are easier ways, why did you have to learn the "hard ways" in chapter 9? The reason is that if you are not able to format numbers in the traditional way, it is unlikely you will be able to successfully format the numbers in all of your worksheets.

FIRST COMMENTS

At this point, you should feel fairly comfortable with the concepts in chapter 9. If you aren't, it would be a good idea to reread chapter 9 before you begin this chapter. When you are ready to proceed, begin by opening the REPORT.XLS worksheet that you created in Exercise 7.

FORMATTING CONVENTIONS

Before you format any worksheets, you should be aware of a universally followed formatting convention. If your worksheet consists largely of financial data, it is customary not to use dollar signs throughout the worksheet. Figure 10.1 is an example of a worksheet that uses dollar signs throughout. Notice that all the dollar signs make the worksheet look a little confusing.

	A	B	C	D	E	F
1	Sales of Widgets					
2	By Division					
3						
4						
5		Jan	Feb	Mar	Apr	Total
6	North	$1,000.00	$1,500.00	$ 2,000.00	$ 2,500.00	$ 7,000.00
7	South	$1,500.00	$2,000.00	$ 2,500.00	$ 3,000.00	$ 9,000.00
8	East	$2,000.00	$2,500.00	$ 3,000.00	$ 3,500.00	$11,000.00
9	West	$2,500.00	$3,000.00	$ 3,500.00	$ 4,000.00	$13,000.00
10	Total	$7,000.00	$9,000.00	$11,000.00	$13,000.00	$40,000.00
11						

Figure 10.1.

Standard practice is to include the dollar signs in the top row, and also in any rows that contain totals. Figure 10.2 shows how the same worksheet looks using the standard formatting convention. Notice how much better the second worksheet looks.

	A	B	C	D	E	F
1	Sales of Widgets					
2	By Division					
3						
4						
5		Jan	Feb	Mar	Apr	Total
6	North	$1,000.00	$1,500.00	$ 2,000.00	$ 2,500.00	$ 7,000.00
7	South	1,500.00	2,000.00	2,500.00	3,000.00	9,000.00
8	East	2,000.00	2,500.00	3,000.00	3,500.00	11,000.00
9	West	2,500.00	3,000.00	3,500.00	4,000.00	13,000.00
10	Total	$7,000.00	$9,000.00	$11,000.00	$13,000.00	$40,000.00
11						

Figure 10.2.

CREATING A NEW WORKSHEET

You are now ready to create and format a worksheet.

1. Create a worksheet from figure 10.3.

	A	B	C	D	E	F
1	Faculty Salaries					
2	2003 Academic Years					
3						
4	First	Last	Department	Basic	Extra	Total
5	Name	Name		Salary	Pay	Salary
6	John	Adams	English	35000	2000	
7	Denise	Baker	Math	37000	5000	
8	Maria	Chavez	English	39000	0	
9	Edith	Davis	Music	41000	1000	
10	Barbara	Eaton	Math	43000	6000	
11	Edward	Franklin	English	45000	15000	
12						
13			Total			

Figure 10.3.

2. Type a formula in cell F6 to calculate the first faculty member's Total Salary.
3. Copy the formula to the range of cells F7:F11.
4. Type a formula in cell D13 to calculate the total Basic Salary of all faculty members.
5. Copy the formula to E13:F13.
6. Select Save As from the File menu and name the worksheet FACSAL.

FORMAT THE NUMBERS

Since the numbers in D6:F6 represent currency, you will want to apply currency formatting to these cells.

1. Begin by selecting or highlighting cells D6:F6.
2. Select Format, Cells from the menu, and click on the Number tab.

	A	B	C	D	E	F
1	Faculty Salaries					
2	2003 Academic Years					
3						
4	First	Last	Department	Basic	Extra	Total
5	Name	Name		Salary	Pay	Salary
6	John	Adams	English	35000	2000	37000
7	Denise	Baker	Math	37000	5000	42000
8	Maria	Chavez	English	39000	0	39000
9	Edith	Davis	Music	41000	1000	42000
10	Barbara	Eaton	Math	43000	6000	49000
11	Edward	Franklin	English	45000	15000	60000
12						
13			Total	240000	29000	269000

Figure 10.4.

3. From the categories at the left of the Number Formatting dialog box, select Currency.
4. Two decimal places are selected. Since you want two decimal places, do not change that.
5. Under Symbol, you will see a dollar sign ($). Do not change this.
6. Select a format that you feel is appropriate for negative numbers.
7. Click OK.

A PROBLEM!

Depending on the version of Excel you are using, some of your numbers may have been replaced with a series of number signs ####### (Fig. 10.5).

Do not be concerned if this has happened. Your worksheet has not been damaged. Click on any cell containing #######. Look at the formula bar at the top of your screen to see the cell content. You data are still intact (Fig. 10.6).

What has happened is that your cell entry, formatted as you requested it, is too big to fit in the cell.

	A	B	C	D	E	F
1	Faculty Salaries					
2	2003 Academic Years					
3						
4	First	Last	Department	Basic	Extra	Total
5	Name	Name		Salary	Pay	Salary
6	John	Adams	English	#########	$ 2,000.00	#########
7	Denise	Baker	Math	37000	5000	42000
8	Maria	Chavez	English	39000	0	39000
9	Edith	Davis	Music	41000	1000	42000
10	Barbara	Eaton	Math	43000	6000	49000
11	Edward	Franklin	English	45000	15000	60000
12						
13			Total	240000	29000	269000

Figure 10.5.

D6 | fx 35000

	A	B	C	D	E
1	Faculty Salaries				
2	2003 Academic Years			Cell Content	
3					
4	First	Last	Department	Basic	
5	Name	Name		Salary	
6	John	Adams	English	#########	
7					
8					
9					
10					Cell Display

Figure 10.6.

CHANGING THE COLUMN WIDTH

The simple solution is to change the width of any cells that contain ########. However, you cannot change the width of a single cell. It would look confusing if different cells in a column were of different widths. So if you want to change the width of a cell, Excel requires you to change the width of all the cells in that column.

It is easy to manually change the width of all the cells in a column.

1. Using your mouse point the cursor to the line between B and C at the top of your worksheet. The cursor will appear as a two-sided arrow.
2. Hold down the left mouse button, and drag to the right to increase the width of the column, or to the left to decrease its width.
3. Release the mouse button and the column will assume the width you have specified.

	A	B	C	D	E	F
1	Faculty Salaries					
2	2003 Academic Years					
3						
4	First	Last	Department	Basic	Extra	Total
5	Name	Name		Salary	Pay	Salary
6	John	Adams	English	$35,000.00	$ 2,000.00	$37,000.00
7	Denise	Baker	Math	37000	5000	42000
8	Maria	Chavez	English	39000	0	39000
9	Edith	Davis	Music	41000	1000	42000
10	Barbara	Eaton	Math	43000	6000	49000
11	Edward	Franklin	English	45000	15000	60000
12						
13			Total	240000	29000	269000

Figure 10.7.

If your version of Excel automatically adjusted the widths of the cells, use this technique to reduce the width of one of your columns so that you can see a cell with ########. Then increase the width of the column to make the number visible again.

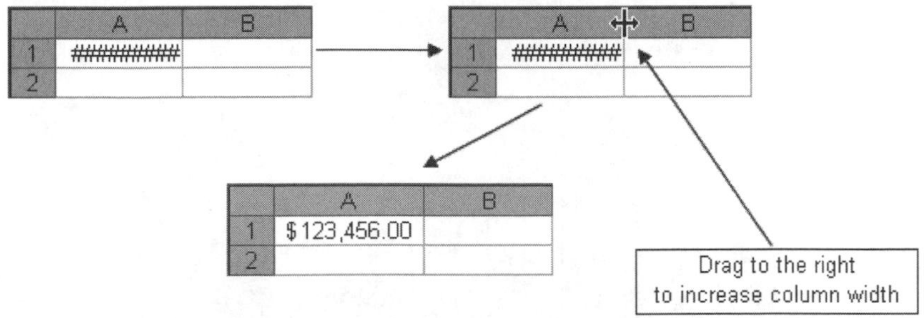

Figure 10.8.

Another way to change the width of the cells in a column is to let Excel select the best column width for you.

1. Choose the column whose width you want Excel to autoadjust. Point the cursor to the line between the letter of that column and the column to its right. The cursor will appear as a two-sided arrow.
2. Double click the left mouse button to adjust the column width to the best fit for your data.

CHANGING THE WIDTHS OF SEVERAL COLUMNS AT ONE TIME

Suppose you want to change the widths of Columns A through F at one time.

1. Position the cursor to point to the letter A at the top of Column A.
2. Hold down the left mouse button—all the cells in Column A will be selected.
3. Still holding down the left mouse button, move the pointer across to the letter F at the top of Column F. This will select Columns A through F.
4. Now point to the division marker between Columns A and B. Drag it to the left or right. The widths of all the columns you selected will change together.

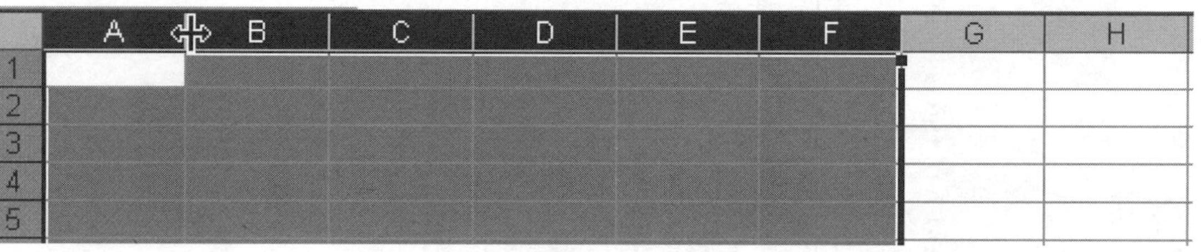

Figure 10.9.

FORMAT CELLS

You will want to format cells D7:F10 for currency format *without* the dollar signs. This format is called *comma format.* That is, you want thousands separated by commas, and you want two decimal places.

1. Select or highlight cells D7:F10.
2. From the menu, select Format, Cells.
3. If the Number tab is not selected, click on the tab to select it.
4. Select the category Currency. You will want two decimal places, but change the Symbol from $ to None. Select an appropriate format for Negative Numbers.
5. Click OK.

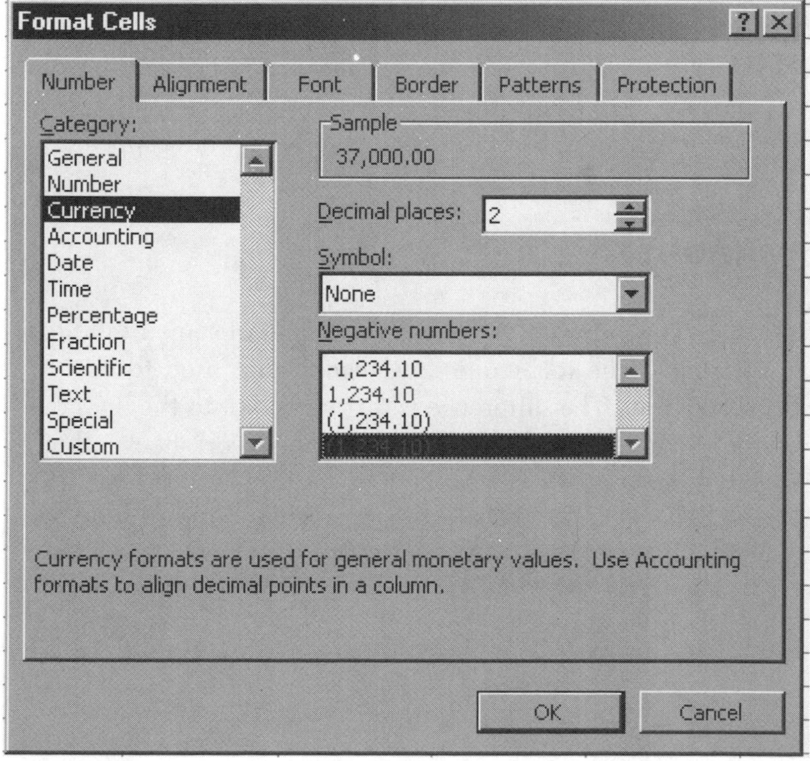

Figure 10.10.

COMPLETE THE FORMATTING

Finally, apply Currency formatting *with* the dollar sign to row 13, and resave the worksheet.

	A	B	C	D	E	F
1	Faculty Salaries					
2	2003 Academic Years					
3						
4	First	Last	Department	Basic	Extra	Total
5	Name	Name		Salary	Pay	Salary
6	John	Adams	English	$ 35,000.00	$ 2,000.00	$ 37,000.00
7	Denise	Baker	Math	37,000.00	5,000.00	42,000.00
8	Maria	Chavez	English	39,000.00	0.00	39,000.00
9	Edith	Davis	Music	41,000.00	1,000.00	42,000.00
10	Barbara	Eaton	Math	43,000.00	6,000.00	49,000.00
11	Edward	Franklin	English	45,000.00	15,000.00	60,000.00
12						
13			Total	$240,000.00	$ 29,000.00	$269,000.00

Figure 10.11.

Notice how much more professional the worksheet now appears.

ROW HEIGHTS

Occasionally, you will want to change the height of some of the rows in your worksheet. The technique is similar to that used to change the width of a column. The difference is that you point to the divisions between the row numbers at the left side of your worksheet rather than the divisions between the column letters.

	A	B	C
1			
2			
3			
4			

Figure 10.12.

FORMATTING NUMBERS FROM THE TOOLBAR

Now that you know the traditional way to format a worksheet, here is an even easier way. You can also format text by using toolbar buttons.

1. Select (highlight) the cells you want to format.
2. Click on the appropriate toolbar button.

Using the Increase and Decrease Decimal Places Buttons

If you wanted to use the toolbar buttons to format a cell for currency with zero decimal places (Fig. 10.13), simply follow this procedure:

1. Click on the cell you want to format for currency format with zero decimal places.
2. Click on the Dollar Sign button to format the cell for currency with two decimal places.
3. Click on the Decrease Decimal Places button twice to remove both decimal places.

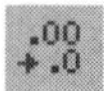

Figure 10.14.

	A	B
1	123	
2		

	A	B
1	$ 123.00	
2		

	A	B
1	$ 123	
2		

Figure 10.15.

You may be wondering why, if there is an easy way to format numbers in cells, we began by showing you the complicated way in the previous chapter. There are two reasons:

1. If you don't learn the standard way to format a cell, you are likely to encounter problems at some point that you will not know how to resolve.
2. There are some formatting options that are not available from the toolbar.

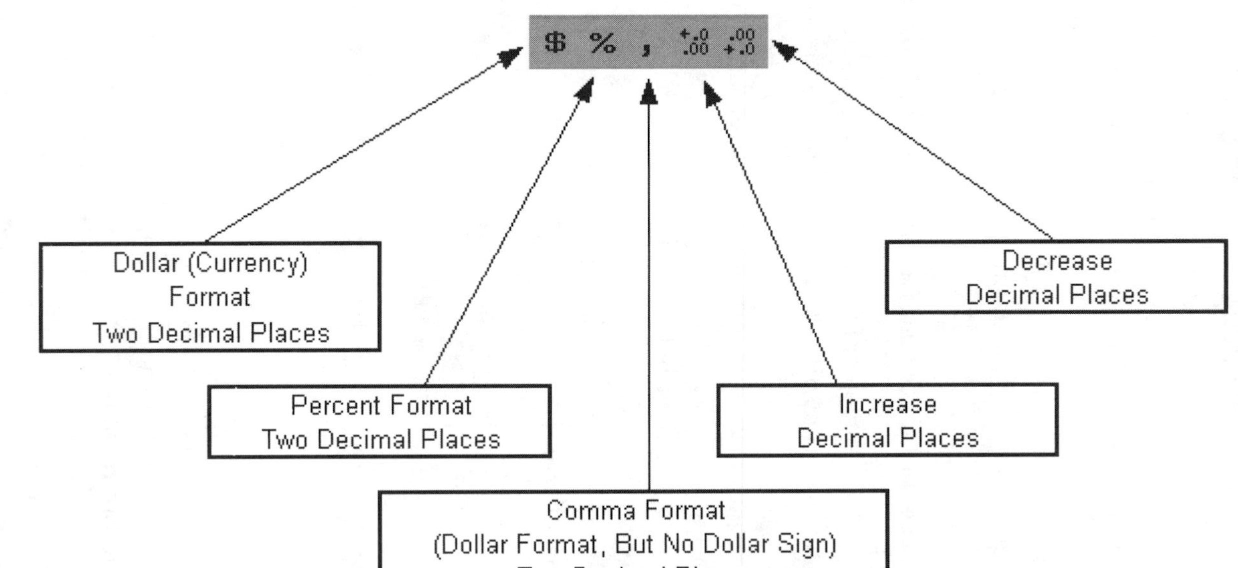
$ % , +.0 .00 .00 +.0
Dollar (Currency)
Format
Two Decimal Places
Percent Format
Two Decimal Places
Comma Format
(Dollar Format, But No Dollar Sign)
Two Decimal Places
Increase
Decimal Places
Decrease
Decimal Places

Figure 10.13.

But as a practical consideration, you will probably do most of your formatting from the toolbar.

EXERCISE 10

1. Explain the convention that is generally observed when formatting a worksheet for currency.
2. What is indicated when the number in a cell is replaced by #######?
3. How would you resolve this problem?
4. Describe two ways to change the width of a column.
5. Explain how to change the widths of several columns simultaneously.
6. What are the five number formatting buttons on the toolbar? Explain how to use each.
7. Explain the process you would use to format a cell for currency format, with zero decimal places, using the toolbar.
8. Create a worksheet from figure 10.16.

	A	B	C	D	E
1	Teacher Salary Analysis				
2					
3		2001	2002	2003	Average
4	Adams	28000	29200	31300	
5	Baker	42000	44500	46800	
6	Chin	37900	39400	42000	
7	Davis	52000	55000	57500	
8	Average				
9	Highest				
10	Lowest				
11					

Figure 10.16.

9. Write formulas where necessary.
10. Copy the formulas as appropriate.
11. Assign appropriate number formatting.
12. Save the worksheet as SalAnal.

11

FORMATTING TEXT

Now that you know how to format numbers in your worksheets, you will probably agree that your worksheets have a much more professional-looking appearance. This chapter explains how to format the text in your worksheets.

OPEN THE WORKSHEET

Begin by opening the STUDPOP.XLS worksheet you created in chapter 3 and updated in chapter 7.

1. Select File, Open from the menu.
2. Select STUDPOP.XLS.
3. Click OK.

ADJUSTING COLUMN WIDTHS

Note that some of the text entries in Column A have been *truncated* or cut off because there is not enough room to display them fully. You can remedy this problem easily by widening Column A. You have already learned how to do this by dragging the division marker between Columns A and B to the right, or by double clicking on the division marker between Columns A and B to let Excel determine the best column width.

	A	B	C	D	E	F
1	Student Population					
2						
3						
4	Grade	1999	2000	2001	2002	Total
5	One	325	375	425		1,125
6	Two	300	350	400		1,050
7	Three	275	325	375		975
8	Four	250	300	350		900
9	Five	225	275	325		825
10	Six	200	250	300		750
11						
12	Total	1,575	1,875	2,175	-	5,625
13						
14	Free Milk	315	375	435	-	1,125
15						
16	Free Lunch	158	188	218	-	563
17						
18	Free Transportation	1,024	1,219	1,414	-	3,656
19						

Figure 11.1.

A WORD OF CAUTION

Don't make your columns too wide! Always remember the universal law, *TANFL*. Don't know about TANFL? Think about it for a minute . . . TANFL stands for: *There Ain't No Free Lunch*! How does TANFL apply to changing column widths?

You can increase the width of any column in an Excel worksheet. But, you obviously cannot increase the width of your computer screen. So the more you increase the width of the columns in your worksheet, the fewer columns will be visible on your computer screen. Yes, you can make your columns as wide as you want. But as with almost everything else, you pay a price. Increase the widths of your columns when you need to. But always keep in mind TANFL!

TEXT ALIGNMENT

Text alignment refers to where your text is located in a particular cell. Text may be left aligned, center aligned, or right aligned.

Remember:

1. The default alignment for text is left alignment.
2. The default alignment for numbers is right alignment.

The default alignment works most of the time, but there are cases in which it does not. In this case, right align the entries in cells A5:A10:

1. Drag across the range of cells A5:A10 to select (highlight) them.
2. From the menu, select Format, Cells. Click on the Alignment tab, select Right, then click OK.

You will probably want to center align the years, in cells B4 through E4, and the word Total in cell F4.

1. Drag on the range of cells B4:F4 to select (highlight) them.
2. From the menu, select Format, Cells. Then select Alignment, Center, OK.

	A	B	C	D	E	F
1	Student Population					
2						
3						
4	Grade	1999	2000	2001	2002	Total
5	One	325	375	425		1,125
6	Two	300	350	400		1,050
7	Three	275	325	375		975
8	Four	250	300	350		900
9	Five	225	275	325		825
10	Six	200	250	300		750
11						
12	Total	1,575	1,875	2,175	-	5,625
13						
14	Free Milk	315	375	435	-	1,125
15						
16	Free Lunch	158	188	218	-	563
17						
18	Free Transportation	1,024	1,219	1,414	-	3,656
19						
20						

Figure 11.2.

TEXT ALIGNMENT FROM THE TOOLBAR

You can also align text from the toolbar by using the Left, Center, and Right Alignment toolbar buttons shown in figure 11.3.

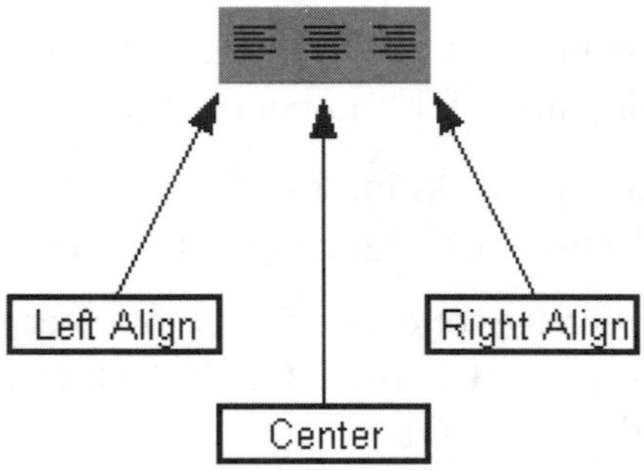

Figure 11.3.

Use the toolbar alignment buttons to experiment with different cell alignments in your worksheet.

FONTS

Look at text and numbers in different places: newspapers, magazines, advertisements, posters, signs, and invitations. You will see that the design of the letters and numbers varies from one document to another.

A *font* is simply a set of letters and numbers with a particular design. There are thousands of different styles or designs of type, each of which conveys a different feeling. Each of these fonts is referred to by its individual name.

Because there are so many different fonts, fonts are usually divided into three groups: *decorative*, *serif*, and *sans serif*.

Decorative Fonts

Decorative fonts are fancy. The type used on wedding invitations, for example, or diplomas, or garage sale posters is usually a decorative font. Decorative fonts are eye-catching. They get your attention. But in bodies of text, decorative fonts are often difficult to read. With very few exceptions, decorative fonts are not appropriate for spreadsheets.

Serif Fonts

A serif font is one in which all the letters and numbers have serifs. That is a fine definition—if you know what a serif is. Serifs are little hooks or extensions on the ends of all the letters and numbers in a serif font. Serif fonts are very popular for what is called *body text*. That is, they are used for large blocks of text in relatively small sizes. The body text in most newspapers, books, and magazines is generally set in a serif font.

ABCDEFabcdef123456 ABCDEFabcdef123456

ABCDEFabcdef123456

Figure 11.4. Examples of three serif fonts

Sans Serif Fonts

The word *sans* in French means without. Sans serif fonts are those in which the letters and numbers do not have serifs or extensions. Sans serif fonts are very popular in large sizes such as headlines and posters. Because they are cleaner looking than serif fonts, sans serif fonts are generally used in spreadsheet work. Excel is usually configured to display your text and numbers in a sans serif font called Arial.

ABCDEFabcdef123456

Figure 11.5. The Arial sans serif font.

Generally, sans serif fonts work best in Excel spreadsheets.

FONT SIZES

In addition to selecting a font for your work, you can also vary the size of the type. Type size is usually expressed in points. Technically, 1 point = 1/72 inches. It is not necessary to remember that number, but remember the larger the point size, the larger the type. Generally, you will use a 10-point font in your worksheets. If you want larger text and numbers, simply select a larger point size.

This is 8-point type.
This is 10-point type.
This is 12-point type.
This is 14-point type.
This is 18-point type.
This is 24-point type.

SETTING THE FONT AND SIZE FROM THE MENU

The standard way to change the font and font size is from the Format menu.

1. Click on the cell that contains the entry whose font and/or size you want to change. If you want to change the entries in a range of cells, hold down the left mouse button and drag the mouse pointer across all the cells to select all the cells in the range.
2. Select Format, Cells from the menu. Then click on the Font tab.
3. Click on the name of a font. Notice that the font you have chosen is displayed in the Preview box.
4. Click on a font size. Notice that the font size is displayed in the Preview box.
5. When you have selected an appropriate font and size, click OK.

Note: Some fonts cannot be resized. However, fonts that are called *TrueType fonts* can all be resized. You can tell if a font is a TrueType font by the letters TT that appear just to the left of its name.

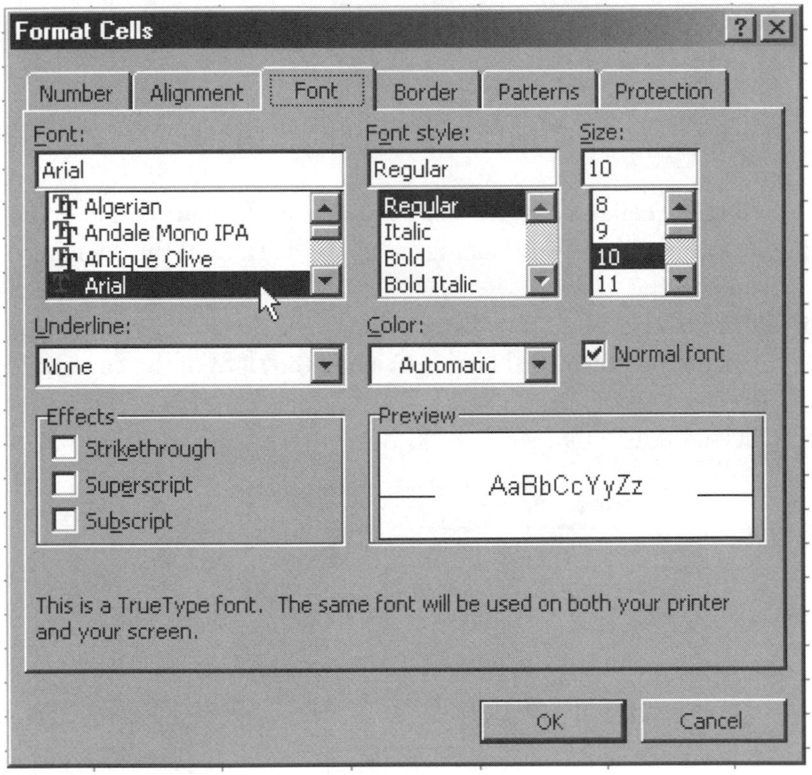

Figure 11.6.

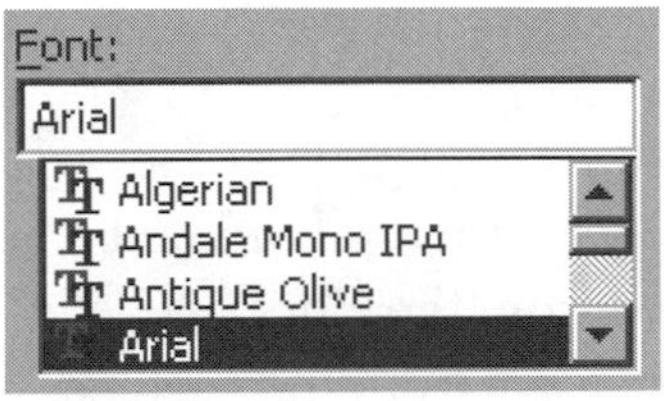

Figure 11.7.

SETTING THE FONT AND FONT SIZE FROM THE TOOLBAR

You can also set the font and font size from the toolbar.

1. Select the cell or cells whose font and font size you want to change.
2. Click on the downward facing arrow to the right of the current font name on the toolbar.
3. Click on a new font to select it.
4. Click on the downward facing arrow to the right of the current font size on the toolbar.
5. Click on a new font size.

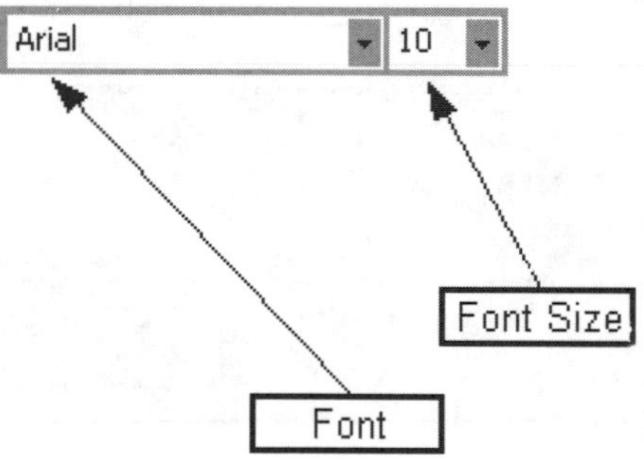

Figure 11.8.

In most cases you will find that changing the font and font size from the toolbar is quicker and easier than using the Format, Font menu.

FONT STYLES

Finally, each font can be displayed in one of several different styles. The most common styles you will use are bold, italic, and underline. While font styles can be changed from the Format, Cells, Font menu, the easiest way to change font styles is from the toolbar.

To change the font style of a cell or range of cells from the toolbar:

1. Select the cell or cells whose font style you want to change.
2. Click on the bold, italic, or underline button on the toolbar.

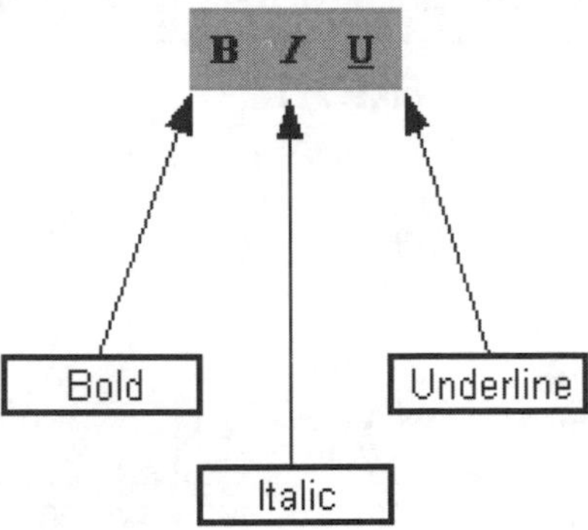

Figure 11.9.

Note that when you have applied a style to a cell entry and that cell is selected, the corresponding button on the toolbar will be surrounded by a dark border or will appear lighter in color. This gives the impression that the tool or button is depressed.

You can also remove a style that is inappropriate. For example, suppose you have bolded the entry in a cell or a range of cells, and you now want to remove the bold style.

1. Select the cell or range of cells. Note that the Bold button on the toolbar is surrounded by a dark border, or is lighter in color, indicating that the bold style has been applied to the entry in the cell or cells.
2. Click on the Bold button on the toolbar. Bold will no longer be applied to the cell entry.

PUTTING IT INTO PRACTICE

Use the concepts you have learned to format text in the STUDPOP worksheet. Change alignments, fonts, font sizes, and font styles. Obviously, there is no one right way to format the text in a worksheet. Your worksheet may, or may not, look like the example in figure 11.10.

	A	B	C	D	E	F
1	**Student Population**					
2						
3						
4	Grade	1999	2000	2001	2002	Total
5	*One*	325	375	425		**1,125**
6	*Two*	300	350	400		**1,050**
7	*Three*	275	325	375		**975**
8	*Four*	250	300	350		**900**
9	*Five*	225	275	325		**825**
10	*Six*	200	250	300		**750**
11						
12	**Total**	**1,575**	**1,875**	**2,175**	-	**5,625**
13						
14	**Free Milk**	**315**	**375**	**435**	-	**1,125**
15						
16	**Free Lunch**	**158**	**188**	**218**	-	**563**
17						
18	**Free Transportation**	**1,024**	**1,219**	**1,414**	-	**3,656**

Figure 11.10.

CENTERING THE TITLE

You will now center the worksheet title across the top of the worksheet. You have seen how easy it is to center text within a cell using the Center Alignment button on the toolbar. But here, you will want to center a text entry across a range of cells. You cannot use the center text button to do this.

1. Highlight cells A1:F1, the range of cells across which you want to center the worksheet title that appears in cell A1.
2. Select Format, Cells from the menu, and then click on the Alignment tab.
3. Select Center Across Selection.
4. Click OK.

Note: You can also center text across a range of cells by highlighting the range of cells and clicking on the *Merge and Center* button on the toolbar (note that in some versions of Excel this button is called the *Center Across Selection* button).

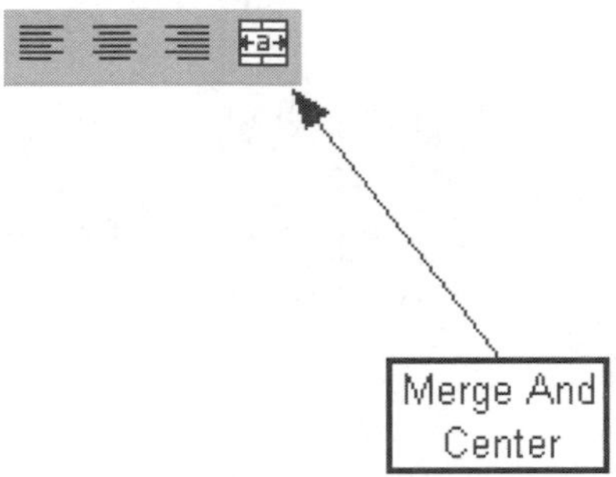

Figure 11.11.

	A	B	C	D	E	F
1	Student Population					
2						
3						
4	Grade	1999	2000	2001	2002	Total
5	*One*	325	375	425		1,125
6	*Two*	300	350	400		1,050
7	*Three*	275	325	375		975
8	*Four*	250	300	350		900
9	*Five*	225	275	325		825
10	*Six*	200	250	300		750
11						
12	Total	1,575	1,875	2,175	-	5,625
13						
14	Free Milk	315	375	435	-	1,125
15						
16	Free Lunch	158	188	218	-	563
17						
18	Free Transportation	1,024	1,219	1,414	-	3,656
19						
20						
21						

Figure 11.12.

OUTLINING AND SHADING

1. Click on cell A1. When you centered Student Population across the range of cells A1:F1, you also merged all these cells into cell A1. So the entire section is selected.
2. Select Format, Cells from the menu. Then click on the Border tab.
3. Select Outline.
4. Select a Line Style for your outline.
5. Now click on the Patterns tab.
6. Click on the downward facing arrow next to the Pattern box.
7. Select a fairly light pattern or color (a darker color or pattern will obscure your text).
8. Click OK.

LEFT, RIGHT, TOP, AND BOTTOM LINES

You can also draw lines at the left, right, top, and bottom of selected cells.

1. Select the appropriate cells.
2. Select Format, Cells from the menu, and then select the Borders tab.
3. Click on Left, Right, Top, Bottom, or any combination of these.
4. Select a style for your lines.
5. Click OK.

SAVE THE WORKSHEET

Notice how much more attractive and professional looking your worksheet now appears. Resave the completed worksheet.

1. Select File, Save from the menu.

	A	B	C	D	E	F
1	Student Population					
2						
3						
4	Grade	1999	2000	2001	2002	Total
5	*One*	325	375	425		**1,125**
6	*Two*	300	350	400		**1,050**
7	*Three*	275	325	375		**975**
8	*Four*	250	300	350		**900**
9	*Five*	225	275	325		**825**
10	*Six*	200	250	300		**750**
11						
12	Total	**1,575**	**1,875**	**2,175**	-	**5,625**
13						
14	Free Milk	**315**	**375**	**435**	-	**1,125**
15						
16	Free Lunch	**158**	**188**	**218**	-	**563**
17						
18	Free Transportation	**1,024**	**1,219**	**1,414**	-	**3,656**
19						
20						

Figure 11.13.

EXERCISE 11

1. Why is it sometimes not practical to adjust column width by double clicking?
2. Explain the term *text alignment.*
3. What three text alignment options are available to you in Excel?
4. What is the default alignment for text entries in cells?
5. What is the default alignment for number entries in cells?
6. Explain how to change the alignment of a cell entry from the menu.
7. Explain how to change the alignment of a cell entry from the toolbar.
8. What is a font?
9. What are the three types of fonts?
10. Explain how the font types differ and the general uses for each.
11. How are font sizes measured?
12. Explain how to change the font and font size of a cell entry using the Excel menu.

13. Explain how to change the font and font size of a cell entry using the Excel toolbar.
14. What are the advantages of changing font and size from the menu? From the toolbar?
15. What are the three major font styles?
16. What is the advantage of using TrueType fonts?
17. Explain how to change the font style of a cell entry.
18. Explain how to center text across a range of cells.
19. Explain how to outline and shade cells.
20. How can you ensure that the entry in a cell you shaded will be legible?
21. Explain how to add lines to the left, right, tops, and bottoms of cells.
22. Create a worksheet from figure 11.14.

	A	B	C	D
1	Textbook Inventory			
2	English Department			
3				
4		2001	2002	2003
5	English 9 Grammar	200	223	
6	English 10 Grammar	250	248	
7	English 11 Grammar	250	246	
8	English 12 Grammar	250	247	
9	Catcher in the Rye	60	58	
10	Silas Marner	60	55	
11	Hamlet	75	75	
12	Macbeth	75	71	
13				

Figure 11.14.

23. Format the worksheet appropriately, and then save the worksheet.

12

PAGE SETUP AND PRINTING

You are now ready to print your worksheet. Of course, you can just click on the Print button on the toolbar—and you have probably been doing that all along. But if you have special print needs, or if want to take advantage of some of Excel's special print options, you will need to print your worksheet using the Excel menu. Additionally, the Page Setup command allows a considerable number of options so you can further tailor your printout to your specific needs.

PAGE SETUP

Page setup allows you to specify how your worksheet will appear when you print it. You can change the default page setup options from the File, Page Setup menu.

1. Select File, Page Setup from the menu.
2. Notice that the Page Setup window has several tabs: Page, Margins, Header/Footer, Sheet.

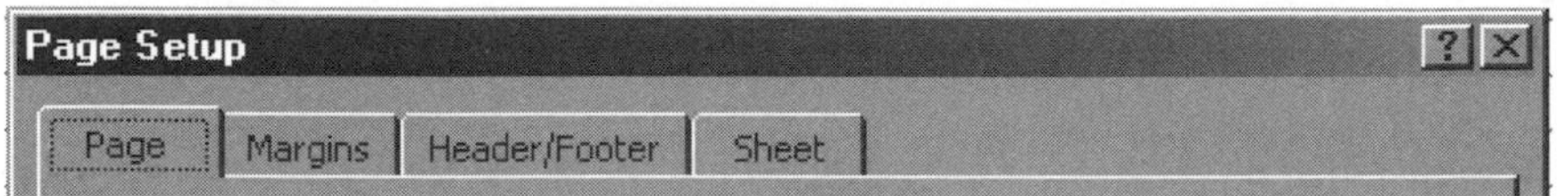

Figure 12.1.

The Page Tab

When you select File, Page Setup from the menu, you will usually find the Page tab displayed. If the Page tab is not selected, click on it now to choose it. The options shown in figure 12.2 are available from the Page tab.

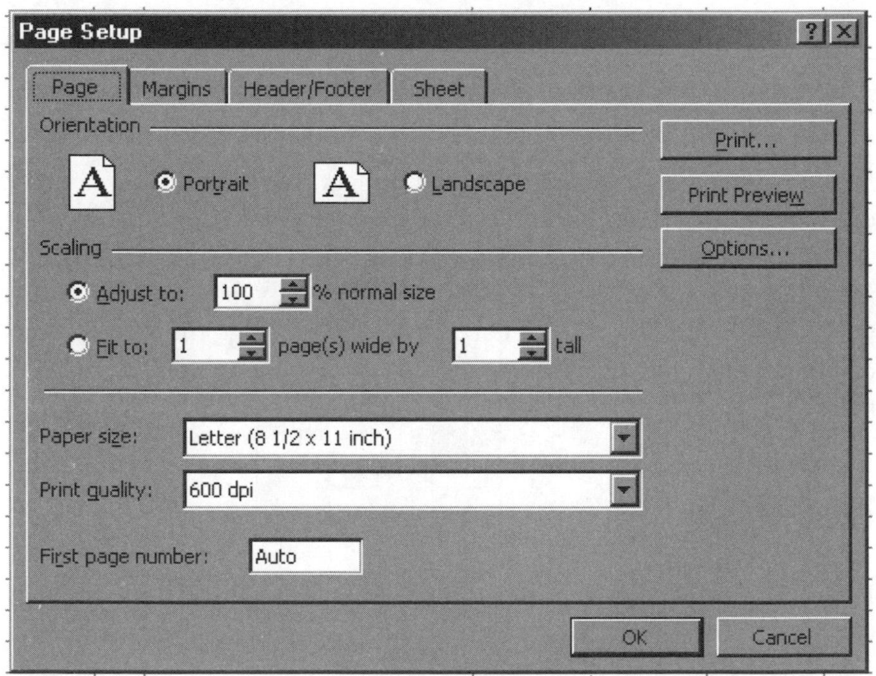

Figure 12.2.

Portrait and Landscape Orientation

Portrait orientation positions your worksheet in the most common page format—that is, the page is positioned so it is taller than it is wide. But you may also select *Landscape* orientation, which positions the page so it is wider than it is tall. Portrait orientation is the default. But if your worksheet is wider than it is tall, as most worksheets are, click on Landscape orientation to select it.

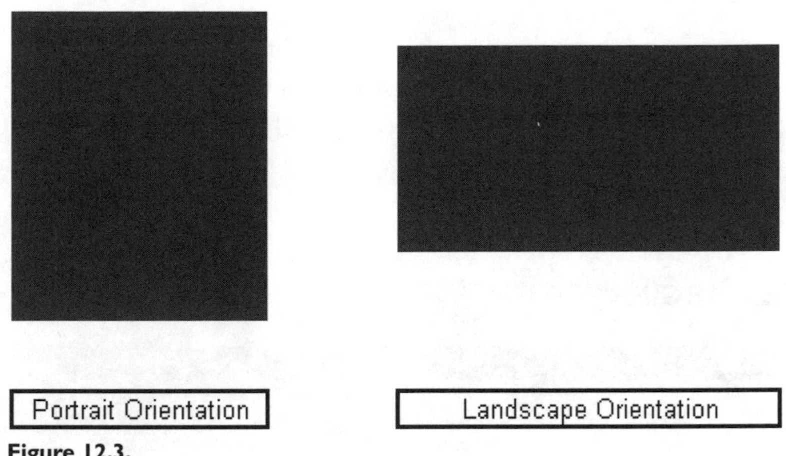

Figure 12.3.

Adjust to 100% Normal Size

Adjust to 100% Normal Size is the default option. That is, your printed worksheet will be approximately the same size as your worksheet appears on your screen. If you change 100% to another number, say 90%, your worksheet and all the text and numbers in it will appear at 90% of the size of your on-screen worksheet.

If your worksheet is just a little too big to fit on the page, try 95%, or 90%, or even a smaller number. Of course, the more you reduce the size of your worksheet, the smaller your text and numbers will be, and consequently the harder it will be to read them.

Another way to achieve the same end is to select the *Fit to 1 page wide by 1 tall*. This option will automatically scale your worksheet to fit on one single page. You can change this setting to print your worksheet on the number of pages you specify.

Paper Size

The default is 8 1/2" × 11" paper. If you are using a different size paper, change it here. For worksheets that are a little too large to fit on one page it is convenient to have some legal size paper on hand. Legal size paper is 8 1/2" × 14".

Print Quality

With most printers, the default print quality is generally 300 or 600 dpi (dots per inch), which is usually what you want. A higher number, if your printer can handle it, will produce slightly better quality output, but your page will print more slowly. And a lower number will produce much less acceptable print quality.

THE MARGINS TAB

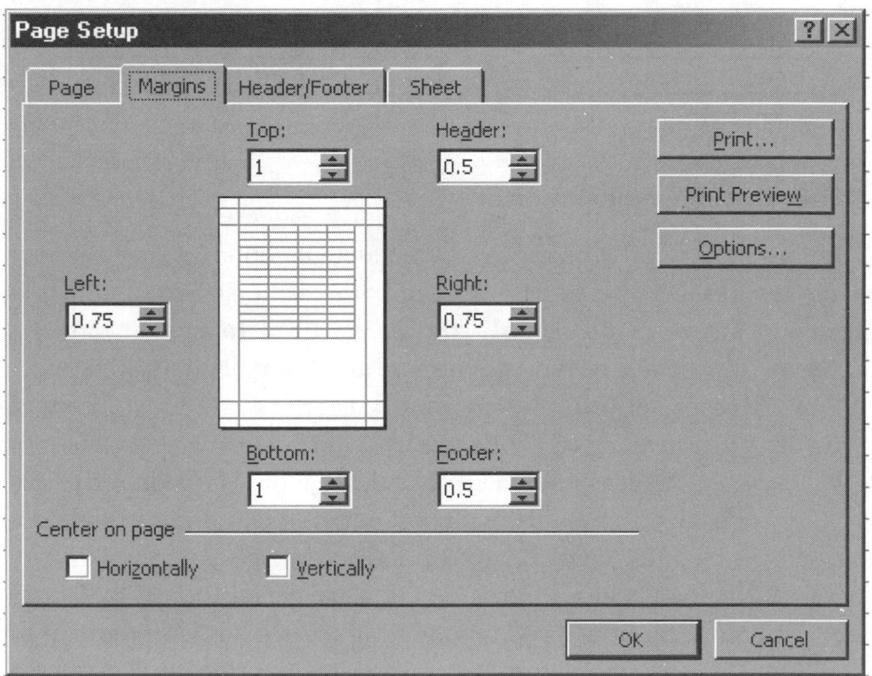

Figure 12.4.

Margins

The default margins are:

Top:	1"
Bottom:	1"

Left: 0.75"
Right: 0.75"

You can change these, but keep in mind that most printers cannot print closer than .25" from the top, bottom, left, or right edge of the page.

Center on Page

Down near the bottom of the Margins dialog box you will see two checkboxes, Horizontally and Vertically.

1. Click on Horizontally to center your worksheet horizontally on the page.
2. Click on Vertically to center your page vertically on the page.

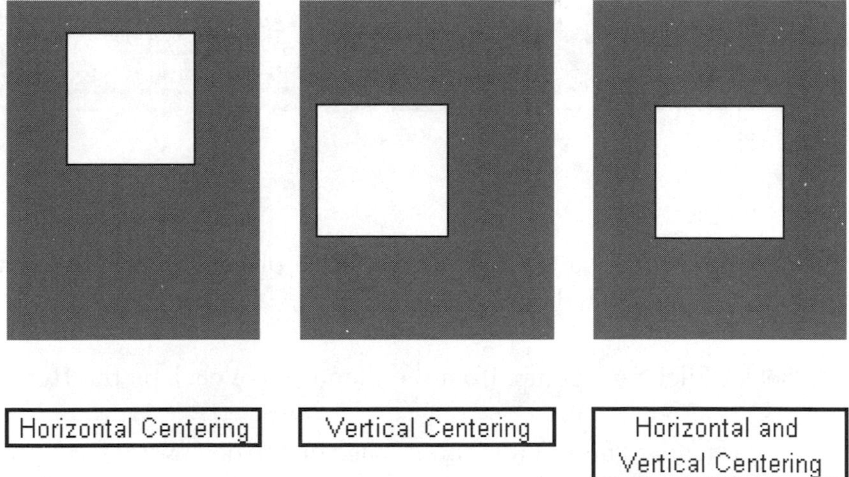

Figure 12.5.

Although horizontal centering is more commonly used with worksheets, sometimes you will also find vertical centering useful. You also have the option of centering your worksheet completely on the page, by selecting both horizontal and vertical centering.

THE HEADERS AND FOOTERS TAB

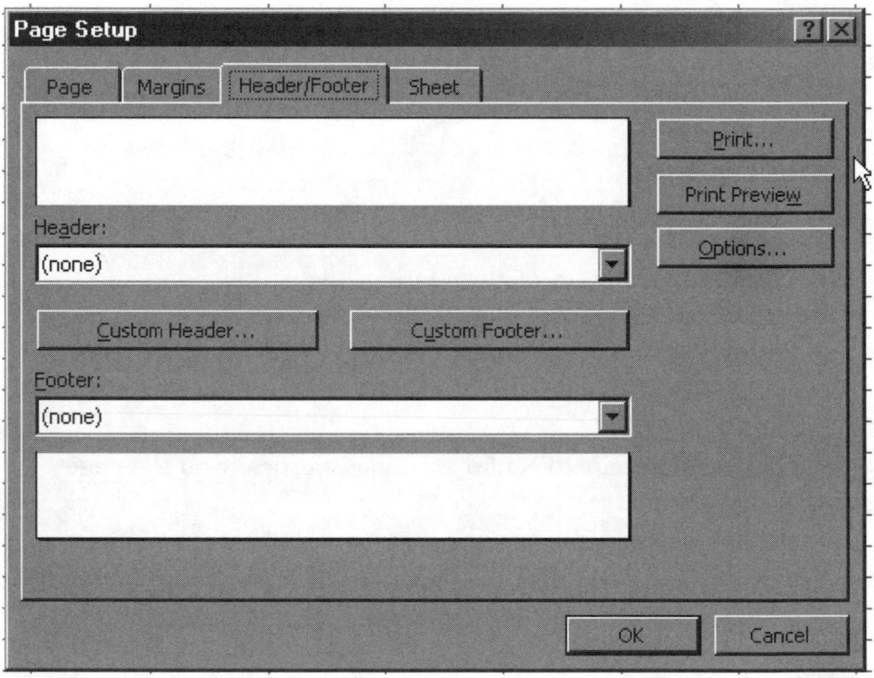

Figure 12.6.

A header is a section at the top of each page of your printout, and a footer is a section at the bottom of each page of your printout.

1. Select File, Page Setup, from the menu. Then click on the Headers and Footers tab.
2. For a standard header (or footer), click on the downward facing arrow next to the Header (or Footer) box.
3. Select a standard header (or footer).

You can also create a custom header and/or footer by typing it into the Header or Footer box. You will probably find that the standard headers and footers meet most of your needs.

SHEET (THE FOURTH TAB)

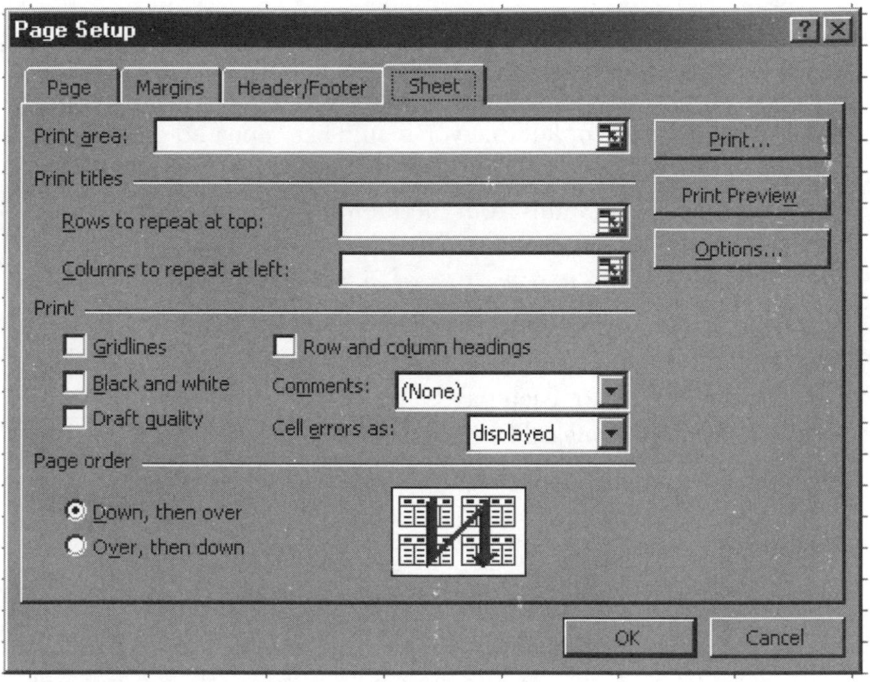

Figure 12.7.

Print Area

This section allows you to print only part of a worksheet.

1. Select File, Page Setup from the menu.
2. Click on the Sheet tab.
3. Notice that at the right side of the Print Area box there is a downward facing arrow. Click on the downward facing arrow.
4. Point to the first cell you want to appear in your printout.
5. Hold down the left mouse button, and drag across the range (area) that you want to print. Release the mouse button.
6. Click on the downward facing arrow again.

7. Click on the Print button to print the section of your worksheet you have selected.

Rows to Repeat at Top

This option is useful if you have a worksheet that spans many pages and has titles at the top or left that you would like repeated on each page.

1. Select File, Page Setup from the menu.
2. Click on the Sheet tab.
3. To the right of the *Rows to Repeat at Top* you will see a downward facing arrow. Click on the downward facing arrow.
4. Highlight the row or rows that contain the titles you would like repeated at the top of each page.
5. Click on the downward facing arrow again.
6. Click Print.

Gridlines

In recent versions of Excel, when you print your worksheet the gridlines you see on your screen will not print (in older versions of Excel, the opposite was true). If you prefer the gridlines to print, you can easily turn that feature on.

1. Select Format, Page Setup from the menu, and then click on the Sheet tab.
2. Click on the checkbox next to Gridlines. When you print your worksheet, all gridlines will print.

A FEW WORDS ABOUT GRIDLINES

Most often, you will not want gridlines to appear throughout your worksheet. Rather, you are likely to want gridlines to appear only in some parts of your worksheet. You can easily accomplish this.

1. Select File, Page Setup from the menu, and then select the Sheet tab.

2. If there is a checkmark in front of gridlines, click on it to turn gridlines off, and then click OK.
3. Next, use your mouse pointer to drag across the range of cells that you want to be surrounded by gridlines.
4. Select Format, Cells, Border from the menu.
5. Select Outline and Inside in the Presets section.
6. Click OK.

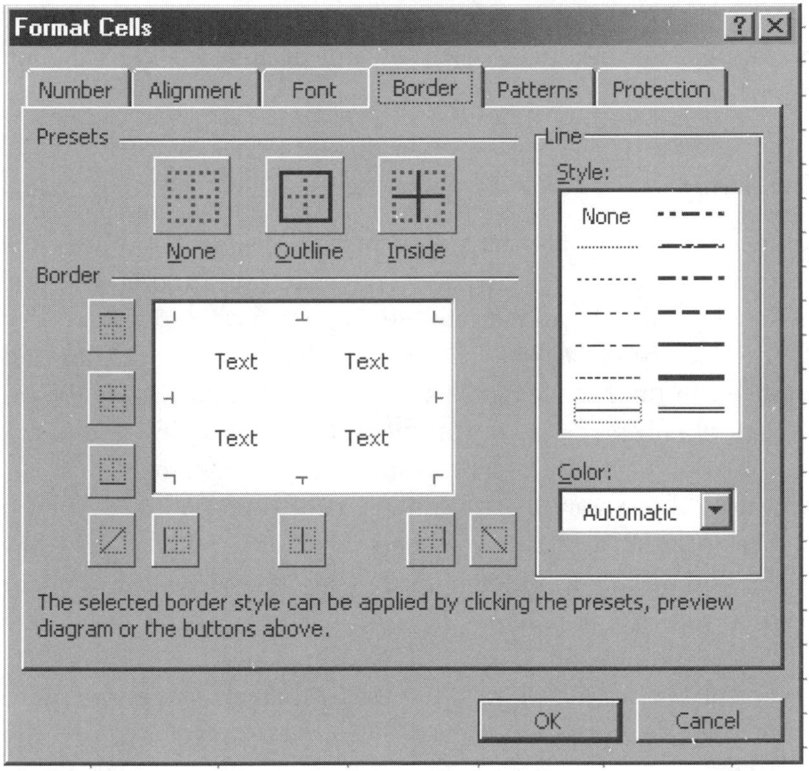

Figure 12.8.

BASIC PRINTING

Printing an Excel worksheet is accomplished in much the same way as printing in most other Windows programs.

1. From the menu, select File, Print. The Print dialog box will appear on your screen.
2. Click OK in the Print dialog box.

Printer

In some office settings, you will have the ability to print on one of two or more printers—often a monochromatic laser printer and a color ink jet printer. One printer will be displayed next to the word Printer. If you want to print your worksheet on the other printer, click on the downward facing arrow next to the name of your printer and select the other printer.

Print Range

By default, Excel will print your entire worksheet. However, if you have a multiple page worksheet and you want Excel to print only some pages, select Page(s), and indicate the pages you want to print.

Print What?—Selection By default, Excel will print your entire worksheet. In the Page Setup section you learned how to set the print area to print only part of your worksheet. If you make this choice, it will be in effect permanently, or at least until you change it again.

However, if you want to print only part of your worksheet now, but will want to print the entire worksheet at other times, the Print menu provides you with a way to temporarily select the section of your worksheet that you want to print.

1. Select the section of your worksheet that you want to print by holding down the left mouse button and dragging across those cells.
2. Select File, Print from the menu.
3. Click on Selection.
4. Click OK.

Print What?—Entire Workbook If you have a workbook that consists of multiple worksheets, this option will enable you to print all the worksheets in one operation.

Print What?—Active Sheet If your workbook consists of multiple worksheets, this option, which is the default, will print only the worksheet that is currently displayed on your screen.

Copies By default, Excel will print only one copy of your worksheet. However, you can direct Excel to print multiple copies of a worksheet. As a practical matter, you will most often print one copy of your worksheet, and make photocopies of it as needed.

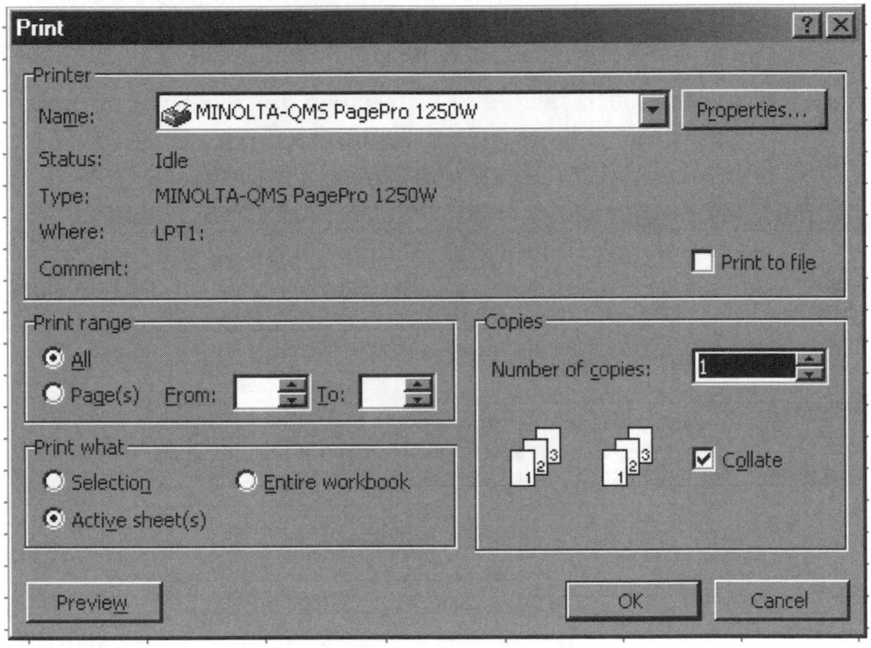

Figure 12.9.

FAST AND EASY PRINTING

Of course, the fastest and easiest way to print your worksheet if you do not have special print needs is to simply click on the Print button on the toolbar.

Figure 12.10.

EXERCISE 12

1. Explain the difference between portrait and landscape orientation. Which is the default? Explain how to change the page orientation.
2. Explain when you would be likely to use, Adjust to 100% Normal Size.
3. What are Excel's default margins? How do you change them?
4. What is the smallest margin that most printers can accommodate?
5. What are the default header and footer in Excel?
6. Why might you want to set print titles? Explain how to do this.
7. You see gridlines displayed on your screen. But when you print your worksheet, the gridlines are not displayed on your printout. Explain.
8. Explain how to add gridlines to part of a worksheet.
9. Describe how to print a worksheet from the Print menu.
10. Describe how to print only part of a worksheet.
11. What are the advantages and disadvantages of printing a worksheet from the menu? From the Print button on the toolbar?
12. Create a worksheet like figure 12.11.

	A	B	C	D
1	State Achievement Test Analysis			
2	Administered: February 1, 2003			
3	Average Scores by Class			
4				
5		Verbal	Math	Mean
6	Class 101	1.2	1.1	
7	Class 102	1.6	1.4	
8	Class 103	1.3	1.3	
9	High			
10	Low			
11	Mean			
12				

Figure 12.11.

13. Write appropriate formulas and copy where necessary, format numbers and text, specify appropriate page setup options, save, and print the worksheet.

13

VIEWS AND PRINT PREVIEW

Suppose you are working on a worksheet that is just a little too big to fit on your screen. Did you know that you can shrink the worksheet so that it will fit neatly on the screen? Or suppose you are ready to print your worksheet, but you would like to know what your printed worksheet will look like before you print it. You will learn how to accomplish both of these tasks in this chapter.

VIEWS

Excel displays your worksheet on your screen in approximately actual size. That is, what you see on the screen is very similar to what your printed worksheet will look like. But Excel provides you with a number of viewing options.

View, Full Screen

Your view of your worksheet is somewhat limited by the title bar and the toolbars, both of which take up room on your screen. You can direct Excel not to display the title bar and toolbars, and by doing so, display more of your worksheet on your screen.

1. Select View, Full Screen from the menu.
2. When you are in Full Screen view, one button will be displayed on your screen. Click on the Close Full Screen button, and you will be immediately returned to the traditional view of your worksheet.

Figure 13.1.

View, Zoom

The View, Zoom option allows you to change the magnification of the worksheet to greater or less than actual size (100%). You can use one of the preset magnifications, or you can specify any custom magnification of your choice. Note that you can make entries in the worksheet, and changes to it, at whatever magnification you choose.

1. Click on the downward arrow to the right of the Zoom button.

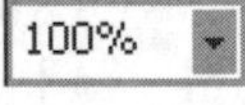

Figure 13.2.

2. Select a magnification.

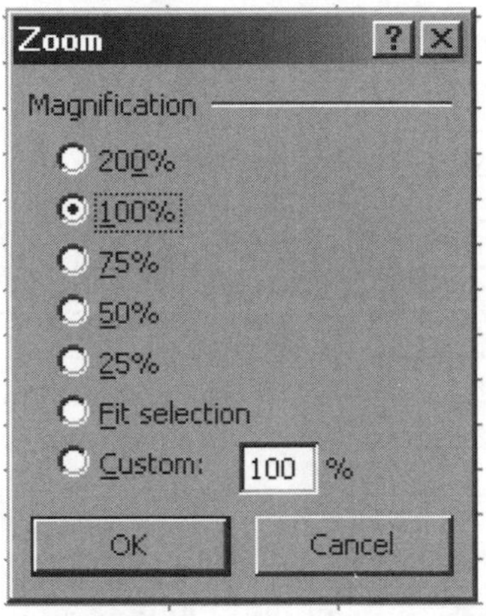

Figure 13.3.

3. Click OK.

Or, you can select a custom magnification.

1. Click on the downward arrow to the right of the Zoom button.

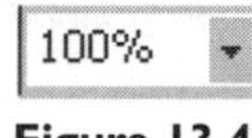

Figure 13.4.

2. Type a magnification.

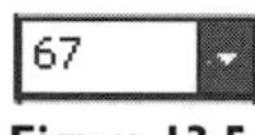

Figure 13.5.

3. Press [Enter].

FORMULA BAR, STATUS BAR, AND TOOLBARS

You can use the View menu to display the formula bar and status bar if they are not displayed, and to remove them if they are displayed. Traditionally, you will want the formula bar and status bar to be displayed—they provide valuable information and use very little screen space. However, if you do not want them displayed, you can easily hide them:

1. Select View, from the menu.
2. If the formula bar and/or status bar are displayed, there will be checkmarks next to each of them. Click on either to deselect it, and that toolbar will be removed from your display.
3. To turn the formula bar and/or status bar on again, follow the same procedure. Click on the item that is not displayed to checkmark it and display it.

Although the standard and the formatting toolbars are the most commonly used Excel toolbars, Excel also provides a number of other tool-

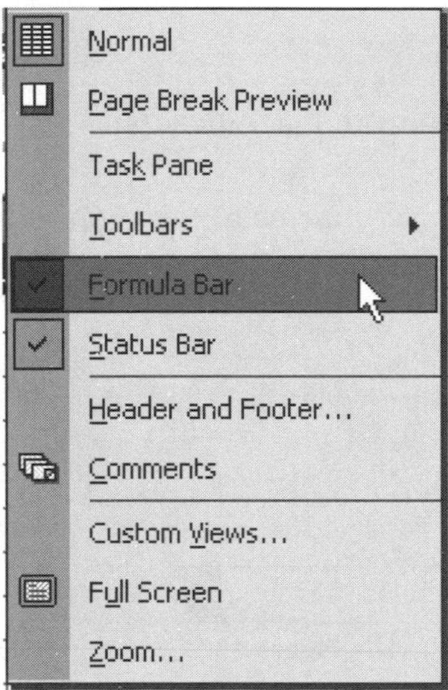

Figure 13.6.

bars. You can use the View menu to determine which toolbars will be displayed.

1. Select View, Toolbars from the menu.
2. The toolbars that are displayed will have checkmarks next to them.
3. Click on a selected toolbar to deselect it.
4. Click on a toolbar that is not selected to display it.
5. Click OK.

You will probably find it convenient to always have the formatting and standard toolbars visible.

If you frequently create drawing objects in your worksheets, you will probably also find it useful to have the Drawing toolbar visible. For certain kinds of work, you may also find it useful to have some of the other specialized toolbars displayed. Remember, however, that the more toolbars you display, the less room is available for your worksheet. If you don't need a toolbar, it is generally best not to display it. Also note that most people find it confusing to display several toolbars in one place, such as at the top of the screen. If you have more than two toolbars dis-

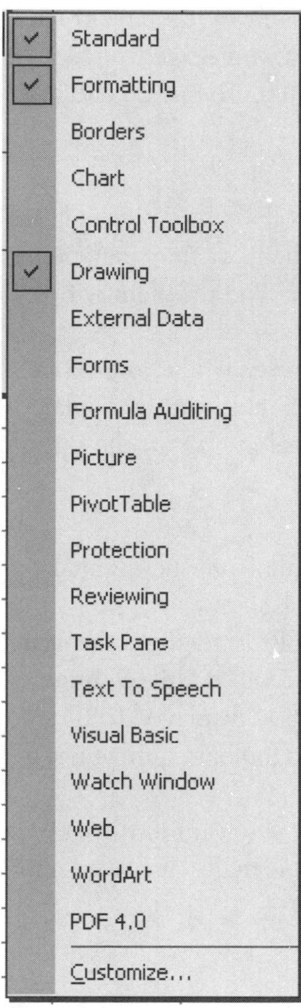

Figure 13.7.

played and they are all located at the top of the screen, you may find it difficult to find a specific tool.

Most people display the formatting and standard toolbars at the top of the screen. If they display the Drawing toolbar, its most common location is either at the bottom or at the left or right side of the screen.

If you do not like the location of a toolbar, it is fairly easy to reposition it.

1. With your cursor point to the faint vertical line at the left edge of the toolbar that you want to move (Fig. 13.8).
2. Hold down the left mouse button and drag the toolbar to a new location.

Remember that the toolbars may be displayed at the top, bottom, left, or right edge of a worksheet, or they may be allowed to "float" over the surface of the worksheet. The problem with a floating toolbar is that it obscures part of the worksheet.

Now, suppose that you really like to use one or two buttons on a particular toolbar, but you do not want to display the entire toolbar for just one or two buttons. Excel gives you the option of customizing one or more toolbars.

1. Select View, Toolbars from the menu.
2. Select Customize.
3. You will see a list of the toolbars displayed on the left side of the screen. One toolbar will be highlighted, and the tools that appear on that toolbar will be displayed to the right (Fig. 13.9).
4. Click on the various toolbars until you see the button that you want to display.
5. Point to the button you want to display, and drag it to the name of the toolbar that is normally displayed and on which you want it to appear.
6. Click OK.

Of course, you have the option of returning the toolbars to their original or default configurations at any time.

1. Select View, Toolbars from the menu.
2. Click on the Customize button.
3. Click Reset.
4. Click OK.

Figure 13.8.

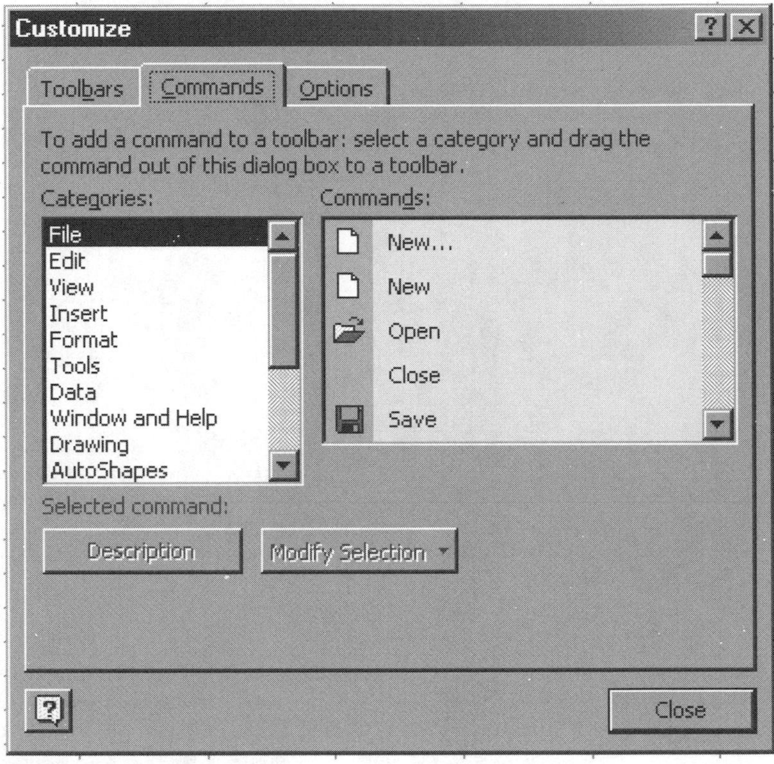

Figure 13.9.

PRINT PREVIEW

The Print Preview option allows you to see what your worksheet will look like when you print it.

1. Select File, Print Preview from the menu.

You can also display a print preview from the toolbar by clicking on the Print Preview button on the standard toolbar.

Figure 13.10.

You can print your worksheet directly from the Print Preview mode. You can also zoom in on a small part of the worksheet, access the page setup dialog box, or change margins directly from the Print Preview screen. However, it is important to understand that you cannot enter new data or change existing data in your worksheet when you are in Print Preview mode. Should you want to see your entire worksheet at one time and still have the ability to edit the worksheet, use the Zoom control, which you learned to use earlier in this chapter. The Print Preview screen has its own toolbar, which provides you with a number of Print Preview options.

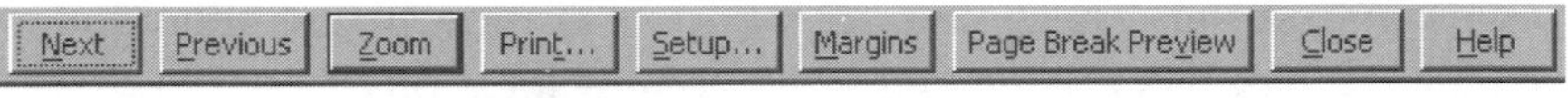

Figure 13.11.

Next and Previous

If your document has more than one page, you can use the Next and Previous buttons to move from one page to the next. You can also accomplish this from the keyboard by pressing the [Page Down] and [Page Up] keys to move down or up, respectively. And, you can also use the scrollbar to move from one page to the next.

Zoom Control

Your document is most likely displayed in whole page view—that is, you can see an entire page. Click on the Zoom button, and your document will be displayed in actual size. Of course, in actual size, you will not be able to see the entire page. Click on Zoom again, and you will be returned to a view of your document in full-page view. Remember that even in actual size, you cannot edit your worksheet while you are in Print Preview mode.

Print

If your document looks good you can print it directly from the Print Preview screen. Click on the Print button to display the Print dialog box.

Now you can select your print options, and then click on the Print button to print your worksheet.

Setup

The Setup button takes you to the Page Setup dialog box. You have access to all the Page Setup options: Page, Margins, Header/Footer, and Sheet.

Margins

This button will display the current margins and will also allow you to change the margins by dragging them to new locations.

Page Break Preview

This button displays page breaks and allows you to manually determine where page breaks will occur.

Close

The Close button closes Print Preview and returns you to your worksheet. You may also press the [Esc] key on your keyboard to close Print Preview and return to your worksheet.

Help

Clicking on the Help button will bring you immediate help with Print Preview options. But once you have selected Help, you will also have access to all the Excel help topics.

SPLITTING THE SCREEN

Have you ever wanted to work in two different parts of your worksheet at the same time? Or suppose you would like to work on one part of your worksheet while still being able to view another part of your worksheet. You can easily accomplish this by splitting the screen.

1. Look at the vertical scroll bar at the right side of your worksheet. Look specifically at the upward facing arrow at the top of the scroll bar. Now look just above the arrow. Notice the very small rectangle that is located just above the arrow.

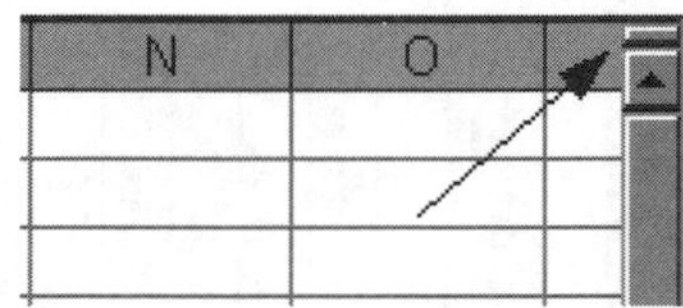

Figure 13.12.

2. Position the tip of your mouse pointer directly on the small rectangle. Your mouse pointer will change to a double line, with upward and downward facing arrows extending from it.

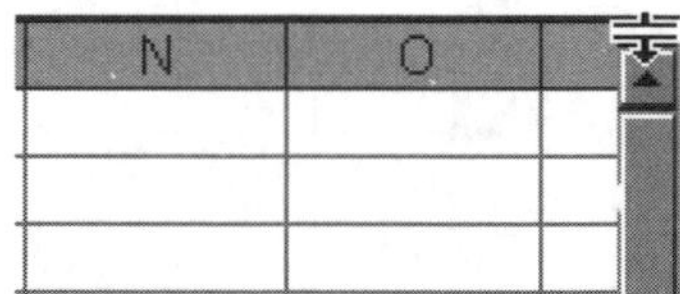

Figure 13.13.

3. Hold down the left mouse button and drag the rectangle downward. As you do so, you will split the screen into two separate panes or windows. Each pane will have its own scroll bar.

Note that in this example splitting the screen enables you to see rows 1, 2, and 3, and also rows 25 through 29.

In split screen view, you can select any cell in either pane by clicking on it. You can also move to other parts of the worksheet by using the scroll bars. And you can do anything to your worksheet that you can do in normal view. Of course, you can return to a single pane view of your worksheet at any time. Simply drag the small rectangle to its original location at the top of your screen.

There is also a small rectangle on the horizontal toolbar, just to the right of the right facing arrow. You can drag that rectangle to divide your worksheet view into two vertical panes.

	A	B	C	D	E	F	G	H	I
1	Student Grades								
2									
3	First	Last	English	Social St.	Math	Science	For. Lang.	Phys. Ed.	
23	Malcolm	Tunis	85	75	95	85	75	95	
24	David	Usher	75	95	85	75	95	85	
25	Barbara	Vance	95	85	75	95	85	75	
26	Edna	Williams	85	75	95	85	75	95	
27	Bob	Adams	95	85	75	95	85	75	
28	Denise	Baker	85	75	95	85	75	95	

Figure 13.14.

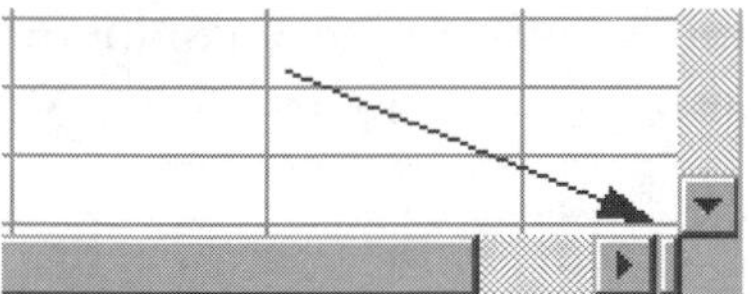

Figure 13.15.

And, if you need to see four parts of your worksheet at one time, you can create two horizontal and two vertical panes at the same time. Obviously, with four separate frames, each frame will be relatively small, and you may find the four-pane view confusing.

You can also divide your worksheet into two horizontal panes from the menu.

1. Select Window, Split from the menu.

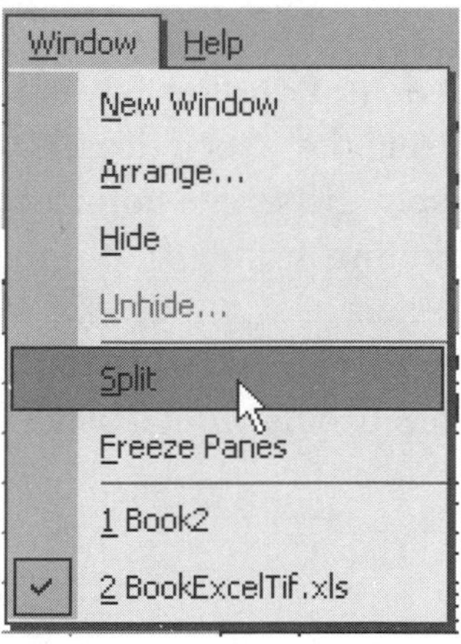

Figure 13.16.

EXERCISE 13

1. What is the advantage of viewing your worksheet in Full Screen view? What is the disadvantage of Full Screen view?
2. Explain how to select Full Screen view. Explain how to return to regular view.

3. Assume that you are working on a computer in which the Excel formula and status toolbars are not visible. Explain how to display them.
4. Which two Excel toolbars do most users display?
5. Explain how to display additional toolbars.
6. What is the disadvantage of displaying all the toolbars at one time?
7. Explain what is meant by customizing a toolbar and how to accomplish this.
8. What are the different locations in which you can display toolbars?
9. Describe how to move a toolbar from one location on your screen to another.
10. Why might you use the Print Preview screen?
11. Describe two ways to select Print Preview.
12. What are the Print Preview options? Describe what each does and how to use it.
13. What can you not do in Print Preview mode?
14. Explain what splitting the screen does.
15. Describe how to split the screen horizontally and vertically.
16. Describe how to return from a split screen view to a one-pane view of your worksheet.
17. Create the Student Grades worksheet displayed in this lesson. Split the screen into two horizontal windows.

14

A CLOSER LOOK AT THE TOOLBARS

You should now be able to create fairly sophisticated worksheets. You have learned how to use some of the tools on Excel's Standard and Formatting toolbars to simplify your work. This chapter explains the most commonly used Excel toolbar buttons, and how to use some of the toolbar buttons you have not yet used.

THE TOOLBARS

It is generally convenient to have the Standard and Formatting toolbars displayed on your screen. You are already familiar with some of the Standard toolbar buttons, such as Create a New Worksheet, Open a File, Save a File, and Print a Worksheet. You have also used some of the Formatting toolbar buttons, such as the Bold, Italicize, and Underline buttons.

If either of these toolbars is not displayed, display it now.

1. Select View, Toolbars from the menu.
2. There should be a checkmark in the boxes in front of Standard and Formatting. If either of these toolbars is not preceded by a checkmark, click on it to display that toolbar.

ONE OR TWO LINES

Beginning with Microsoft Excel version 2000, by default both toolbars are displayed on one line. The problem with having both toolbars displayed on one line is that there is not enough room to display all the buttons on both toolbars on one line. So Excel displays most, but not all, of the toolbar buttons. Specifically, Excel displays the buttons you have used most recently. How does Excel do this? Notice that there is a small downward facing arrow at about the middle of the toolbar, and there is another small downward facing arrow at the right edge of the toolbar.

When you click on one of these arrows, Excel will display the buttons that are not currently visible (Fig. 14.1). Click on one of those buttons, and from that point on that button will appear on the toolbar. Of course, because of space limitations one of the buttons you have not used recently will no longer appear on the toolbar.

Many people do not like this feature. That is, they would prefer to have all the buttons on the Standard and Formatting toolbars visible at one time. Fortunately, there is a very simple way to accomplish this.

1. At the very righthand edge of the toolbar you will see a small downward facing arrow. Click on this arrow.
2. Select, Show buttons on two rows (Fig. 14.2).

The Standard and Formatting toolbars will now be displayed in their entirety on two separate rows.

ADVANCED TOOLS—STANDARD TOOLBAR

There are several buttons on the Standard toolbar (Fig. 14.3) that you may not be familiar with. We will discuss some here, and leave some for subsequent chapters.

Print Preview

Located just to the right of the Print button is the Print Preview button. It is equivalent to selecting File, Print Preview from the menu.

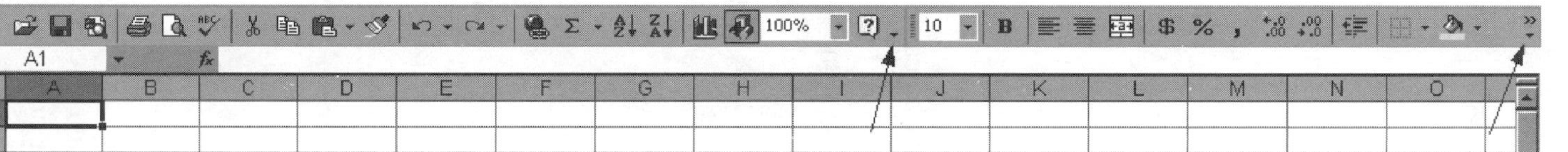

Figure 14.1.

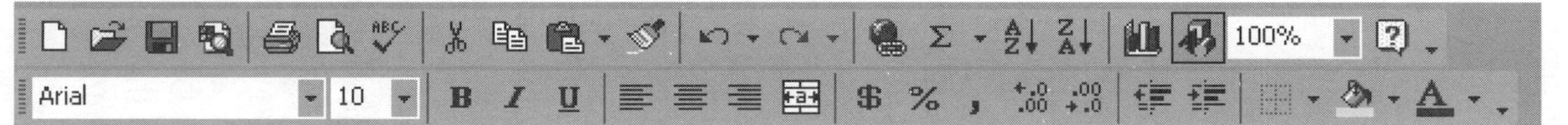

Figure 14.2.

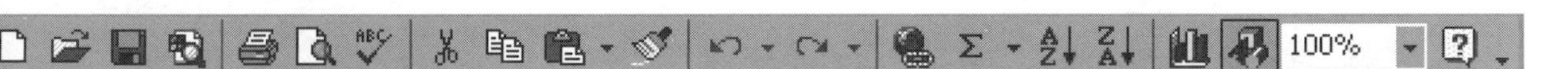

Figure 14.3.

Figure 14.4.

Using Print Preview to view your document before you print it will not only save you paper, but it will also save you time.

While you can change the page setup and margins, zoom in to see your worksheet close up, and even print your worksheet from the Print Preview screen, Print Preview does not allow you edit or change your worksheet. If you want to change your worksheet, you must close Print Preview and return to your worksheet.

Format Painter

The Format Painter tool looks like a paintbrush, and is usually located just to the right of the Paste (clipboard) button. It is useful if you have formatted a cell or a range of cells in your worksheet and you want to apply exactly the same format to another cell or range of cells.

Figure 14.5.

An example will make clear how to use the Format Painter button.

1. Open a new worksheet and type **Mon** in cell B2.
2. Now apply the following formatting to cell B2.
   a. Increase the font size to 14 point.
   b. Apply bold style.
   c. Apply italic style.
   d. Establish an outline border around the cell.
   e. Apply a shading pattern or color to the cell.
3. Now type **Tue** in cell D2 and press [Enter].
4. Suppose that you want to apply the same formatting that you have applied to cell B2 to cell D2.
5. Click on cell B2, the cell that has the formatting you want to copy.
6. Click on the Format Painter tool. Note that the pointer now looks like a paintbrush.

7. Click on cell D2, the cell you want to apply the formatting to.
8. You have used the Format Painter tool to apply the formatting in cell B2 to cell D2. There is no need to exit from Format Painter mode. When you click on the destination cell, the formatting from the source cell is transferred to the destination cell, and the Format Painter automatically turns itself off.

Undo and Redo

You are familiar with the Undo command, which reverses the action you have most recently taken. Clear a cell, for example, and select Edit, Undo from the menu to get it back. The Undo button on the toolbar has the same effect as selecting Edit, Undo from the menu.

Figure 14.6.

The companion to the Undo button is the Redo button.

Figure 14.7.

1. Click on a cell that contains an entry. Do something to the contents of the cell (for example, clear the contents of the cell, or format the cell).
2. Click on the Undo button to undo the last action you have performed.
3. Click on the Redo button. What you have undone will be redone.

Function Wizard

The *Function Wizard* helps you to write functions in Excel.

Figure 14.8.

1. Click on the cell you want to write a function in.
2. Click on the Function Wizard button.
3. From the Function Wizard dialog box select the category of the function you are interested in. Then, from the list that appears, select the specific function you want to use.
4. Click on Next, and Excel will prompt you for the information it needs to write the function.
5. When you have entered the requested data, click on the Finish button.

It sounds like a terrific idea. The problem with the Function Wizard is that it is difficult to use if you are not already familiar with the function you are interested in using. But the Function Wizard can be really useful if you have used a function before, but you cannot remember exactly how it works. You will find the Function Wizard to be more useful as you become familiar with more of Excel's functions.

Drawing

The Drawing button enables you to quickly display, or hide, the Drawing toolbar.

Figure 14.9.

Many people find the drawing toolbar to be extremely useful, but do not want to display it when they do not need it.

1. Click on the Drawing button, and the Drawing toolbar will be displayed.
2. Click again, and it will be hidden.

You will learn how to use the tools on the Drawing toolbar in a subsequent chapter.

Zoom

Your worksheet is normally displayed in 100 percent or actual size—approximately the size your worksheet will appear when you print it. You can use the Zoom button to display your worksheet larger or smaller than 100 percent size.

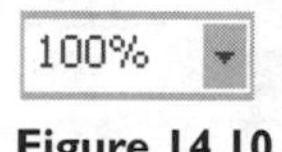

Figure 14.10.

1. Click on the downward facing arrow next to 100%.
2. Select the magnification you prefer.

Do not confuse the Zoom control with Print Preview:

1. Zoom allows you to see what your worksheet will look like in smaller (or larger) size. While it does not show you exactly what your worksheet will look like when you print it. Zoom has the advantage of allowing you to edit your worksheet in smaller (or larger) size.
2. Print Preview shows you almost exactly what your worksheet will look like when you print it. But you cannot edit your worksheet in Print Preview mode.

Help

The Help button looks like a question mark and provides help about virtually any operation in Excel.

Figure 14.11.

1. Click on the Help button.
2. Excel provides you with the Answer Wizard, which will help you find the information you are looking for. With the Answer Wizard, simply type a question using ordinary language in the "What would

you like to do?" box, and then click on the Search button. For example, you could ask, "How do I backup a worksheet?" Excel will automatically find the most appropriate answer to your question.

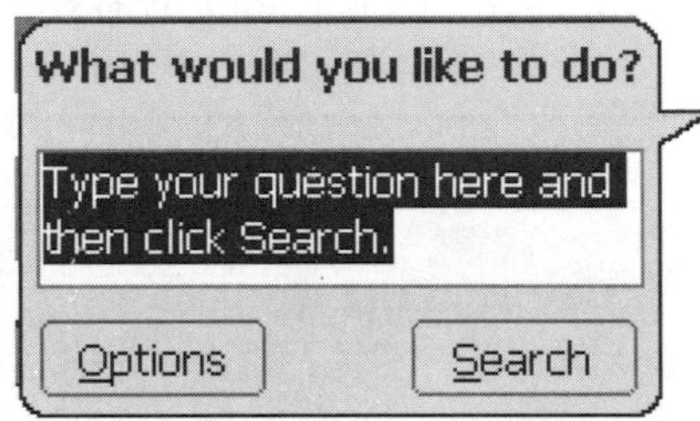

Figure 14.12.

You can also access Microsoft Word help by clicking on Help from the Excel menu.

THE FORMATTING TOOLBAR

The Formatting toolbar can be set above or below the Standard toolbar. You are already familiar with many of the buttons on this toolbar, but because they are so useful, we will briefly review them here.

Alignment

You learned how to use the alignment buttons when you studied text formatting in chapter 11.

1. Click on the cell or range of cells whose alignment you want to change.
2. Click on the appropriate alignment button.

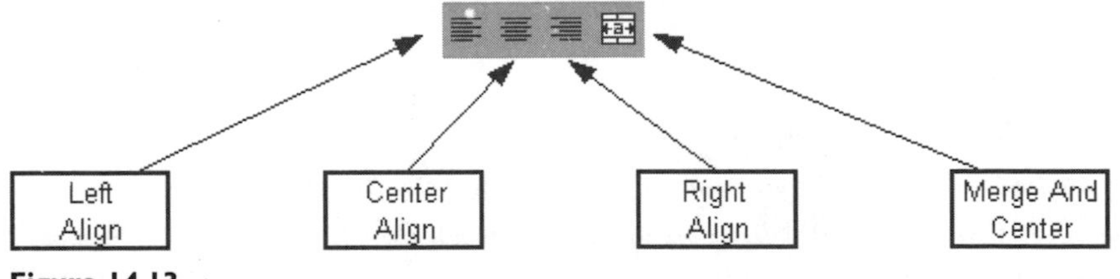

Figure 14.13.

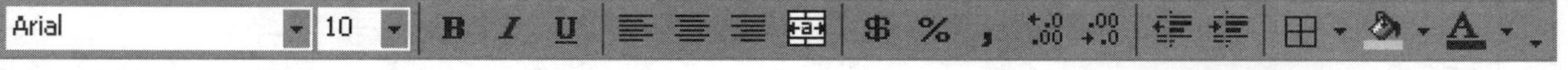

Figure 14.14.

The alignment buttons are generally quite easy to use. The only one that is a little more difficult is the Align Across Selection button.

To align a cell entry across a range of cells:

1. Starting with the cell that contains your entry, drag across the range were you want to center your text.
2. Next click on the Center Across Selection button to center the entry across the range of cells that you selected.

Number Formatting

There are five Number Formatting tools (Fig. 14.15) on the Formatting toolbar that you learned about in chapter 10.

- **Currency** Assigns Currency format, two decimal places, to the value in a cell. It also sets off thousands with commas. That is, 1234.5 will be displayed as $1,234.50.
- **Percent** Assigns Percent format, zero decimal places, to the value in a cell. For example, the number .12 will be displayed as 12%.
- **Comma** Assigns Comma format, two decimal places, to the value in a cell. Comma format is very similar to Currency format, with one difference—Comma format does not display a dollar sign. It does, however, set off thousands with commas. The number 1234.5 in comma format will be displayed as 1,234.50.
- **Increase Decimal** Increases the number of decimal places that are displayed. Each time you click on the button, the number of decimal places will be increased by one. For example, suppose you had entered the number .125 (that is, decimal point, one, two, five) in a cell. Click on the Percent button, and the number will be displayed as 13%. Now click on the Increase Decimal button and the number will be displayed as 12.5%.
- **Decrease Decimal** Decreases the number of decimal places that are displayed. Each time you click on this button, the number of decimal places will be decreased by one. For example, suppose you had entered the number 1234.5 in a cell. Click on the Dollar Sign button, and your number will be displayed as $1,234.50. Now click

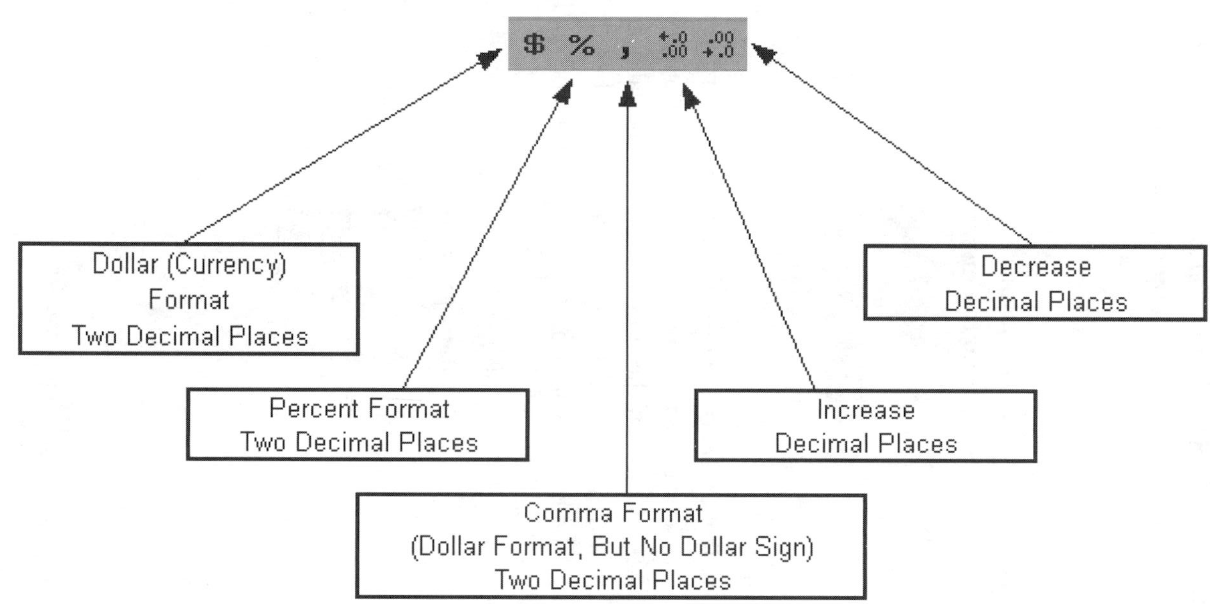
$ % , +.0 .00 .00 +.0
Dollar (Currency) Format Two Decimal Places
Percent Format Two Decimal Places
Comma Format (Dollar Format, But No Dollar Sign) Two Decimal Places
Increase Decimal Places
Decrease Decimal Places

Figure 14.15.

on the Increase Decimal button. The number will be displayed as $1,234.5. Click again, and it will be displayed as $1,235.

Borders

The Borders button allows you to place a border around a cell. You learned how to apply borders from the menu in chapter 11. Here is how to do it from the toolbar.

Figure 14.16.

1. Select the cell or the range of cells you want a border applied to.
2. Click on the downward facing arrow next to the Border button.
3. You will see pictures of the borders that are available to you, such as outline around the cell(s), right side of cells, left side of cells, etc. Select the border you want to use, and it will be applied to the cell or cells you selected.

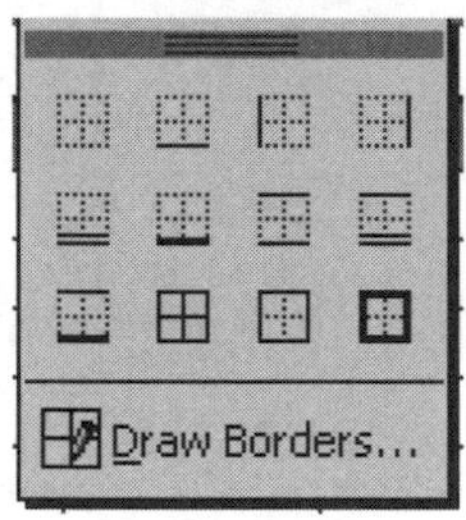

Figure 14.17.

Color

The Color button, which has a picture of a paint can and a color, allows you to apply color to cells in your worksheet.

Figure 14.18.

1. To apply a color to a cell, click on the cell to select it. To apply a color to a range of cells, point to the first cell in the range, hold down the left mouse button, and drag across the range of cells.
2. If you want the color that is displayed on the button, click on the button.
3. If you want a different color, click on the downward facing arrow next to the Color button.
4. Select the color you want to apply to the cells.
5. The color you selected will be applied to the cell or cells that you have selected.

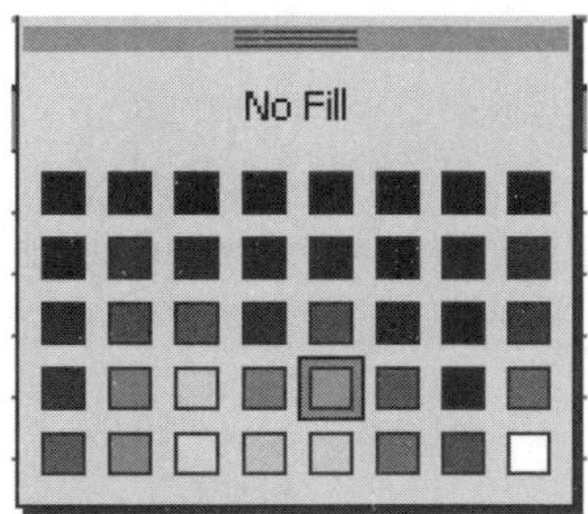

Figure 14.19.

Note that when you drag across a range of cells to select them, the selected cells (except for the first) appear in a color, typically light blue. If you apply color to selected cells, the blue color will alter the color you applied to the cells. Click on any cell to remove the blue highlighting, and you will see the color you applied to the cells.

Font Color

The Font Color button has a picture of the letter A and a colored rectangle. It works just like the Color button, but rather than changing the color of the selected cells, it allows you to change the color of the font in the selected cells.

Figure 14.20.

MOVING TOOLBARS

Remember, you can vary the screen position of any toolbar.

1. Top
2. Bottom
3. Left
4. Right
5. Floating

Whenever you want to move a toolbar:

1. Point your cursor to the faint vertical line at the left edge of the toolbar.
2. Hold down the left mouse button and drag the toolbar to its new location.

EXERCISE 14

1. Explain how the Print Preview feature works.
2. What is the advantage of using Print Preview?
3. What can you not do in Print Preview mode?
4. Explain how to use the Format Painter.
5. Explain the difference between Undo and Redo.
6. Give an example of a situation in which you would use Undo and Redo.
7. What is the purpose of the Function Wizard?
8. What is the problem inherent in using the Function Wizard?
9. What does the Drawing button do?
10. Explain how the Zoom control works.
11. What is the difference between Zoom and Print Preview?
12. Explain the advantages and disadvantages of Zoom and Print Preview.
13. Describe how the Help button works.
14. Explain how each of the Number Formatting buttons works.
15. Explain how to use the Borders tool.

16. Explain how to use the Color button.
17. Explain how to use the Font Color button.
18. Describe the different toolbar locations and how to move a toolbar from one location to another.
19. Create a worksheet from figure 14.21.

	A	B	C	D	E	F	G
1	Baseball Team Analysis						
2	Spring, 2003						
3							
4	First	Last	Position	At Bat	Hits	Pct.	
5	Tom	Williams	Pitcher	25	6	0.24	
6	Ed	Eng	Catcher	32	11		
7	Jose	Ramirez	1st Base	35	12		
8							
9						=E5/D5	
10							

Figure 14.21.

20. Write an appropriate formula in cell F5, and then copy it to F6:F7.
21. Use toolbar buttons to format the worksheet.

15

CREATING AND SORTING A DATABASE

A *database* is a collection of data, often a large quantity of data such as a directory of all the telephone numbers in a city or all bank depositors' account numbers and their account histories. Because databases can contain so much data, database management software, which enables you to accumulate and manipulate large quantities of data, must be extremely powerful. But this power often comes at a price and database management programs are often at least somewhat difficult to learn and use.

Excel contains a number of tools that can create and manage a database. While Excel is not nearly as powerful as database management programs, it is much more convenient and much easier to learn and use. Although more powerful databases are a mainstay of most businesses, many people prefer and use Excel for their everyday database work.

This chapter explains how to create an Excel database, how to enter data into your database, and how to sort the data alphabetically or numerically.

IMPORTANT TERMS

Before you actually learn how to create and use a database, you will need to know a few terms related to databases. Most of the terms are fairly straightforward.

Database

A *database* is a collection of related information that is organized in some way. Suppose you had a business, ABC Industries, and you kept information about all your customers on index cards in a file box. That file box and all those index cards would constitute a database. As you can imagine, a computer database is much more convenient than an index card database.

Record

A *record* is information about one item in your database. For example, in your customer database, Robert A. Smith, Apex Corporation, 888 Corporate Way, Denver, CO, might represent one record. Using the index card file analogy, you can think of a record as one index card in the file box.

Field

A *field* is a category of information in your database that appears in every record in that database. This probably sounds confusing, but an example should make it easier to understand. Suppose you have a database that contains information about all your customers. The fields in your customer database might be FIRST NAME, MIDDLE INITIAL, LAST NAME, COMPANY, and TELEPHONE NUMBER.

Every record contains each of these fields. You might argue, for example, that not every one of your customers has a middle initial. That is certainly true. But there is a place in every record for a middle initial. The middle initial field is that place.

Data

Data are the pieces of information you enter into the fields in each of your records. For example, the last name field in one record might contain the data JONES, while the data in the last name field in another record might contain the data SMITH.

EXCEL DATABASE RULES

Creating a database in Excel is easy and very straightforward, but there are a number of rules you must follow. It might seem as if you can *bend* some of these rules and, in fact, many people do just that. But be forewarned—if you do not follow the rules, at some point you will encounter problems with your database. Very significant problems!

1. You must enter the field names in the adjacent cells of one row at or near the top of your worksheet. Note that each field name must appear in a single cell—field names cannot appear in two rows.

Figure 15.1.

2. Each field name must be unique. That is, you cannot have two fields named TELEPHONE. Suppose that some of your customers have two telephone numbers. You would solve that problem by including two fields for telephone numbers in your database, say, TELEPHONE 1, and TELEPHONE 2.
3. The first row below the field names will contain data for the first record. You cannot skip a row between the field names and the first record.
4. Each subsequent record will occupy a separate row in the database.
5. As you are entering data, adjust the column widths as necessary to accommodate your data.
6. You may want to include a consecutive record number for each record. If you later sort the database and want to return it to its original order, you can accomplish that by sorting the database according to the record number.

CREATING A DATABASE

Enter the database title and the field names as indicated in figure 15.2. You can adjust the column widths now, or you can wait until you start entering data.

	A	B	C	D	E	F	G	H	I
1	Faculty Addresses								
2									
3	No.	First	Last	Address	City	ST	Zip	A/C	Telephone
4									
5									

Figure 15.2.

ENTERING A SERIES OF NUMBERS

In creating a database for this project, the first field will contain a consecutive record number for each of your records. Of course, you could type in the consecutive numbers, but Excel provides an easier way by using the Edit, Fill, Series command.

1. In cell A4, type in 1, the first record number. It is important to type the first record number in the first cell that will contain a number.
2. Select (highlight) the range of cells that will contain the record numbers, in this instance, select cells A4:A13.
3. From the menu, select Edit, Fill, Series.
4. The first section of the Series dialog box asks if your series in Columns or Rows, Columns will most likely be selected. If this is not the case, click on Columns to select it. You will be creating your series of numbers in a column, not a row.
5. The second section of the Series dialog box asks you to indicate the type of series. In this case (and most cases) the type of series will be linear, that is, consecutive numbers.
6. The Series dialog box also asks you to indicate the step value. In this case, the step value will be 1 (that is, consecutive numbers, 1, 2, 3 . . .). If you had selected 2, your series would skip every second number (1, 3, 5 . . .).

7. Since you have indicated a *starting value* (the place a search will begin) and a range for your series, you can leave out the *stop value* (the place a search will end). The series will stop when Excel reaches the end of the range you have defined.
8. Click OK, and Excel will enter your series into the database.

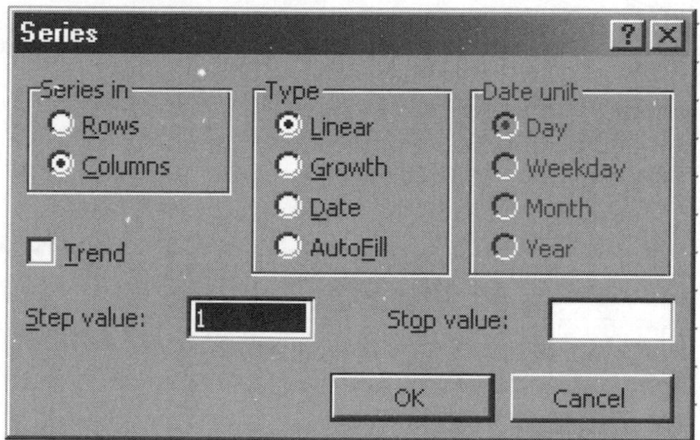

Figure 15.3.

Note: If you followed this procedure and Excel did not enter the series you requested, check that you entered the starting number in the first cell of your range. The most common mistake in using Edit, Fill, Series is forgetting to enter the starting number in the first cell.

ENTERING DATA

Now enter the data from figure 15.4 into your database.

Important note: Excel cannot understand the data in your database. So it is important that you are consistent as you enter your data. If you enter NJ in one cell and N.J. in another, *you* will understand that both represent New Jersey. But, as you have already seen, Excel is not as smart as you are, so Excel will not understand that NJ and N.J. both refer to the same state. In the same way, Excel will even see SMITH, Smith, and smith as three completely different people.

	A	B	C	D	E	F	G	H	I
1	Faculty Addresses								
2									
3	No.	First	Last	Address	City	ST	Zip	A/C	Telephone
4	1	Esther	Eng	123 First Street	New York	NY	10001	212	111-1111
5	2	William	Adams	234 Second Avenue	Fort Lee	NJ	22222	201	222-2222
6	3	Carlos	Rivera	345 Third Road	New York	NY	10002	212	333-3333
7	4	John	Adams	456 Fourth Street	New York	NY	10003	212	444-4444
8	5	Denise	Hunter	567 Fifth Avenue	Fort Lee	NJ	22222	201	555-5555
9	6	Mary	Baker	678 Sixth Court	New York	NY	10004	212	666-6666
10	7	David	Franklin	789 Seventh Street	New York	NY	10005	212	777-7777
11	8	Edith	Davis	890 Eighth Avenue	Fort Lee	NJ	22222	201	888-8888
12	9	Edward	Chin	901 Ninth Road	New York	NY	10006	212	999-9999
13	10	Barbara	Adams	1000 Tenth Street	New York	NY	10007	212	123-4567
14									
15									

Figure 15.4.

SAVE YOUR DATABASE

You have already learned how to save a worksheet and how important it is to save your worksheets frequently. Although saving worksheets is important, it is even more important with databases. Save your database now.

1. From the menu, select File, Save As. . . .
2. In this case, type FACULTY as your file name.
3. Click the Save button.

PREPARING TO SORT AN EXCEL DATABASE

Once you have created an Excel database, you can easily sort your data alphabetically or numerically. But before you learn how to do this, there are a few more terms you will need to understand.

Header Row

Your database *header row* is nothing more than the field names that appear in the top row of your database.

Ascending and Descending Order

Ascending order indicates that the items in the database will be sorted from smaller to larger, alphabetically (A, B, C, D . . .), or numerically (1, 2, 3, 4 . . .). *Descending order*, on the other hand, indicates that the items in the database will be sorted from larger to smaller, alphabetically (Z, Y, X, W . . .), or numerically (10, 9, 8, 7 . . .).

A WORD OF CAUTION

Sorting changes the entire structure of your worksheet. Although the process generally progresses flawlessly, problems do occasionally occur.

To prevent a problem from destroying your database, always save your worksheet before you sort it! That way, if anything goes wrong you can simply open the worksheet as it was saved and try again.

SORTING THE DATABASE

If you set up your database according to the rules indicated above ("Excel Database Rules"), sorting will be very easy and will almost always work perfectly. In this regard, *traditionally* means that the database contains field names in one row, that the first row below the field names contains the first record, and that each successive row contains another record.

1. Always begin by saving the worksheet.
2. Click on any cell in the field you want to sort by. In this case, you will sort by last name. So click on any cell that contains a last name.
3. Select Data, Sort from the menu. You will notice that Excel has highlighted all your data, but not the field names. You will also notice that the Sort dialog box has opened. It indicates that Excel is prepared to sort your data by last name, in ascending order.
4. Note that the Sort dialog box also indicates that your database has a *header row*—that is, it has field names.
5. Since you want to sort your database by last name (Fig. 15.5), in ascending order, simply click OK, and Excel will sort your database as you directed (Fig. 15.6).

NONTRADITIONAL SORTS

If your database is not traditional, Excel may not be able to correctly determine the data range. A *nontraditional* database is one in which you did not completely follow the rules governing its creation. For example, if you skipped a row between your field names and your first record, your database would be considered nontraditional. In these cases, Excel will be unable to accurately define your database. Consequently, you will need to select or highlight the data before you select Data, Sort from the menu.

	A	B	C	D	E	F	G	H	I	J
1	Faculty Addresses									
2										
3	No.	First	Last	Address	City	ST	Zip	A/C	Telephone	
4	2	William	Adams	234 Second Avenue	Fort Lee	NJ	22222	201	222-2222	
5	4	John	Adams	456 Fourth Street	New York	NY	10003	212	444-4444	
6	10	Barbara	Adams	1000 Tenth Street	New York	NY				
7	6	Mary	Baker	678 Sixth Court	New York	NY				
8	9	Edward	Chin	901 Ninth Road	New York	NY				
9	8	Edith	Davis	890 Eighth Avenue	Fort Lee	NJ				
10	1	Esther	Eng	123 First Street	New York	NY				
11	7	David	Franklin	789 Seventh Street	New York	NY				
12	5	Denise	Hunter	567 Fifth Avenue	Fort Lee	NJ				
13	3	Carlos	Rivera	345 Third Road	New York	NY				
14										
15										
16										
17										
18										
19										
20										
21										
22										

Database Just Prior
To Sorting

Sort

Sort by

Last

(none)
No.
First
Last
Address
City

Ascending
Descending

Ascending
Descending

Then by

Ascending
Descending

My list has

Header row
No header row

Options...
OK
Cancel

Figure 15.5.

	A	B	C	D	E	F	G	H	I
1	Faculty Addresses								
2									
3	No.	First	Last	Address	City	ST	Zip	A/C	Telephone
4	2	William	Adams	234 Second Avenue	Fort Lee	NJ	22222	201	222-2222
5	4	John	Adams	456 Fourth Street	New York	NY	10003	212	444-4444
6	10	Barbara	Adams	1000 Tenth Street	New York	NY	10007	212	123-4567
7	6	Mary	Baker	678 Sixth Court	New York	NY	10004	212	666-6666
8	9	Edward	Chin	901 Ninth Road	New York	NY	10006	212	999-9999
9	8	Edith	Davis	890 Eighth Avenue	Fort Lee	NJ	22222	201	888-8888
10	1	Esther	Eng	123 First Street	New York	NY	10001	212	111-1111
11	7	David	Franklin	789 Seventh Street	New York	NY	10005	212	777-7777
12	5	Denise	Hunter	567 Fifth Avenue	Fort Lee	NJ	22222	201	555-5555
13	3	Carlos	Rivera	345 Third Road	New York	NY	10002	212	333-3333
14									
15									
16				Database After					
17				Sorting					
18									

Figure 15.6.

1. Begin by saving your worksheet.
2. Use your mouse to select all the data in your database, but do not include the field names. In this case, select cells A4:H13.
3. Select Data, Sort from the menu. Excel will open the Sort dialog box.
4. At the bottom of the Sort dialog box, indicate that your list has *No header row*.
5. Click on the down arrow next to the Sort dialog box. Indicate that you want to sort Column C.
6. Select Ascending or Descending order. In this case, select Ascending order.
7. Click OK.

SORTING WITH MULTIPLE SORT KEYS

The *sort key* is the field you use to sort. In the sort you that have just performed, the sort key was Last. But sometimes, you will want to sort by more than one key. For example, in this database notice that you have three faculty members named Adams. In a case such as this, you will want to sort the three faculty members named Adams by their First names. In other words, Last would be the first sort key, and First would be the second sort key.

Remember, the second sort key only comes into play when there are several items in the primary sort key with the same data. The second sort key acts as a kind of tie-breaker.

In this database, you have several records in NJ and several in NY. Suppose you want to sort by state. Because several records are in each state, you will probably want to sort within State by using Last. And since there may be instances in which there are more than one person in one state with the same last name, you will want to sort within Last by First (Figs. 15.7 and 15.8).

1. Begin by saving the database.
2. Click on any cell that contains a state in the ST field.
3. Select Data, Sort from the menu. Excel will open the Sort dialog box.

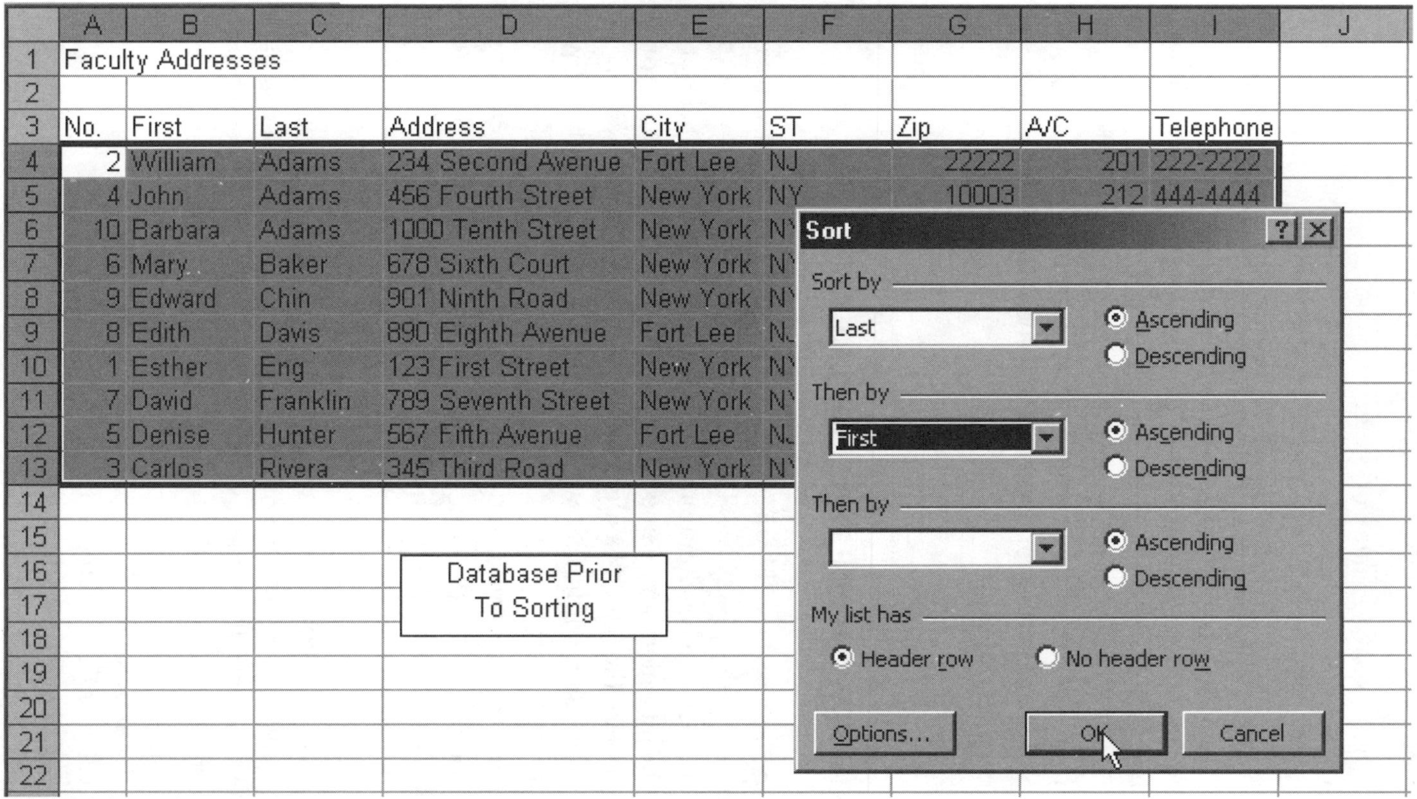

	A	B	C	D	E	F	G	H	I	J
1	Faculty Addresses									
2										
3	No.	First	Last	Address	City	ST	Zip	A/C	Telephone	
4	2	William	Adams	234 Second Avenue	Fort Lee	NJ	22222	201	222-2222	
5	4	John	Adams	456 Fourth Street	New York	NY	10003	212	444-4444	
6	10	Barbara	Adams	1000 Tenth Street	New York	N				
7	6	Mary	Baker	678 Sixth Court	New York	N				
8	9	Edward	Chin	901 Ninth Road	New York	N				
9	8	Edith	Davis	890 Eighth Avenue	Fort Lee	N				
10	1	Esther	Eng	123 First Street	New York	N				
11	7	David	Franklin	789 Seventh Street	New York	N				
12	5	Denise	Hunter	567 Fifth Avenue	Fort Lee	N				
13	3	Carlos	Rivera	345 Third Road	New York	N				
14										
15										
16				Database Prior						
17				To Sorting						
18										
19										
20										
21										
22										

Sort
Sort by
Last
Ascending
Descending
Then by
First
Ascending
Descending
Then by
Ascending
Descending
My list has
Header row
No header row
Options...
OK
Cancel

Figure 15.7.

	A	B	C	D	E	F	G	H	I
1	Faculty Addresses								
2									
3	No.	First	Last	Address	City	ST	Zip	A/C	Telephone
4	10	Barbara	Adams	1000 Tenth Street	New York	NY	10007	212	123-4567
5	4	John	Adams	456 Fourth Street	New York	NY	10003	212	444-4444
6	2	William	Adams	234 Second Avenue	Fort Lee	NJ	22222	201	222-2222
7	6	Mary	Baker	678 Sixth Court	New York	NY	10004	212	666-6666
8	9	Edward	Chin	901 Ninth Road	New York	NY	10006	212	999-9999
9	8	Edith	Davis	890 Eighth Avenue	Fort Lee	NJ	22222	201	888-8888
10	1	Esther	Eng	123 First Street	New York	NY	10001	212	111-1111
11	7	David	Franklin	789 Seventh Street	New York	NY	10005	212	777-7777
12	5	Denise	Hunter	567 Fifth Avenue	Fort Lee	NJ	22222	201	555-5555
13	3	Carlos	Rivera	345 Third Road	New York	NY	10002	212	333-3333
14									
15									
16				Database After					
17				Sorting					
18									

Figure 15.8.

4. The dialog box indicates that you will Sort by ST, and that the sort order will be Ascending. That is, the first sort key is ST.
5. Notice the box next to Then By. This is where you will indicate the second sort key. Click on the downward facing arrow next to the Then By box. Select Last, and select Ascending order.
6. Since you might have two or more people in the same state with the same last name, you will want to indicate a third sort key, in this case First (Fig. 15.9). Indicate your third sort key in the second Then By box. Click on the downward facing arrow next to the second Then By box, and indicate that you want the third sort key to be First. Indicate that you want Ascending sort order.
7. Click OK to perform the sort.

Sorting is so easy, you will probably do it often. Just remember to follow the rules when you create your database and to always save your worksheet before you perform a sort.

PRACTICE

Practice sorting this database by different sort keys and in different sort orders.

EXERCISE 15

1. Define the following terms:
   Database
   Record
   Field
   Data
2. Review the rules that must be followed when you create a database. Do not memorize the rules. Just explain each in your own words.
3. Why might you want to enter a series of consecutive numbers in one field of your database?

	A	B	C	D	E	F	G	H	I	J
1	Faculty Addresses									
2										
3	No.	First	Last	Address	City	ST	Zip	A/C	Telephone	
4	10	Barbara	Adams	1000 Tenth Street	New York	NY	10007	212	123-4567	
5	4	John	Adams	456 Fourth Street	New York	NY	10003	212	444-4444	
6	2	William	Adams	234 Second Avenue	Fort Lee	NJ				
7	6	Mary	Baker	678 Sixth Court	New York	N				
8	9	Edward	Chin	901 Ninth Road	New York	N				
9	8	Edith	Davis	890 Eighth Avenue	Fort Lee	NJ				
10	1	Esther	Eng	123 First Street	New York	N				
11	7	David	Franklin	789 Seventh Street	New York	N				
12	5	Denise	Hunter	567 Fifth Avenue	Fort Lee	NJ				
13	3	Carlos	Rivera	345 Third Road	New York	N				
14										
15										
16										
17										
18										
19										
20										
21										
22										

Figure 15.9.

4. Explain how to enter a series of consecutive numbers into a range of cells using the Edit, Fill, Series command.
5. Why is consistency so important when you are entering data into a database? Give a few examples in which problems might occur because you were not consistent.
6. Define the following terms:
   Header
   Ascending order
   Descending order
7. Why is it so important to save your database before you sort it?
8. Explain how to sort a database.
9. Give an example of a nontraditional database.
10. What problem is likely to occur if your database is nontraditional?
11. How would you resolve this problem?
12. Why might you want to sort by more than one sort key?
13. Explain how to sort a database with multiple sort keys.
14. Create the database as shown in figure 15.10.

	A	B	C	D	E	F	G
1	New Staff						
2	Certification and Degrees						
3							
4	First	Last	Grade	Prov Cert	Perm Cert	BA	MA
5	Mary	Jones	1	X		X	X
6	David	Adams	3		X	X	
7	Edward	Walker	2		X	X	X
8	Denise	Williams	1	X		X	
9	Barbara	Eaton	2		X	X	X
10							
11							

Figure 15.10.

15. Sort the database by Grade, and within Grade by Last.
16. Describe three databases you could create in Excel for school use. Create one of these databases and sort it appropriately.

16

FILTERING A DATABASE AND OTHER ADVANCED DATABASE TOPICS

You now know how to create a database and sort it. This chapter explains some additional techniques for working with Excel databases. Most importantly, you will learn how to search your database for specific information. For example, you might want to find a specific record, say John Smith, or you might want to find a group of records that meet specific criteria, say all people who are over thirty-five years of age or women living in California who earn more than $60,000. This process is called *filtering* your database. That is, you are filtering out the data that meet your specific needs.

CREATE A DATABASE

Create a database based on figure 16.1, being certain to enter the data into the cells indicated.

	A	B	C	D	E
1	Cafeteria Analysis				
2					
3	Week Beginning	Studs Present	Hot Meals	Cold Meals	Total Meals
4	9/1/2003	625	250	185	435
5					
6					

Figure 16.1.

USING EDIT, FILL SERIES TO ENTER DATES

In chapter 15, you learned how to use the Edit, Fill, Series command to enter a series of consecutive numbers into your worksheet. In this example you will use Edit, Fill, Series to enter a series of dates that are exactly one week apart.

1. Select (highlight) A4:A8.
2. Select Edit, Fill, Series.
3. If Columns is not selected, click on Columns to select it.
4. If Date is not selected, click on Date.
5. If Day is not selected, click on Day.
6. Change the step value to 7 (7 days = 1 week).
7. Click OK.

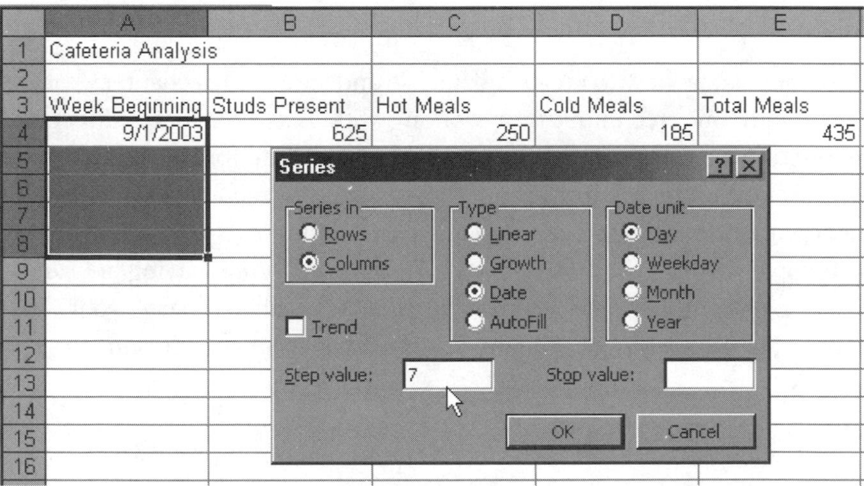

Figure 16.2.

Excel has entered a series of dates exactly one week apart.

COMPLETE THE DATABASE

Now enter data for the rest of the worksheet from figure 16.3.

	A	B	C	D	E
1	Cafeteria Analysis				
2					
3	Week Beginning	Studs Present	Hot Meals	Cold Meals	Total Meals
4	9/1/2003	625	250	185	435
5	9/8/2003	723	325	253	578
6	9/15/2003	718	323	251	574
7	9/22/2003	696	313	243	556
8	9/29/2003	731	328	255	583
9					
10					

Figure 16.3.

FILTERING THE DATABASE

Suppose that you wanted to see only the data for the week in which 718 students were present.

1. Click on any cell within your database.
2. Select Data, Filter, Auto Filter from the menu. Notice the downward facing arrows that appear next to each field name.
3. Click on the downward facing arrow next to Students Present.
4. Click on 718.

	A	B	C	D	E
1	Cafeteria Analysis				
2					
3	Week Beginni	Studs Present	Hot Meals	Cold Meals	Total Meals
4	9/1/2003	(All)	250	185	435
5	9/8/2003	(Top 10...)	325	253	578
6	9/15/2003	(Custom...) 625	323	251	574
7	9/22/2003	696	313	243	556
8	9/29/2003	718	328	255	583
9		723			
10		731			

Figure 16.4.

5. Click OK.

	A	B	C	D	E
1	Cafeteria Analysis				
2					
3	Week Beginni	Studs Present	Hot Meals	Cold Meals	Total Meals
6	9/15/2003	718	323	251	574
9					

Figure 16.5.

The week in which 718 students were present has been filtered from your database. Now close the Auto Filter.

1. Select Data, Filter from the menu.
2. Click on Auto Filter to close it.

MORE COMPLEX FILTERS

In order to perform more complex filters, you will choose from among a variety of *logical operators*. Fortunately, recent versions of Excel make this easy by listing the logical operators in everyday language, rather than using symbols which can be a little more confusing. The most common logical operators are:

- greater than,
- less than,
- not equal to,
- greater than or equal to,
- less than or equal to.

Suppose you wanted to see the weeks in which more than 700 students were present—that is, Students Present was greater than 700 (Fig. 16.6).

1. Click on any cell in the Studs Present column of your database.
2. Select Data, Filter from the menu, and then select Auto Filter.
3. Click on the downward facing arrow next to Students Present.
4. Click on Custom.
5. Click on the downward facing arrow next to "is equal to."
6. Select "is greater than."
7. Type 700 in the box next to "is greater than."
8. Click OK.

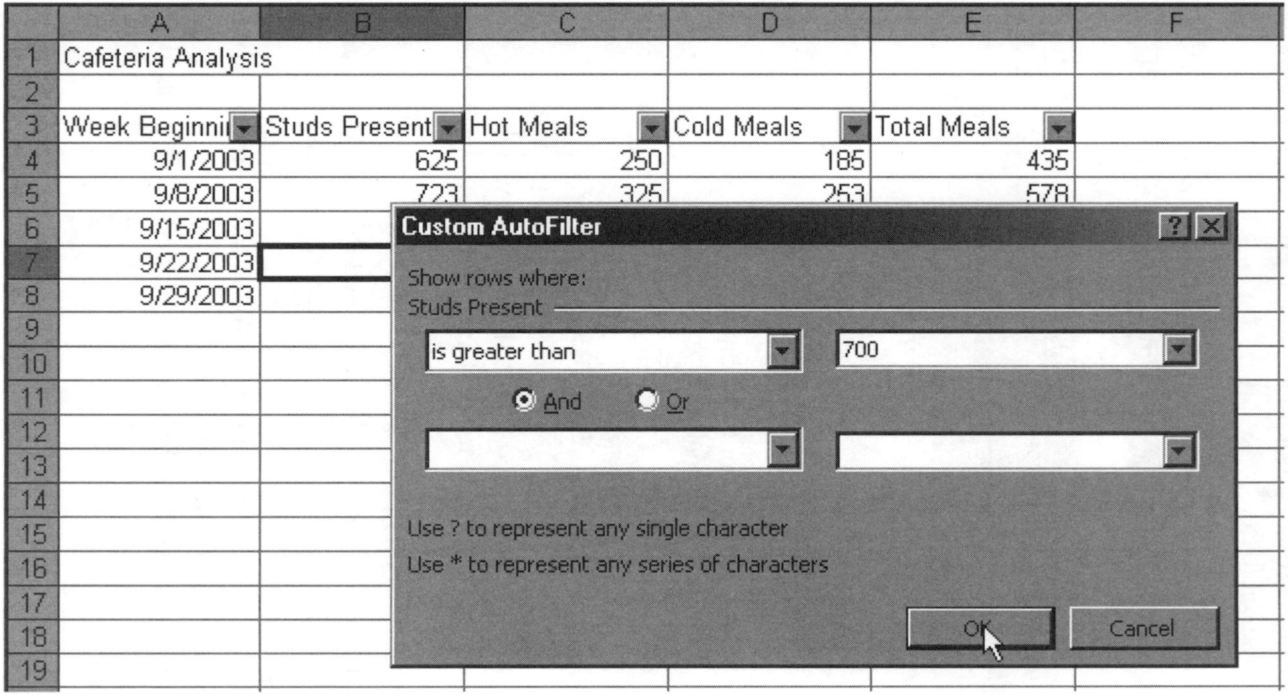

	A	B	C	D	E	F
1	Cafeteria Analysis					
2						
3	Week Beginni	Studs Present	Hot Meals	Cold Meals	Total Meals	
4	9/1/2003	625	250	185	435	
5	9/8/2003	723	325	253	578	
6	9/15/2003					
7	9/22/2003					
8	9/29/2003					
9						
10						
11						
12						
13						
14						
15						
16						
17						
18						
19						

Custom AutoFilter

Show rows where:

Studs Present

is greater than | 700

And | Or

Use ? to represent any single character

Use * to represent any series of characters

OK | Cancel

Figure 16.6.

All the weeks in which Students Present is greater than 700 will be filtered from the database.

	A	B	C	D	E
1	Cafeteria Analysis				
2					
3	Week Beginni	Studs Present	Hot Meals	Cold Meals	Total Meals
5	9/8/2003	723	325	253	578
6	9/15/2003	718	323	251	574
8	9/29/2003	731	328	255	583
9					

Figure 16.7.

Now close the filter.

1. Select Data, Filter from the menu.
2. Click on Auto Filter to close it.

STILL MORE COMPLEX FILTERS

Now suppose that you wanted to find the weeks in which more than 700 students were present AND fewer than 730 students were present.

1. Click on any cell in the database.
2. Select Data, Filter from the menu, and then select Auto Filter.
3. Click on the downward facing arrow next to Studs Present.
4. Select Custom.
5. Select "is greater than" and type 700 in the appropriate box.
6. Be certain that "And" is selected.
7. In the lower section of the dialog box, select "is less than" and type 730.
8. Click OK.

The results of applying your custom filter will be automatically displayed for you.

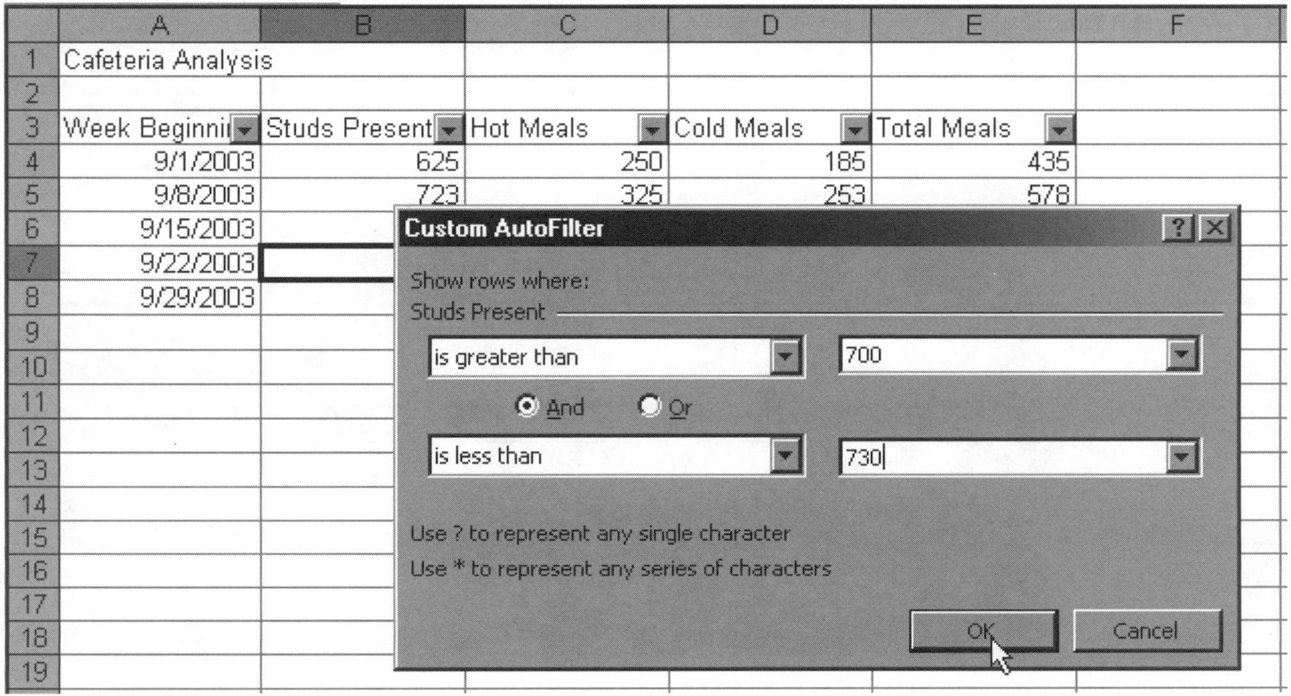

	A	B	C	D	E	F
1	Cafeteria Analysis					
2						
3	Week Beginni	Studs Present	Hot Meals	Cold Meals	Total Meals	
4	9/1/2003	625	250	185	435	
5	9/8/2003	723	325	253	578	
6	9/15/2003					
7	9/22/2003					
8	9/29/2003					
9						
10						
11						
12						
13						
14						
15						
16						
17						
18						
19						

Custom AutoFilter

Show rows where:

Studs Present

is greater than | 700

And | Or

is less than | 730

Use ? to represent any single character

Use * to represent any series of characters

OK | Cancel

Figure 16.8.

	A	B	C	D	E
1	Cafeteria Analysis				
2					
3	Week Beginning	Studs Present	Hot Meals	Cold Meals	Total Meals
5	9/8/2003	723	325	253	578
6	9/15/2003	718	323	251	574
9					

Figure 16.9.

SIMPLIFYING DATABASE OPERATIONS

You have learned how to create a database, how to sort your data, and now, how to filter it. Next, you will learn some shortcuts that will make it even easier for you to work with databases.

Data Forms

Once you create a database, you can use a data form to simplify data entry.

1. Begin by entering field names for your database, and one record directly below the field names.

	A	B	C	D
1	Emergency School Closing			
2	Telephone Chain List			
3				
4	First	Last	A/C	Telephone
5	Mary	Jones	212	987-6543
6				
7				

Figure 16.10.

2. Click on any cell that contains data.
3. Select Data, Form from the menu.

Note that Excel has created a data entry form for you, and that the form is displaying the data in your first record (Fig. 16.11).

Using the Data Form

1. Click on New, or press [Enter] to clear the data entry form so that you can enter a new record.
2. Enter the data for the new record, pressing [Tab] to move from one field to the next.

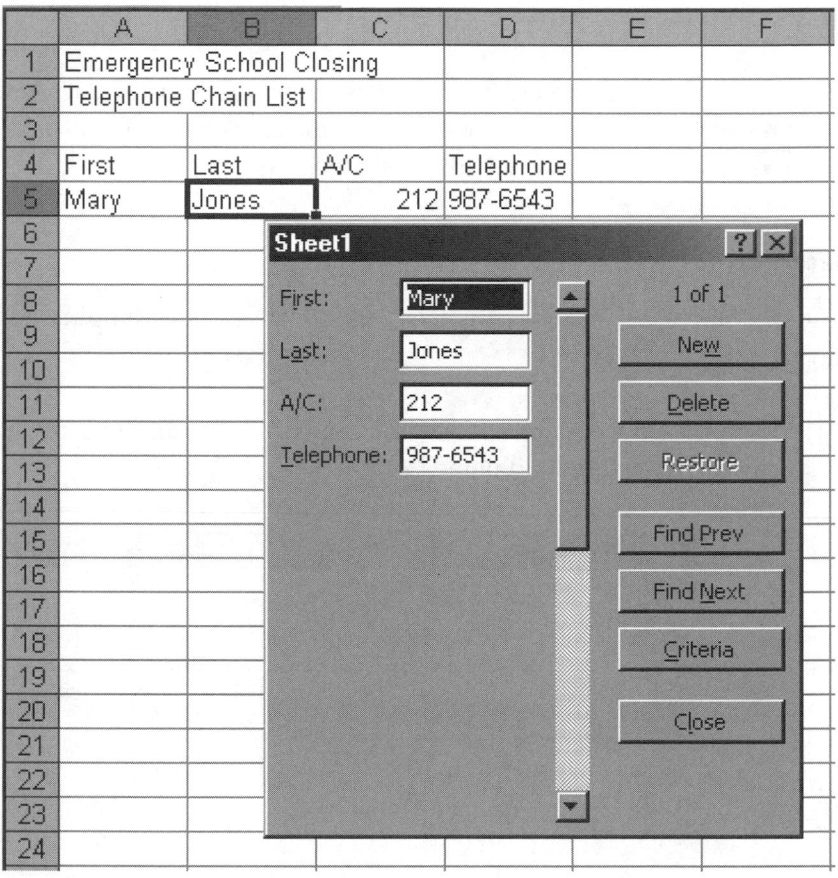

Figure 16.11.

3. Using this method, enter several new records into your database.
4. When you have finished, click on Close to close the data form.

Using a Data Form in an Established Database

Once you have an established database, you can use a data form at any time.

1. Click on any cell in your database.
2. Select Data, Form from the menu to open a data form.

ADDITIONAL DATA FORM OPTIONS

The following options are available when you use a data form. To use any option, simply click on the appropriate data form button.

- **Find Prev** Click on this button to display the previous record in your database.
- **Find Next** Click on this button to display the next record in your database.
- **Delete** This button will delete the record that is currently displayed.
- **Restore** If you start to make changes and want to return to the original information, click the Restore button. Note, however, that the Restore button will *not* restore a record you have deleted.
- **New** The New button will present you with a blank form, so that you can enter a new record.

In addition to the Find Prev and Find Next buttons, you may also use the scroll bar to move from one record to another.

NAVIGATING WITHIN A DATABASE

In regular view, you will usually move from one field or record to another by using the keyboard arrow keys. However, you can sometimes speed the process by using the following combination keyboard shortcuts to maneuver within your database.

- **[Ctrl] [Right Arrow]** Last field in the selected record.
- **[Ctrl] [Left Arrow]** First field in the selected record.
- **[Ctrl] [Up Arrow]** First record in the database.
- **[Ctrl] [Down Arrow]** Last record in the database.
- **[Tab]** Enter data and move one cell to the right.
- **[Shift] [Tab]** Enter data and move one cell to the left.

EXERCISE 16

1. Give two examples of situations in which you might want to filter a database.
2. Explain how to enter a series of dates that are exactly one week apart into a database.
3. Explain how to filter a database using the Auto Filter feature.
4. Describe how to perform a more complex filtering operation.
5. How would you create a data form for an existing database?
6. Explain how to use a data form.
7. Describe what each of the buttons in a data form does.
8. Describe the keystrokes you can use to navigate within a database.
9. Create a database and enter one record. Create a data form for the database. Enter several additional records using the data form. Close the data form.
10. Practice using the navigation keys that you have learned.

17

ADDITIONAL DATABASE OPERATIONS

This is the third and final chapter about using Excel for database management. You will learn some additional techniques for simplifying data entry, as well as some new database operations.

ENTERING DATES AND TIMES

It is likely you will be making some kinds of entries in your databases much more often than others. Two of the most common entries are the current date and the current time.

- To enter the current date into a cell, press [Ctrl] [;]—that is, Ctrl + semicolon.
- To enter the current time into a cell, press [Ctrl] [:]—that is, Ctrl + colon.

REPEATING PREVIOUS ENTRIES

You will also often find that as you enter records, you will frequently enter data into a cell that is identical to the data in the cell directly above.

For example, you have just entered a record of a client in New York. The next client also lives in New York.

- To repeat data that appears in the cell above, press [Ctrl] [‘] or [Ctrl] [“]—that is, Ctrl + apostrophe, or Ctrl + quotation mark.

Note that this shortcut, and also the date and time shortcuts in the section above, will work not only in databases, but also in any Excel worksheet.

AUTOFORMATTING A DATABASE

You can quickly format a database (this technique will also work with any type of Excel worksheet).

1. Click on any cell in the database (or worksheet).
2. Select Format, Auto Format from the menu (Fig. 17.1).
3. Select a format from the samples that are displayed.
4. Click OK, and the format you have chosen will be applied to your worksheet.

Of course, if Excel has not formatted the worksheet exactly as you want it formatted, you can modify it using the standard formatting techniques you have previously learned.

SORTING FROM THE TOOLBAR

There are two buttons on the toolbar you can use to simplify sorting a database—A-Z sort button and Z-A sort button.

1. To sort a database, click on any cell in the column that you want to sort by.
2. Click on the A-Z sort button to perform a sort in ascending order.
3. Or, click on the Z-A sort button to perform a sort in descending order (Fig. 17.2).

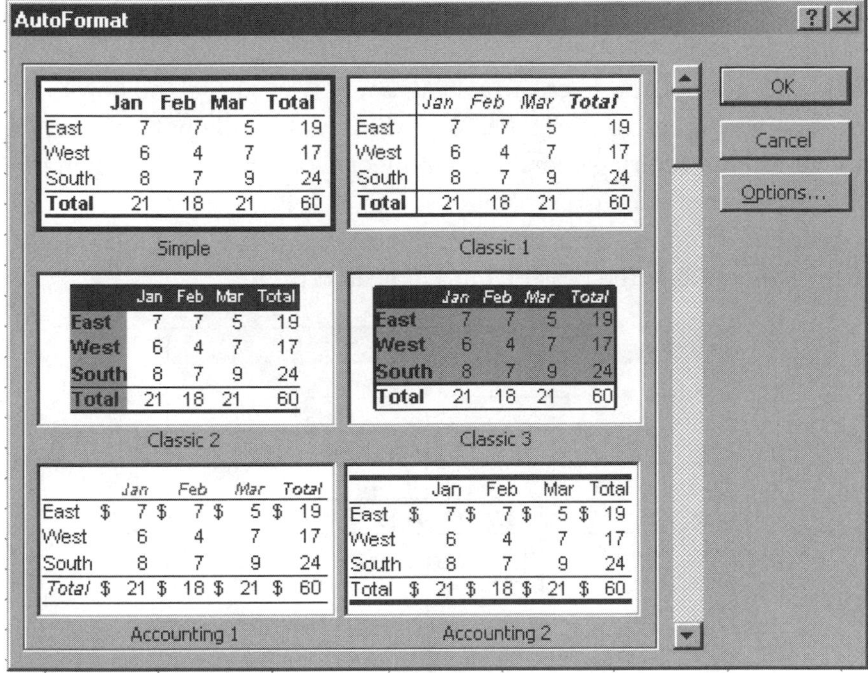

Figure 17.1.

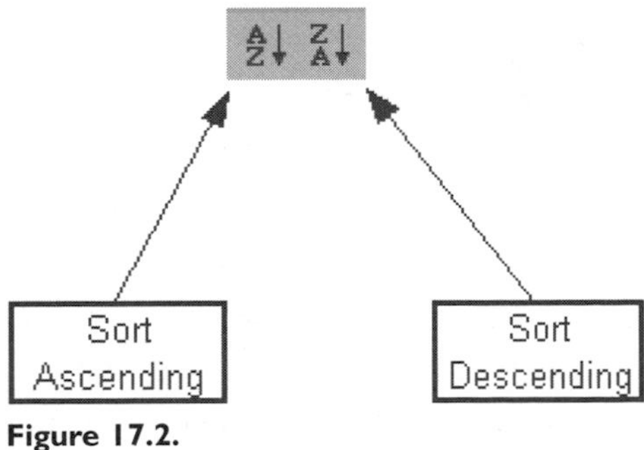

Figure 17.2.

In most cases, Excel will be able to determine that your field names are field names rather than data. But rarely, Excel will inadvertently sort your field names in with your data. If this happens, it will be necessary for you to sort your database in the traditional way. Select Edit, Undo to return your database to its original state, and then sort the database the way you have previously learned.

DATA EXTRACT

You have learned how to create a database, how to sort it, and how to filter data that meet your criteria. You will now learn how to perform a special kind of filtering operation that meets your criteria, and then display the filtered data in a separate list.

Create a database of faculty salaries using figure 17.3. Be certain to enter the data into the cells that are indicated there.

	A	B	C	D
1				
2				
3				
4				
5	Last	First	Age	Salary
6	Adams	Tom	45	52000
7	Eng	Ted	35	44000
8	Ortiz	Maria	40	41000
9	Smith	John	25	34000
10	Walker	Barbara	30	42000
11				

Figure 17.3.

CREATE A CRITERIA RANGE

Previously, you filtered a database using the Data, Filter, Auto Filter command. In this case, you will accomplish the same thing without using Excel's Auto Filter. You will do this by first creating a criteria range. A *criteria range* is a section in your worksheet where you will indicate what you are searching for. It consists of a copy of the field names, and one row below the copied field names. Your first step is to copy the field names to a blank section of your worksheet. In this case, copy the field names to cells A1:D1.

1. Drag across cells A5:D5 to select them.
2. Select Edit, Copy from the menu.
3. Click on cell A1.
4. Select Edit, Paste from the menu.

CREATE AN EXTRACT RANGE

The extract range is where you want the data that will be filtered from your database to be displayed. Copy the field names to any blank area of the worksheet. Just be certain there is nothing below this copy of the field names. You do not want the data you extract to overwrite part of your worksheet. In this case, you will copy the field names to cells A12:D12.

1. Drag across cells A5:D5 to select them.
2. Select Edit, Copy from the menu.
3. Click on cell A12.
4. Select Edit, Paste from the menu.

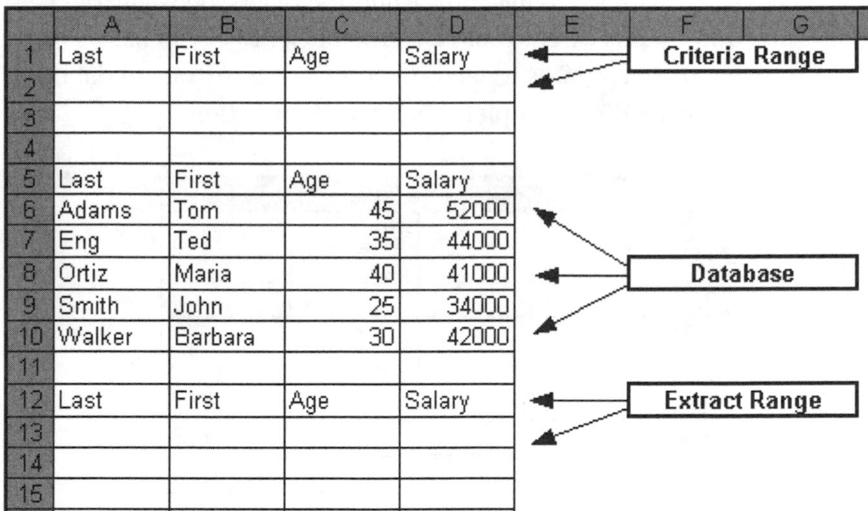

	A	B	C	D
1	Last	First	Age	Salary
2				
3				
4				
5	Last	First	Age	Salary
6	Adams	Tom	45	52000
7	Eng	Ted	35	44000
8	Ortiz	Maria	40	41000
9	Smith	John	25	34000
10	Walker	Barbara	30	42000
11				
12	Last	First	Age	Salary
13				
14				
15				

Figure 17.4.

THE CRITERIA RANGE AND EXTRACT RANGE

Note that the *criteria range* will consist of the first copy of your field names and one row below them. In this case, the criteria range consists of the range of cells A1:D2. The *extract range* will consist of the second copy of your field names. In this case, the extract range consists of the range of cells A12:D12. Excel will include as many additional rows as it needs below A12:D12 to contain your extracted data.

Perform the Extract Operation

Begin by entering your search criteria. In this case, type >35 in cell C2. You are now ready to perform the extract operation.

1. Click on any cell in your database that contains data.
2. Select Data, Filter, Advanced Filter from the menu.
3. In this situation, Excel refers to the field names and the data as the list range. Note that the list range $A$5:$D$10 has been entered for you, and that the database is highlighted (don't be concerned about the dollar signs).
4. Select Copy to Another Location (Fig 17.5).
5. Enter the criteria range, in this case A1:D2.
6. Click on the Copy to Range box. Enter the range you want your data copied to. In this case A12:D12 (remember, Excel will use as many rows below A12:D12 as it needs to contain your extracted data).
7. Finally, click OK to complete the extract operation.

	A	B	C	D
1	Last	First	Age	Salary
2			>35	
3				
4				
5	Last	First	Age	Salary
6	Adams	Tom	45	52000
7	Eng	Ted	35	44000
8	Ortiz	Maria	40	41000
9	Smith	John	25	34000
10	Walker	Barbara	30	42000
11				
12	Last	First	Age	Salary
13	Adams	Tom	45	52000
14	Ortiz	Maria	40	41000
15				
16				
17				
18				
19				

Figure 17.6.

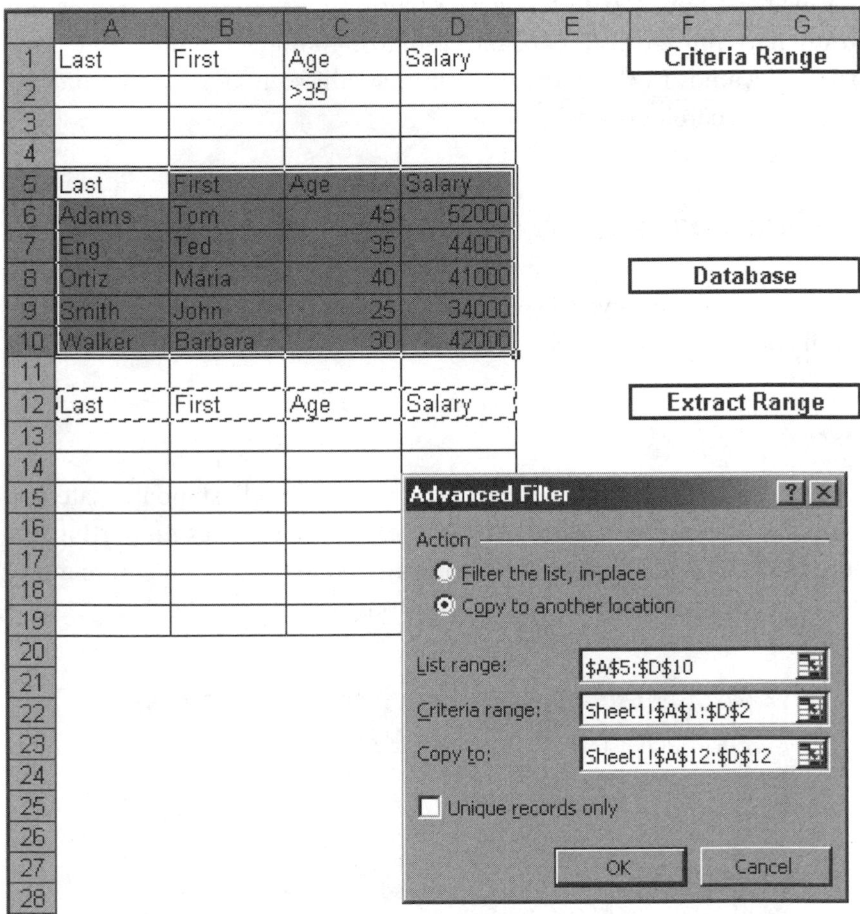

A
B
C
D
E
F
G
Criteria Range
Last
First
Age
Salary
>35
Last
First
Age
Salary
Adams
Tom
45
52000
Eng
Ted
35
44000
Ortiz
Maria
40
41000
Database
Smith
John
25
34000
Walker
Barbara
30
42000
Last
First
Age
Salary
Extract Range
Advanced Filter
Action
Filter the list, in-place
Copy to another location
List range:
$A$5:$D$10
Criteria range:
Sheet1!$A$1:$D$2
Copy to:
Sheet1!$A$12:$D$12
Unique records only
OK
Cancel

Figure 17.5.

Note that the data that have been filtered out of your database have been copied to the extract range. But note also that while the data have been copied to your extract range, the original data still remain in your database.

Finally, if you had not selected Copy to Another Location, Excel would have filtered your data and displayed them where the entire database is located. In this case, it would have hidden all data that did not meet your search criteria.

SPECIAL DATABASE OPERATIONS

Excel can perform several special sort operations that you will find useful in some of your worksheets.

Dates

If you enter dates into a database in any of Excel's standard date formats, Excel can sort by date. The process is the same as for sorting any other kind of data. You can use either the Data, Sort menu command or the Ascending or Descending sort buttons.

	A	B
1	Birthdays	
2		
3	Student	Birthdate
4	John	1/1/1995
5	Maria	2/1/1997
6	David	3/1/1993
7	Alice	4/1/1996
8	Carlos	8/1/1994
9	Denise	6/1/1992
10		
11		
12	Unsorted Dates	
13		

	A	B
1	Birthdays	
2		
3	Student	Birthdate
4	Denise	6/1/1992
5	David	3/1/1993
6	Carlos	8/1/1994
7	John	1/1/1995
8	Alice	4/1/1996
9	Maria	2/1/1997
10		
11		
12	Sorted Dates	
13		

Figure 17.7.

Sorting by Days and Months

Excel can also sort months and days, although the process is just slightly more complicated than an ordinary sort. Create a database based on figure 17.8.

	A	B
1	Bake Sale	
2		
3	Day	Cakes Sold
4	Mon	22
5	Thu	22
6	Tue	25
7	Wed	28
8	Fri	35
9		

Figure 17.8.

You will now sort the database by day—that is, you will put the days in their correct order.

1. Highlight the entire sort range (all the data, but not the field names).
2. Select Data, Sort from the menu.
3. Select Options.
4. Indicate the type of data you are sorting, such as Sun., Mon., Tue., or Jan., Feb., Mar.
5. Click OK to return to the Sort dialog box.
6. Click OK to perform the sort.

Left to Right Sorts

Most often, your data will be in a *horizontal format*. That is, the field names will appear in one row, and each record will appear in a row below the field names. On rare occasions, you will have created a database in which the field names will appear in a column, and each record appears in a column, rather than a row. In these cases, if you want to sort your data it will be necessary to sort from left to right.

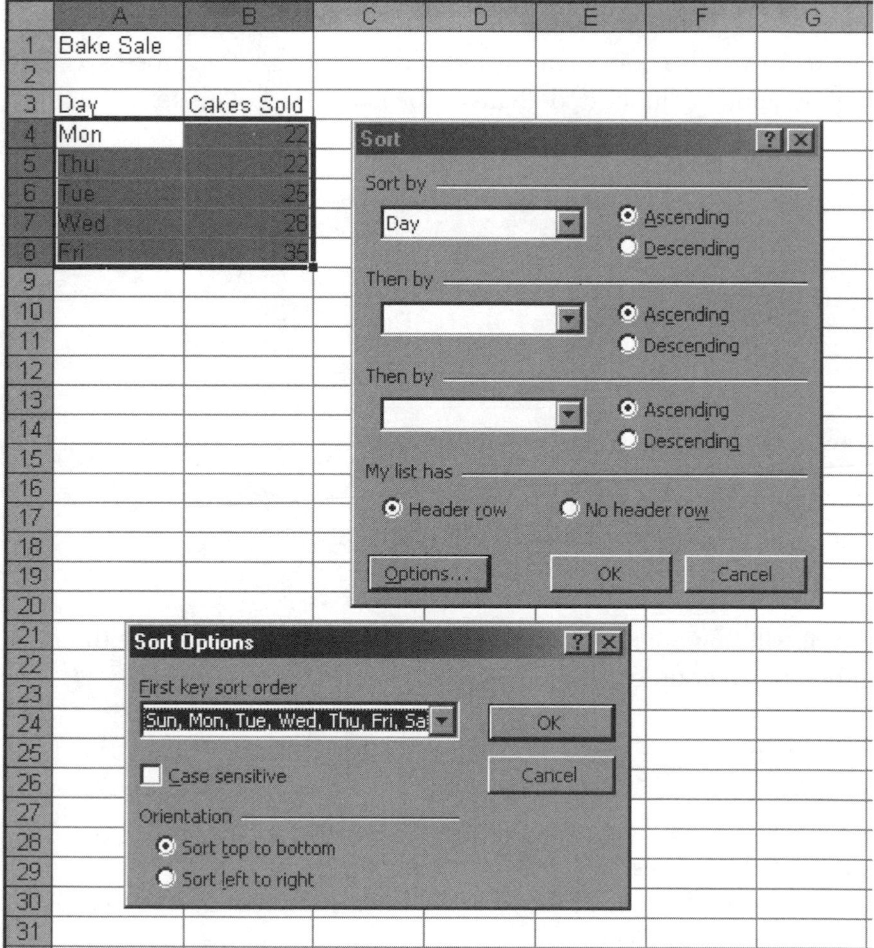

Figure 17.9.

1. Highlight the entire database, both the field names and the data.
2. Select Data, Sort from the menu.
3. Select Options.
4. Indicate you want to sort from Left to Right.
5. Click OK to return to the Sort dialog box.
6. Indicate the row (field) you want to sort by.
7. Click OK to perform the sort.

Try it by creating a worksheet based on figure 17.10.

	A	B	C	D	E	F	G
1							
2							
3							
4							
5							
6	Name	Wilkins	Smith	Adams	Chin	Davis	Barbera
7	Age	15	20	25	30	35	40
8							

Figure 17.10.

Now sort the data in ascending order by name:

1. Select (highlight) the entire database, in this case, A6:G7.
2. Select Data, Sort from the menu.
3. Select Options.
4. Indicate that you want to sort from Left to Right.
5. Click OK to return to the Sort dialog box.
6. Indicate that you want to sort by Name.
7. Click OK to perform the sort (Fig. 17.11).

Sorting on More than Three Fields

Ordinarily, Excel allows you to sort by only three fields. However, you can trick Excel into sorting by more than three fields. Suppose, for example, you have created a database in which the fields are: First Name, Last Name, City, and State, and that you want to sort by State, then by City, and finally by Last Name. But suppose also that you have several people in a particular city who have the same last name. You will want to sort your data, first by state, then by city, then by last name, and finally by first name. In other words, you want to sort your data by four sort keys, but Excel only allows you to sort by three. The trick is to sort by the least important field first, and after you have completed that sort, to sort by the remaining three sort keys. In this case, you would proceed as follows:

1. Begin by sorting by First.
2. Then, after you have completed the sort by First, go back and sort by City, then by State, and then by Last.

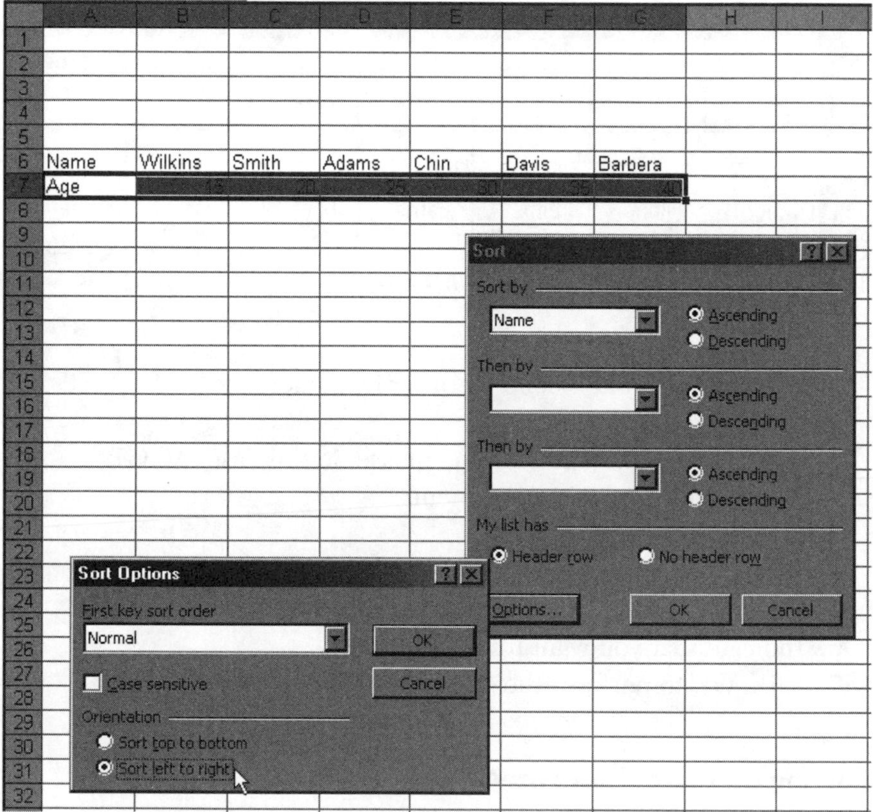

Figure 17.11.

In this way, you will have been able to sort your data by more than three fields.

EXERCISE 17

1. What is the shortcut for entering the current date into a cell?
2. What is the shortcut for entering the current time into a cell?
3. Suppose you wanted to enter data into a cell that are identical to the data in the cell directly above it. What is the easiest way to repeat the data from the cell above to the current cell?
4. Why might you want to autoformat a database or other worksheet?
5. Explain how to autoformat a database or other worksheet.

6. Describe how to sort a database from the toolbar.
7. What does data extract do?
8. Explain the following terms:
   Criteria range
   Extract range
9. Review the steps for performing the data extract operation. Using any database you have previously created, perform the data extract operation.
10. Suppose you had created a database that contains the information given in figure 17.12.

	A	B
1	Suspensions by Month	
2		
3	Month	Suspensions
4	March	10
5	December	20
6	February	30
7	April	40
8	January	50
9		

Figure 17.12.

11. Explain how to sort the database by month.
12. Create the database, and perform the sort operation.
13. Explain how to perform a left to right sort.
14. Create a database in which records appear in columns rather than rows, and perform a left to right sort.
15. Give an example of a database in which you might want to sort by more than three fields. Explain how you would perform the sort.
16. Create any database and apply some of the concepts you have learned in this chapter.

18

CREATING A CHART FROM AN EXCEL WORKSHEET

Worksheets can be a very effective way to display your data. But graphs—Excel calls them *charts*—often make it even easier to see relationships between data and trends. This chapter describes how to create charts from Excel worksheets. Fortunately, Excel makes it very easy to create a wide variety of charts from your worksheets—you can even produce really professional looking three-dimensional charts.

BASIC PRINCIPLES—CHARTS

Before you create your first Excel chart, you should be familiar with the following terms and concepts.

1. Every chart or graph has an X axis and a Y axis. The *X axis* is the horizontal line that usually appears at the bottom of the chart. It is also called the *category* or *time* axis because it most commonly contains the categories of information associated with the chart, or measures progress over a period of time. The *Y axis* is the vertical line that usually appears at the left side of the chart. It is referred to as the *value* axis because it generally represents numerical criteria associated with your data.

2. All charts consist of at least one *data range*, which is made up of the individual data points that are to be plotted. In your worksheet, the data ranges are usually the rows that contain the numerical data you are charting.
3. Your worksheet will usually contain two rows of text, usually column headings and row headings. The *column headings* will generally become your X axis categories. The row headings will generally refer to the individual data ranges.
4. Excel will create a scale along the Y axis. The numbers in the Y axis will be formatted in the same format as that of your worksheet.
5. The default chart format is a column chart. However, you may choose from among a wide variety of charts.
6. If you want, Excel will include a *legend* for your chart that will indicate which columns or lines represent which data.

BASIC PRINCIPLES—WORKSHEETS

If you are going to create a chart from a worksheet, you will find that the process is much easier if you follow a few conventions.

1. Your worksheet will generally include column and row headings. Each heading should appear in only one cell.

Figure 18.1.

2. Do not include blank rows or columns in your worksheet.
3. Format numbers if appropriate.

CREATE A WORKSHEET

Begin by creating a worksheet from which you will create your first chart. Note that each column and row heading occupies only one cell, and there are no blank rows or columns in the worksheet.

1. Create a worksheet from figure 18.2.

	A	B	C	D	E	F
1	Weekly Attendance					
2	By Grade					
3						
4		Mon	Tue	Wed	Thu	Fri
5	10	550	582	585	583	540
6	11	612	626	629	635	618
7	12	508	512	518	522	518
8						
9						

Figure 18.2.

2. Then save it as WeekAtt.

CREATING A CHART

1. Begin by selecting (highlighting) the data that you want to chart. In this case, select the range A4:F7. Note that you have selected the numerical data, and also the headings at the top and to the left of the numerical data.
2. Select Insert, Chart from the menu, or click on the Chart Wizard button on the toolbar.

Figure 18.3.

3. In either case, the Excel Chart Wizard will appear. It will ask you what kind of chart you want to create. Choose a type of chart on the left side of the Chart dialog box, and you will see subtypes displayed to the right. In this case, select Column chart, and within Column charts, select the first subtype.

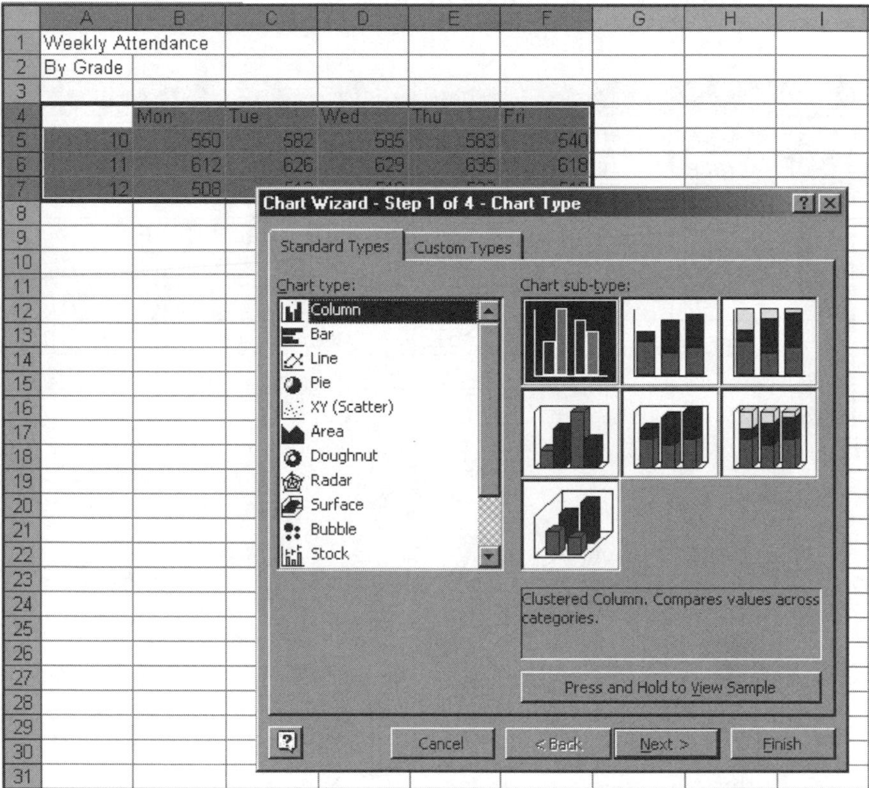

Figure 18.4.

4. Click Next.
5. You will now see a display of what your completed chart will look like. Excel has assumed that your series are in rows. If you wanted to create a chart from a worksheet in which the series are in columns, simply select Series in Columns. Try it here, but then return to Series in Rows.

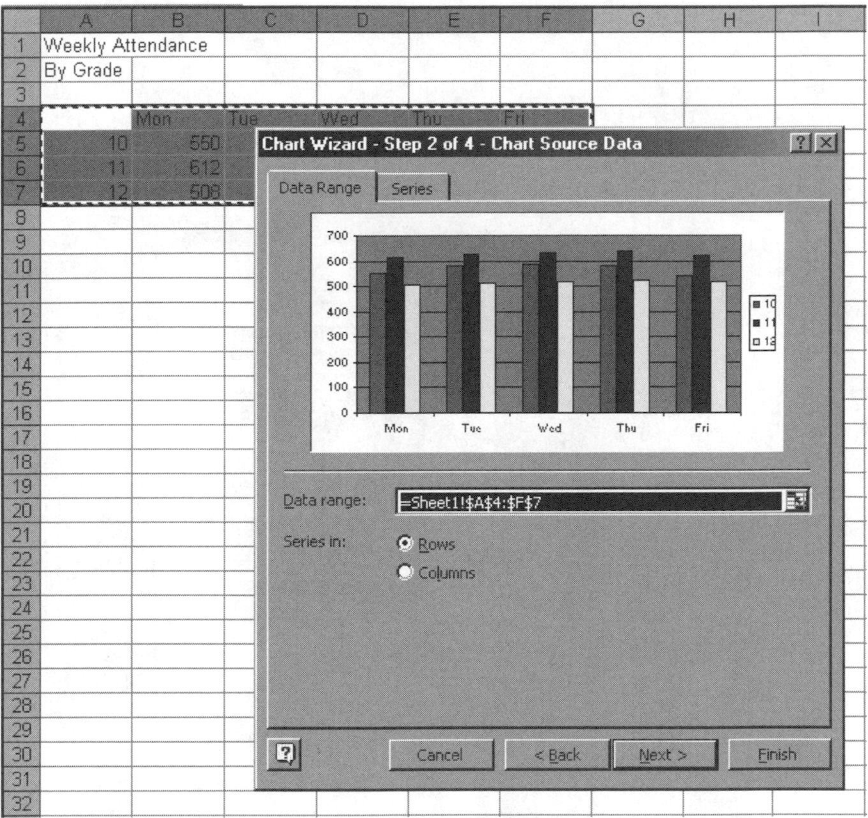

Figure 18.5.

6. Click Next.
7. Click in the Chart Title box. Type a chart title, in this case, Weekly Attendance. You may also enter titles for the X and Y axes in the same way.
8. Most of the other options in this dialog box (Axes, Gridlines, Legend, Data Labels, Data Table) are self-explanatory. Experiment with them if you would like.
9. Click Next.
10. You must now tell Excel if you want your chart to be included on the same sheet as your worksheet (As Object In), or as a separate sheet (As New Sheet) in the workbook. In this case, select, As Object In.

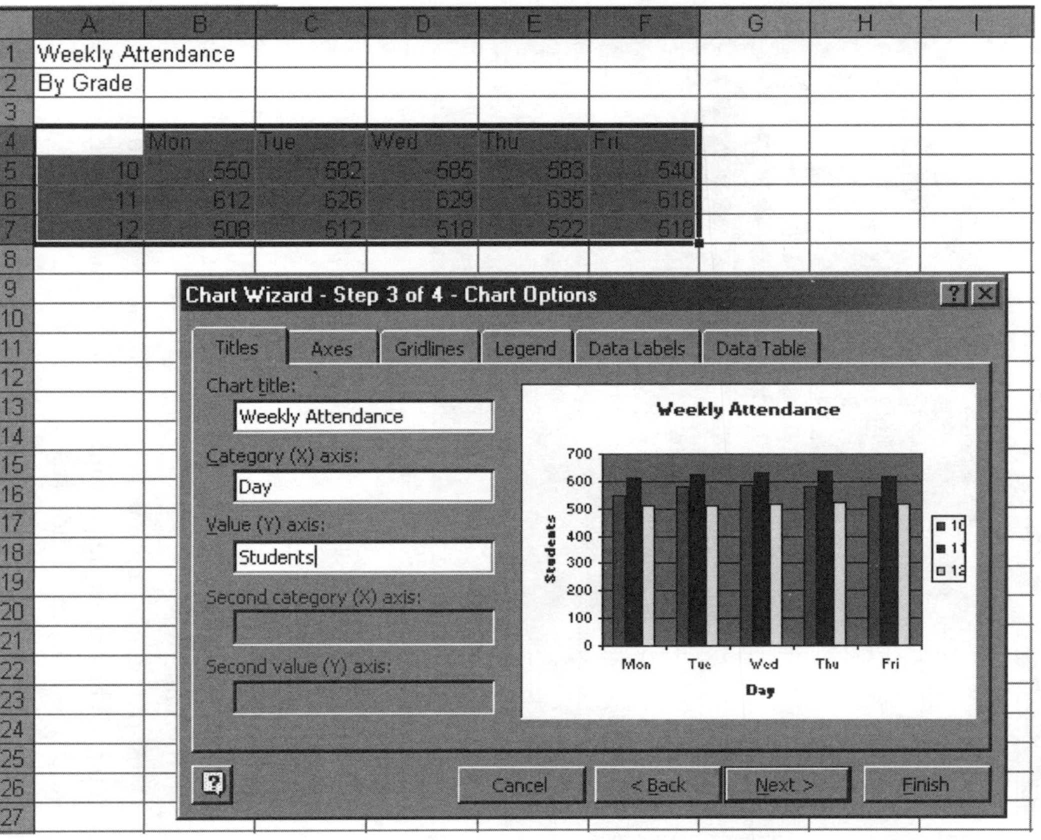
A
B
C
D
E
F
G
H
I
Weekly Attendance
By Grade
Mon Tue Wed Thu Fri
10 550 582 585 583 540
11 612 626 629 635 618
12 508 512 518 522 518
Chart Wizard - Step 3 of 4 - Chart Options
Titles
Axes
Gridlines
Legend
Data Labels
Data Table
Chart title:
Weekly Attendance
Category (X) axis:
Day
Value (Y) axis:
Students
Second category (X) axis:
Second value (Y) axis:
Weekly Attendance
700
600
500
400
300
200
100
0
Students
Mon
Tue
Wed
Thu
Fri
Day
Cancel
< Back
Next >
Finish

Figure 18.6.

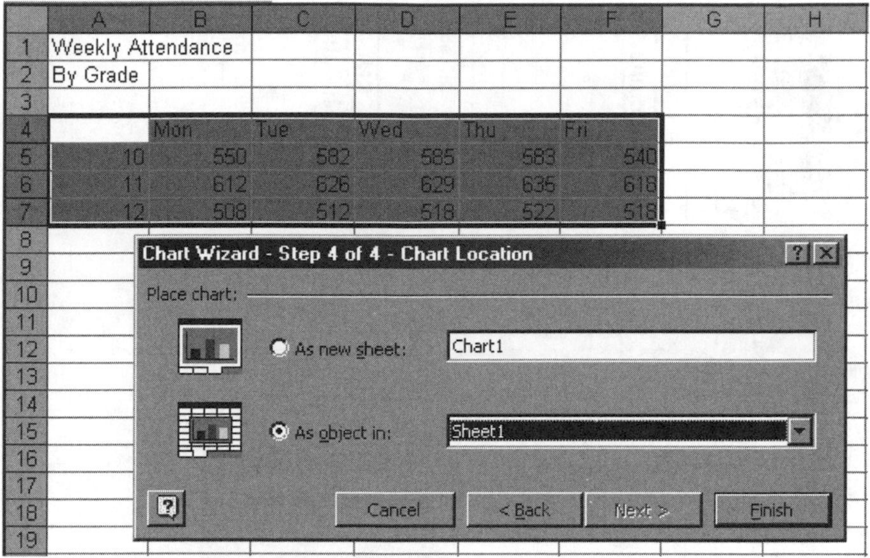

Figure 18.7.

11. Click Finish. You will see your completed chart displayed on the same page as your worksheet.

Notice that your chart is selected. That is, there are eight *sizing handles*, small boxes at the corners and centers of the lines that surround the chart. Notice also that there is a new toolbar visible on the screen. This is the Chart toolbar, which should be visible whenever the chart is selected (Fig. 18.8).

If you click on a part of the worksheet outside the chart, the sizing handles will disappear, indicating that the chart is no longer selected. In that case, the Chart toolbar will also no longer be displayed.

1. Click on the chart to select the chart.
2. Click outside the chart to select the worksheet.

CHANGING THE CHART SIZE

You can modify the size of the chart at any time.

1. If the chart is not selected, click anywhere within the chart to select it.

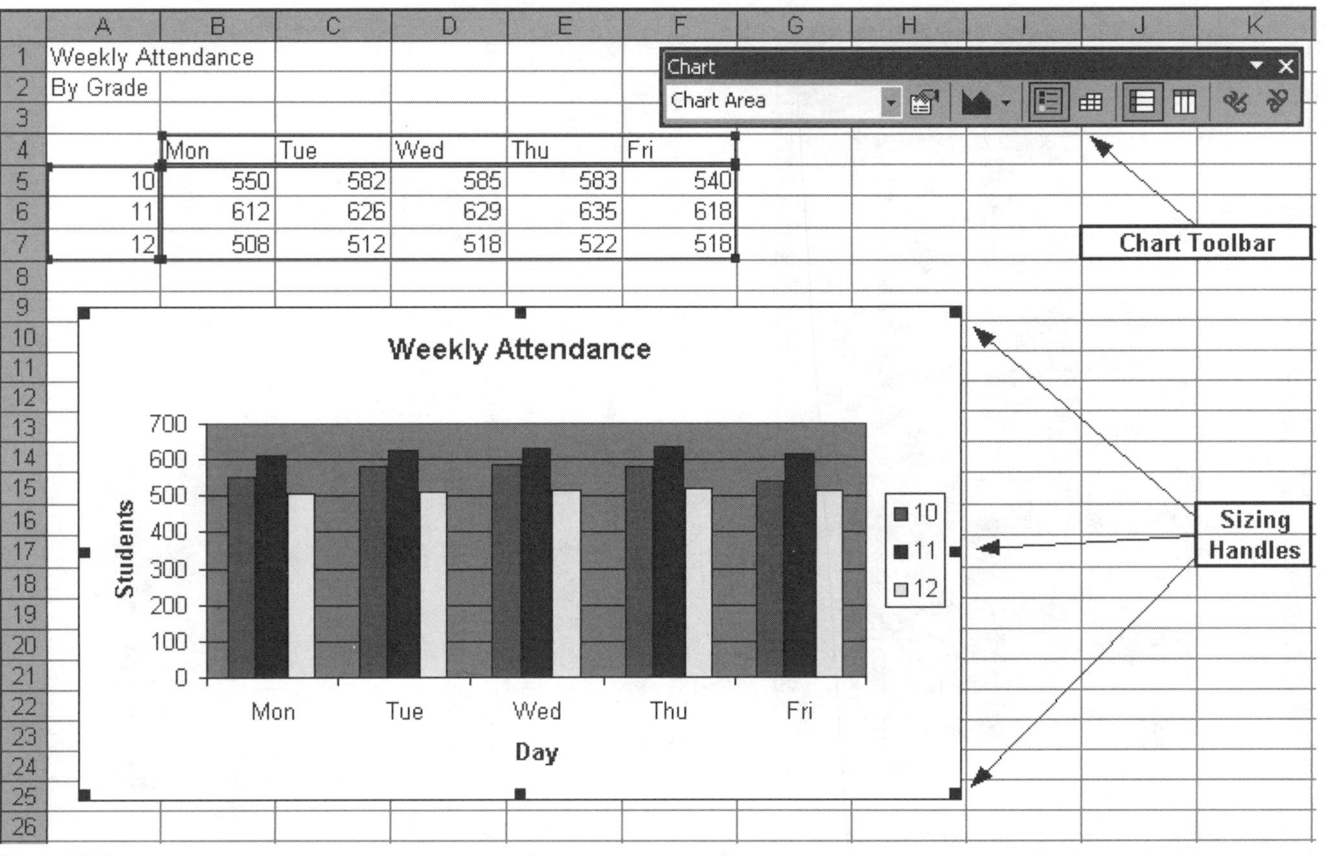
Weekly Attendance
By Grade
Mon Tue Wed Thu Fri
10 550 582 585 583 540
11 612 626 629 635 618
12 508 512 518 522 518
Chart
Chart Area
Chart Toolbar
Weekly Attendance
Students
Day
10
11
12
Sizing Handles

Figure 18.8.

2. Point the cursor to any of the sizing handles, hold down the left mouse button, and drag the handle to increase or decrease the size of the chart.
   a. The handles at the center of the sides of the chart enable you to increase or decrease the horizontal size of the chart.
   b. The handles at the center of the top and bottom of the chart enable you to increase or decrease the vertical size of the chart.
   c. The handles at the corners of the chart enable you to change both the horizontal and vertical size of the chart at one time.

MOVING A CHART

You may also move the chart.

1. Click on the chart to select it.
2. Point the cursor to one of the borders of the chart (but not one of the sizing handles).
3. Hold down the left mouse button, and drag the chart to a new location.

YOUR CHART IS DYNAMIC

Your chart is dynamic in that if you change data in the worksheet, the chart will automatically change to reflect the changed data. Change the Monday attendance figure for Grade 10. Note that when you press [Enter], the appropriate column on the chart will instantly change. If necessary, the scale will change so that it reflects the new data accurately.

THE CHART TOOLBAR

The Chart toolbar should be visible whenever a chart is selected. If you click on the chart to select it and do not see the Chart toolbar displayed, select View, Toolbars from the menu and select the Chart toolbar. The Chart toolbar will now be displayed, and will remain displayed as long as the chart remains selected. It will disappear from view when the worksheet is selected.

The Chart toolbar contains a number of buttons that are useful as you work with charts.

Figure 18.9.

1. The first tool is called the Chart Objects tool. It allows you to select different elements of your chart, such as the Category Axis and the Legend. The *Chart area*, that is, the entire chart, is selected by default.
2. The second tool, the Format Chart Area tool, allows you to format the chart element you selected in item 1.
3. The third tool is the Chart Type tool. It allows you to change the type of chart. That is, for example, you can change a column chart to a line chart.
4. The fourth tool, the Legend tool, allows you to add a legend to your chart, or if there is a legend, to remove it.
5. The fifth tool is called the Data Table tool. It allows you to add a data table to your chart, or if there is a data table, to remove it. A *data table* is a small worksheet that contains the data you have charted.
6. The sixth tool, the By Row tool, allows you to organize data ranges by rows (the default).
7. The seventh tool, the By Column tool, allows you to organize data ranges by columns.
8. The eighth and ninth buttons, Angle Clockwise and Angle Counterclockwise, are available only if you have selected a text item (such as the X axis titles). They allow you to display the text at an angle, which in some instances will improve the appearance of your chart.

Experiment with each of these tools to see how they affect the appearance of your chart.

RESAVE THE WORKSHEET

You originally saved the worksheet before you created your chart. Now, resave the worksheet to save both the worksheet and the chart you have created.

DIFFERENT TYPES OF CHARTS

The kind of chart you choose will depend on the kind of data you are displaying. Different types of charts are better suited to displaying different kinds of data. Because Excel makes it easy to change the type of chart, experiment until you find the kind of chart that works best with your data.

CREATE A NEW WORKSHEET AND CHART

Create a worksheet from figure 18.10 so you can explore some of the many different types of charts that Excel makes available to you.

After you create the worksheet, you will create the same type of column chart you created before. But this time, when the Chart Wizard

	A	B	C	D	E
1	Student Enrollment by Grade				
2					
3		1998	1999	2000	2001
4	Grade 10	500	525	590	635
5	Grade 11	450	540	635	670
6	Grade 12	375	520	425	485
7					
8					

Figure 18.10.

asks where you want to create your chart, indicate that you want to create it on a separate sheet in your workbook.

Your worksheet and your chart will appear on separate sheets, but both will be contained in the same Excel workbook. You can move back and forth from the chart to the worksheet by clicking on the Chart 1 and Sheet 1 tabs at the bottom of your worksheet.

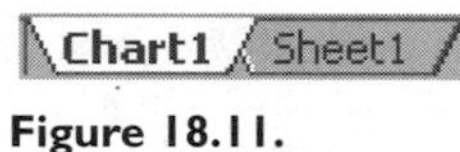

Figure 18.11.

1. Save the workbook as STUDENTS.

TYPES OF CHARTS

Use the Chart Type button on the Chart toolbar to experiment with different types of charts. In some cases, you will not find the particular kind of chart you are looking for on the Chart toolbar. You can view all the different chart types by selecting Format, Chart Type, Options from the menu. The best way to become familiar with the different kinds of charts is to practice creating a variety of different kinds of charts. The following are some of the more commonly used types of charts that Excel makes available to you.

Area Charts

Area charts are like line charts. Both show changes in magnitude over a period of time. The difference is that with an area chart, the second line begins where the first ends. So the chart displays not only the magnitude of each line, but also the total magnitude of all the lines together.

In this case, the first line shows the number of students in Grade 10 over a period of four years. The number of students in Grade 11 is shown above the number of students in Grade 10, and the number of students in Grade 12 is shown above the number of students in Grade 11. The advantage of an area chart in this case is that you can see the relative numbers of students in each grade, but you can also see the total number of students in the three grades by reading the top line.

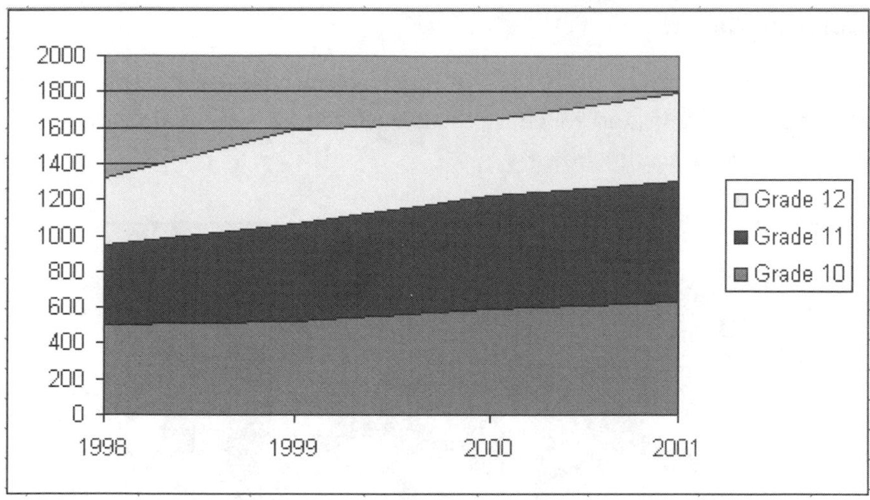

Figure 18.12.

Bar Charts

Bar charts are like column charts, but they use horizontal bars, rather than vertical columns, to display your data graphically. There are no hard and fast rules to help you choose between column charts and bar charts. In each case, use whichever seems to you to display your data most appropriately.

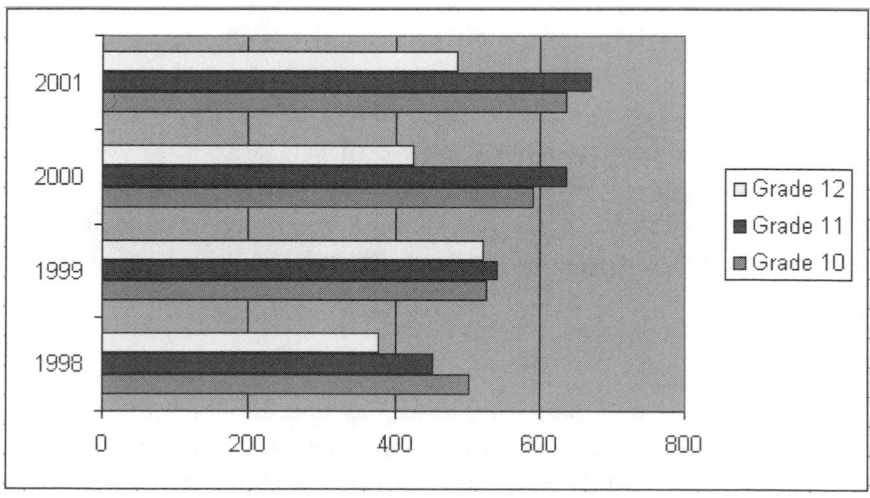

Figure 18.13.

Column Charts

Column charts are probably the most commonly used charts. If you aren't sure which kind of chart to use to display your data, a column chart is usually a safe choice.

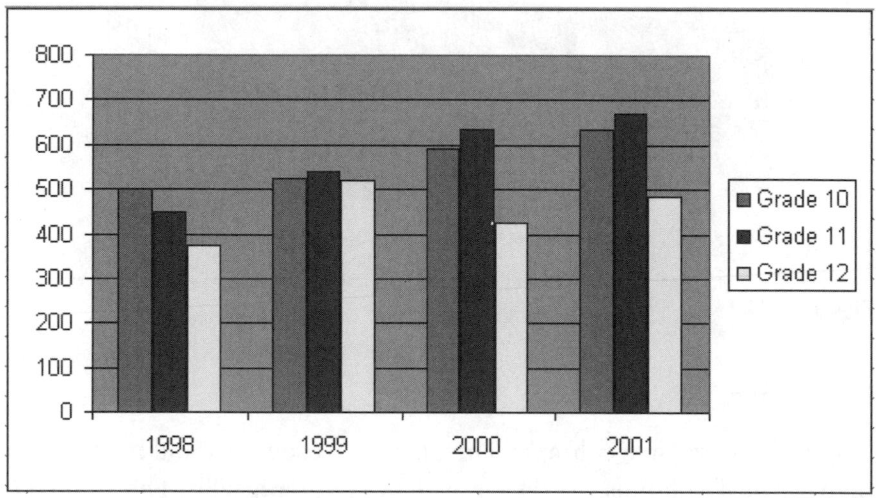

Figure 18.14.

Line Charts

Line charts are most commonly used for displaying data trends over periods of time. A special type of line chart is a high low average or high low close chart. The *high low average* chart is particularly useful for displaying data such as temperature trends (it can be used to display the high and low temperatures for each day over a period of time). And the *high low close* chart is particularly useful for displaying the prices of stocks and other financial instruments (Fig. 18.15).

Pie Charts

Pie charts are commonly used to display data in which there is only one data range. A pie chart compares each part of the data range as it is related to the other parts. You will learn more about pie charts in the next chapter.

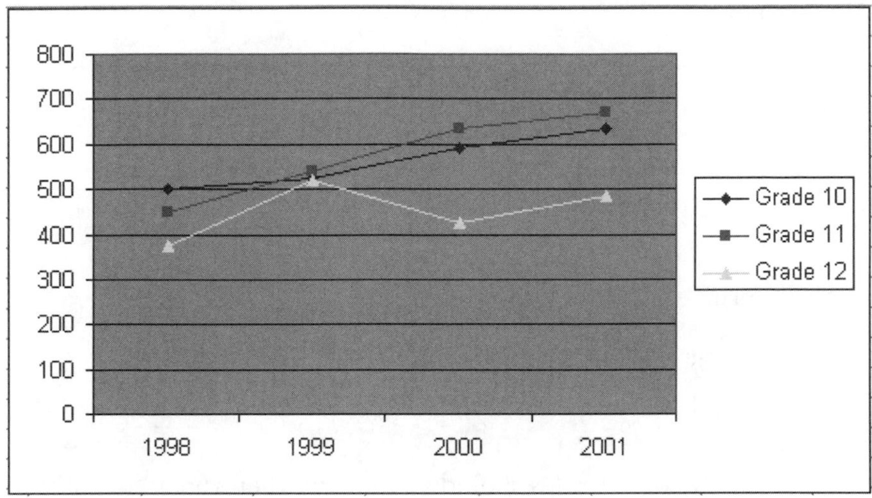

Figure 18.15.

Radar Charts

In a *radar chart*, each category has its own axis, which radiates from the center point.

Scatter Charts

Scatter charts are also called XY charts. They are useful for displaying the relationships between pairs of numbers, where one number is plotted on the X axis, and the other on the Y axis. This type of chart is most commonly used in statistical analyses.

Combination Charts

As the name implies, *combination charts* consist of two different kinds of charts, plotted on the same axis. Combination charts are useful when you are plotting two different kinds of data at one time, for example, workforce and production.

3D Charts

Three-dimensional charts are probably the most impressive looking charts. Use them to make impressive displays and presentations.

EXERCISE 18

1. Explain each of the following terms:
   X axis
   Y axis
   Data range
   Legend
2. What important rules should you follow when you are creating a worksheet from which you intend to create a chart?
3. Explain how to create a chart from a worksheet.
4. How can you tell if a chart is selected?
5. If a chart is selected, explain how to deselect it.
6. If a chart is not selected, explain how to select it.
7. Explain how to change the size of a chart.
8. Explain the statement, "Excel charts are dynamic."
9. If you have created a chart and the chart toolbar is not visible, explain how to display the Chart toolbar.
10. Explain the use of each of the tools in the Chart toolbar.
11. Review the different kinds of charts that Excel makes available to you. Briefly describe each.
12. Create a worksheet of your own choosing. Create a chart from the data in your worksheet using the principles you have learned in this chapter.

19

EXCEL CHARTS: PART 2

This chapter shows how to format your charts to make them even more impressive. You will also learn how to create pie charts, which can be very effective, although they are only appropriate for certain kinds of data.

CREATE A WORKSHEET

Begin by creating a worksheet from figure 19.1.

	A	B	C	D
1	Standardized Test Scores			
2	(Percentiles)			
3				
4		2001	2002	2003
5	Verbal	5	6	7
6	Math	4	4	5
7				
8				

Figure 19.1.

Now create a standard column chart from the data. Do not enter any chart titles, and do not display a legend (Fig. 19.2).

ADD TITLES TO THE CHART

You have already learned that to modify an existing chart, the first step is to select it. And you have also learned that you select a chart simply by clicking on it. *Remember*, you can tell when a chart has been selected by the presence of sizing handles. But if you want to edit an existing chart, rather than selecting the chart, right click on a blank area of the chart.

1. Right click on a *blank area* of the chart. A list box will appear.
2. Select Chart Options from the list box.
3. Click on the Title tab.
4. Type Standardized Test Scores.
5. Now assign a Category (X) axis title Year.
6. In the same way, assign a Value (Y) axis title Percentile.
7. Click OK (Fig. 19.3).

FORMATTING TITLES

1. Now, right click on the chart title.
2. Select Format, Chart Title.
3. Select Patterns.
4. Select a Weight. Choose the heaviest weight (this will put a thick box around the title).
5. Click on the box next to Shadow (a shadow box gives the box you created a three-dimensional appearance).
6. Select Font.
7. Change the font, and change the point size to a slightly larger size.
8. Choose a color (use a light color—a dark color will obscure the text).
9. Click OK (Fig. 19.4).

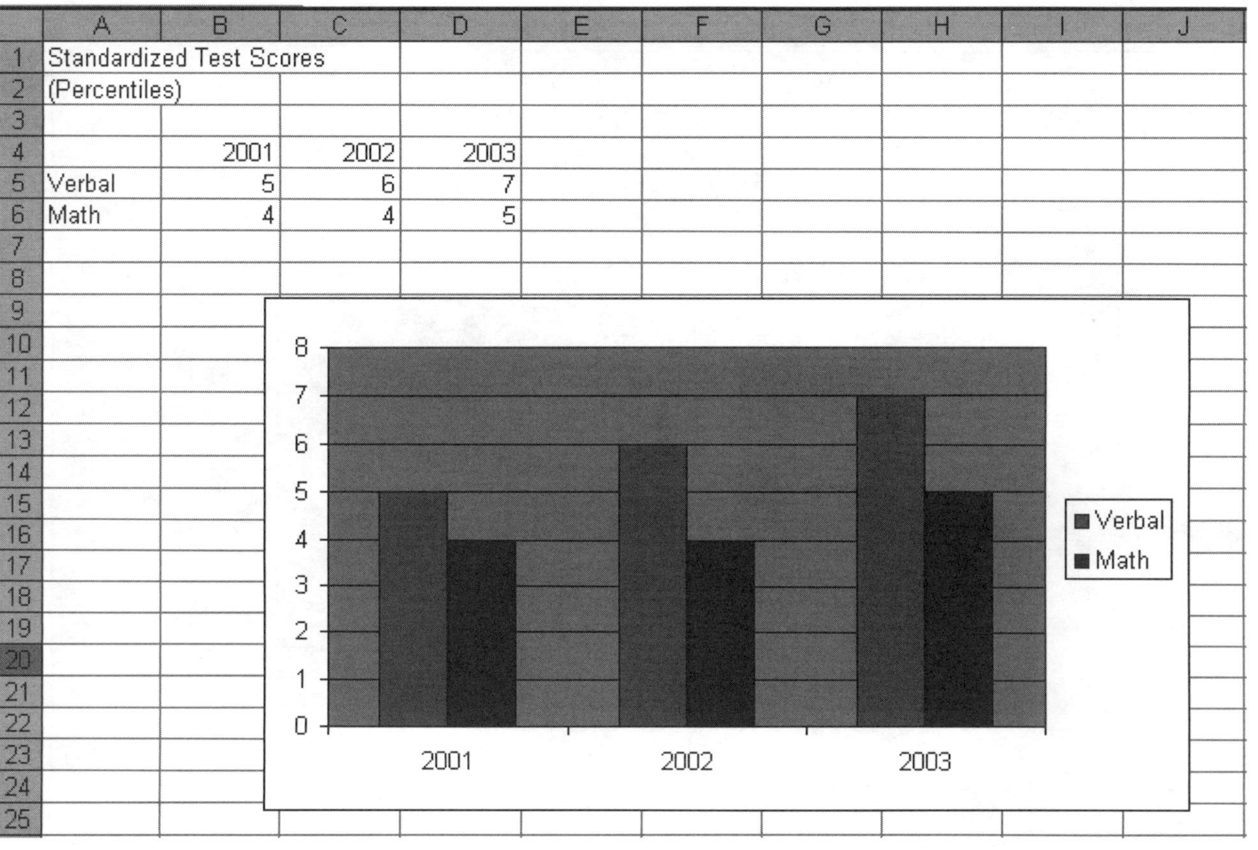
Standardized Test Scores
(Percentiles)
2001
2002
2003
Verbal
5
6
7
Math
4
4
5
8
7
6
5
4
3
2
1
0
2001
2002
2003
Verbal
Math

Figure 19.2.

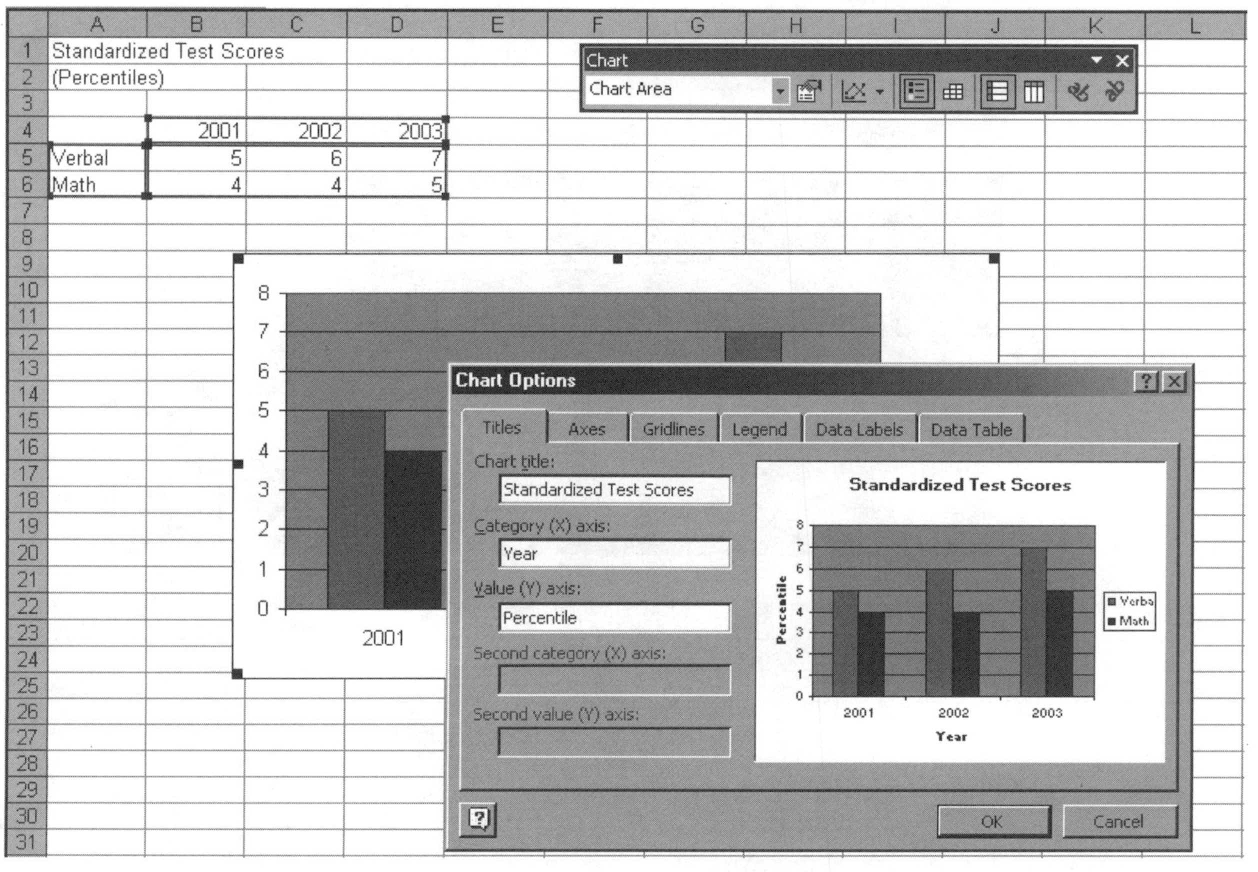
Standardized Test Scores
(Percentiles)
2001
2002
2003
Verbal
Math
Chart
Chart Area
Chart Options
Titles
Axes
Gridlines
Legend
Data Labels
Data Table
Chart title:
Standardized Test Scores
Category (X) axis:
Year
Value (Y) axis:
Percentile
Second category (X) axis:
Second value (Y) axis:
Standardized Test Scores
Percentile
Year
Verba
Math
OK
Cancel

Figure 19.3.

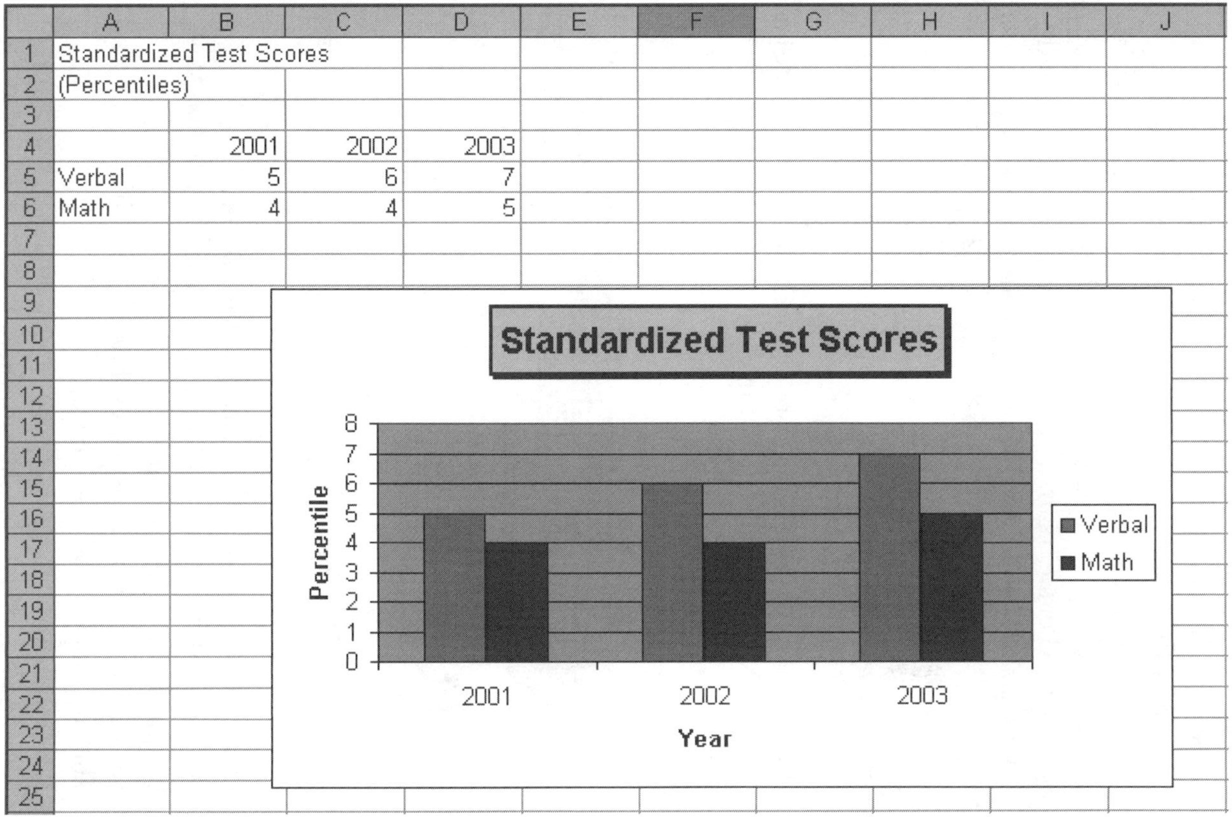

	A	B	C	D
1	Standardized Test Scores			
2	(Percentiles)			
3				
4		2001	2002	2003
5	Verbal	5	6	7
6	Math	4	4	5

Standardized Test Scores

Percentile

8
7
6
5
4
3
2
1
0

2001
2002
2003

Year

Verbal
Math

Figure 19.4.

PIE CHARTS

Pie charts are useful for displaying certain kinds of data. Specifically, *pie charts* show the relationship between the whole of something and its component parts. For example, if you were looking at your January budget, the component parts might be Salary, Utilities, Supplies, and so on. The whole, of course, would be your total January budget. Since there is only one "whole," a pie chart can contain *only one data range*.

CREATE A WORKSHEET

Begin by creating a worksheet based on figure 19.5. Save the worksheet as ENRLGRD. Now create a pie chart from this worksheet.

	A	B	C	D
1	Student Enrollment By Grade			
2				
3				
4		Grade 10	Grade 11	Grade 12
5		1172	1485	1536
6				

Figure 19.5.

1. Drag on B4:D5 to select the data for your pie chart.
2. Select Insert, Chart from the menu, or click on the Chart Wizard button on the Chart toolbar.
3. Select Pie, and then the second subtype of pie chart. Click Next.
4. The chart looks good. Click Next.
5. For the Chart Title, enter Student Enrollment. Click Next.
6. Select As An Object In. Click Finish.

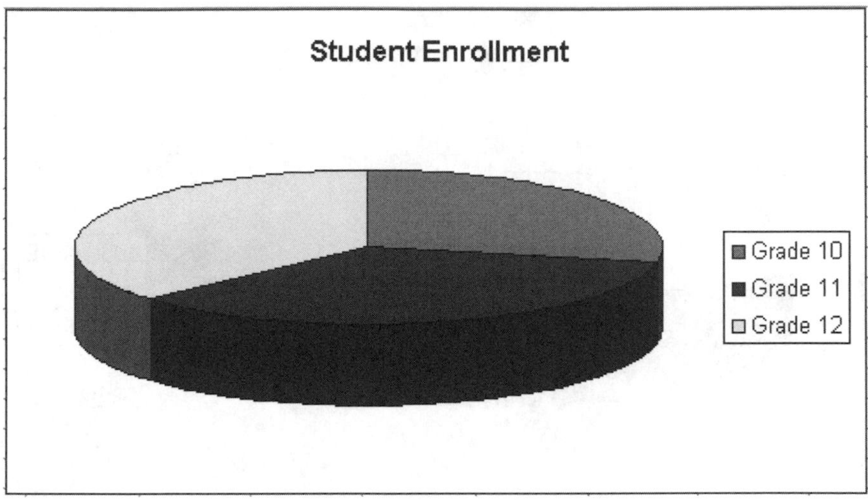

Figure 19.6.

FORMAT THE CHART

You can also format the chart using the techniques you have previously learned.

Exploding a Section

With a pie chart (Fig. 19.6), you can emphasize one or more sections by *exploding* it out from the rest of the pie chart.

1. Point your cursor to the section you want to explode.
2. Click on the section. Handles will appear around the pie chart, indicating that the entire pie chart has been selected.
3. Now click on the section again. This time handles will appear around only the section you were pointing to, indicating that you have selected that section.
4. Point your cursor within the section, hold down the left mouse button, and drag it a small distance away from the pie (Fig. 19.7).

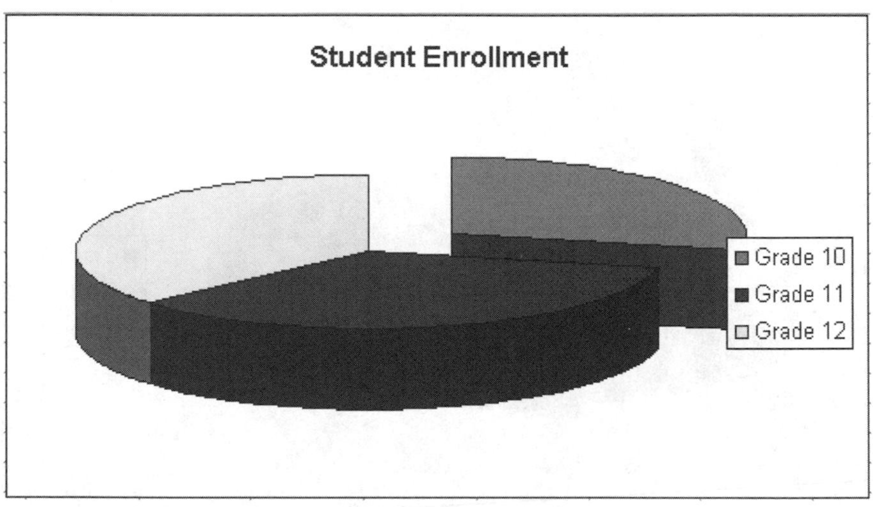

Figure 19.7.

EXERCISE 19

1. Explain how to add a title to a chart after you have created the chart.
2. Describe how to format a chart title.
3. What kind of data lend themselves to being displayed as a pie chart?
4. Describe how to create a pie chart.
5. Why might you want to explode one or more sections of a pie chart?
6. Explain how to explode a section of a pie chart.
7. Create a worksheet from figure 19.8. Create a three-dimensional pie chart from the worksheet. Format the worksheet and chart appropriately.

	A	B	C	D
1	Charity Drive			
2				
3		Grade 10	Grade 11	Grade 12
4		125	178	256
5				

Figure 19.8.

20

THE CONDITIONAL =IF( ) FUNCTION

You have already learned about the most commonly used Excel functions such as =SUM( ) and =AVERAGE( ). The conditional =IF( ) statement is one of the most useful *advanced* Excel functions. Many people use it in almost every worksheet they create.

In fact, =IF( ) will enable you to create some worksheets you otherwise could not have created. But even where it is possible to create worksheets without =IF( ), this function will often enable you to create worksheets that work better and look much more professional than they otherwise would. Consider, for example, a worksheet where:

A1 is a data cell that is currently empty.
A2 is another data cell that is currently empty.
A3 contains the formula =AF1/A2

Now, when you enter data into cells A1 and A2, the formula in cell A3 will divide the number in cell A1 by the number in cell A2. But if there are no data in cell A2, the formula will return an error message because you are, in effect, dividing by zero.

A3 | f_x =A2/A1

	A	B	C
1			
2			
3	#DIV/0!		
4			

Figure 20.1.

You can use the =IF( ) function to write a formula in cell A3 that will perform the calculation only if there is a number in cell A2. If there is no number in cell A2, the formula will not perform the calculation, and consequently, no error message will appear in cell A3.

THE =IF( ) FUNCTION

We frequently make assumptions, check to see if those assumptions are correct, and then act accordingly. For example, suppose the weather was threatening when you went to bed last night. When you awoke this morning, you said to yourself, "If it is raining today, I will wear my raincoat." Then, you looked out the window, saw that it was (or was not) raining, and dressed accordingly.

The conditional =IF( ) function in Excel allows you to do the same thing in a worksheet. You write a statement in one cell based on what you think is happening in another cell. Excel will check to see if your assumption is correct, and will then perform an action based on whether your assumption is, or is not, correct.

The =IF( ) statement is different from the functions previously discussed in that it contains three distinct parts within the parentheses. These parts are technically called *arguments*, and they are separated by commas. The =IF( ) function has the form: =IF (statement, result-if-true, result-if-false)

1. The first argument is a statement of what you believe to be true.
2. The second argument indicates what you want Excel to do if the statement is, in fact, true.

3. Finally, the third argument indicates what you want Excel to do if the statement is false.

This probably sounds really complicated. Rest assured soon it will make perfect sense.

LOGICAL OPERATORS

Before you can learn to use the =IF( ) function, you need to know about *logical operators* in writing an =IF( ) statement. You already learned about the most common logical operators when you studied databases. But here, you will also have to know the symbols used to represent them.

- = equal to
- > greater than
- < less than
- <> not equal to
- >= greater than or equal to
- <= less than or equal to

WRITING AN =IF( ) STATEMENT TO PRINT A TEXT MESSAGE

You can use an =IF( ) statement to print a text message, or to perform a mathematical calculation. You will first learn how to write an =IF( ) statement that prints a text message. Enter the following in cell A5:

=IF(A1>10,"BIG","SMALL")

Note that the arguments are separated by commas, but not spaces.

1. The first argument, the statement A1>10 simply states what you believe to be true, that is, that the number in cell A1 is greater than 10. Note that this statement expresses what you think is the case in cell A1. This statement may be true, but it may just as likely be false.

2. The second argument, "BIG" indicates what the =IF( ) function will do if the statement is true—it will print the message BIG in cell A5. Note that text messages in =IF( ) functions are enclosed in quotation marks.
3. Finally, the third argument, "SMALL" indicates what the =IF( ) function will do if the statement is false—it will print the message SMALL in cell A5.

Initially, you will see the word SMALL in cell A5. Excel has looked at cell A1 and sees there is no number there. Since no number, zero actually, is smaller than 10, the =IF( ) statement indicates the result-if-false, SMALL.

Type the number 2 in cell A1 and press [Enter]. Again, Excel looks at cell A1, sees the number 2 there, and recognizes that 2 is smaller than 10. Because the =IF( ) statement is still false, Excel displays the result-if-false, the word SMALL, in cell A5.

Now type the number 11 in cell A1. Once again, Excel looks at cell A1. But this time, Excel sees the number 11, and recognizes that 11 is greater than 10. Since the =IF( ) statement is now true, Excel displays the result-if-true, BIG, in cell A5 (Fig. 20.2).

USING =IF( ) TO PERFORM A CALCULATION

The =IF( ) statement can also be used to perform a calculation in a cell. The only difference between writing an =IF( ) statement to display a text message and writing one to perform a calculation is that while text messages in =IF( ) statements must be enclosed in quotation marks, formulas are not enclosed in quotation marks.

To see how this works, assume that the school store in a high school offers a 10 percent discount for purchases over $100. You can use an =IF( ) statement to determine whether a discount applies to a particular purchase, and if one does, to calculate the discount.

Begin by creating a worksheet like that in figure 20.3. Now write an =IF( ) statement in cell D10 to calculate a 10 percent discount, but only if the amount in cell D9 is greater than 100. Try it yourself.

	A	B	C
1			
2			
3			
4			
5	=IF(A1>10,"BIG","SMALL")		
6			
7			
8	**Function**		
9			

	A	B
1	2	
2		
3		
4		
5	SMALL	
6		
7		
8	**Result - False**	
9		

	A	B
1	11	
2		
3		
4		
5	BIG	
6		
7		
8	**Result - True**	
9		

Figure 20.2.

	A	B	C	D
1	**School Store Receipt**			
2				
3	**Sold To:**	John Smith		
4				
5	**Quantity**	**Item**	**Unit**	**Total**
6			**Price**	**Price**
7	2	Books	29.95	=A7*C7
8	1	Organizer	14.95	=A8*C8
9				
10			**Subtotal**	=D7+D8
11			**Discount**	
12				
13			**Total**	=D10-D11
14				

Figure 20.3.

1. Begin by typing the following in cell D11: =IF(
2. For the statement, indicate that D10>100: =IF(D10>100
3. Type a comma to separate the first argument from the second: =IF(D10>100,
4. Now write a formula to calculate the discount, the result-if-true, D10*10%: =IF(D10>100,D10*10%
5. Type another comma, and then indicate that no discount will be provided, the result-if-false by typing a zero: =IF(D10>100,D10*10%,0
6. Finally, type a closing parenthesis, and press [Enter] to enter your function into cell D10: =IF(D10>100,D10*10%,0)

Your =IF( ) function will look at cell D10, and based on what it sees there, it will do the following:

1. If the subtotal in cell D10 is greater than $100, the discount will be the subtotal, which appears in cell D10, multiplied by 10 percent.
2. But if the subtotal in cell D10 is not greater than $100, the discount will be 0.
3. In this case, because the subtotal is less than $100, there is no discount (that is, the discount is 0) (Fig. 20.4).

Now, change the number of books purchased in cell A7 to 3, which will result in a subtotal greater than $100. The statement in the =IF( ) function will now be true, and consequently, the =IF( ) statement will calculate the 10-percent discount (Fig. 20.5).

OTHER APPLICATIONS

There are many ways you can use the =IF( ) function. You can write an =IF( ) function to flag data that meet certain criteria. Create a worksheet from figure 20.6 to see how this works.

	A	B	C	D
1	School Store Receipt			
2				
3	Sold To:	John Smith		
4				
5	Quantity	Item	Unit	Total
6			Price	Price
7	2	Books	29.95	59.90
8	1	Organizer	14.95	14.95
9				
10			Subtotal	74.85
11			Discount	-
12				
13			Total	74.85
14				

Figure 20.4.

	A	B	C	D
1	School Store Receipt			
2				
3	Sold To:	John Smith		
4				
5	Quantity	Item	Unit	Total
6			Price	Price
7	3	Books	29.95	89.85
8	1	Organizer	14.95	14.95
9				
10			Subtotal	104.80
11			Discount	10.48
12				
13			Total	94.32
14				

Figure 20.5.

	A	B	C	D	E	F	G
1	Flag Failing Students						
2							
3	Student	Grade 1	Grade 2	Grade 3	Average	Flag	
4	Mary	75	85	75			
5							
6							
7							
8							
9							
10							
11							

=AVERAGE(B4:D4)

Figure 20.6.

Now enter some student names and grades into the worksheet.

	A	B	C	D	E	F
1	Flag Failing Students					
2						
3	Student	Grade 1	Grade 2	Grade 3	Average	Flag
4	Mary	75	85	75	78.33	
5	John	55	65	55	58.33	
6	Denise	85	95	85	88.33	
7	Carlos	45	55	45	48.33	
8	Edward	90	80	90	86.67	
9	Franklin	50	60	50	53.33	
10	Alice	78	85	95	86.00	

Figure 20.7.

You would like an asterisk (*) to appear in cell F4 if the first student has an average below 65 percent. Use the =IF( ) function in cell F4 display an asterisk if the average in cell E4 is less than 65, but to display nothing if that is not the case. Note that Excel considers the asterisk to be a text entry. So to display an asterisk, you must enclose the asterisk within quotation marks ("*"). Note also that to display nothing in a cell, type: (quotation mark-space-quotation mark).

The =IF( ) function you will enter in cell F4 is:

=IF(E4<65,"*"," ")

After you have written the =IF( ) statement in cell F4, copy it to cells F5:F10.

	A	B	C	D	E	F
1	Flag Failing Students					
2						
3	Student	Grade 1	Grade 2	Grade 3	Average	Flag
4	Mary	75	85	75	78.33	
5	John	55	65	55	58.33	*
6	Denise	85	95	85	88.33	
7	Carlos	45	55	45	48.33	*
8	Edward	90	80	90	86.67	
9	Franklin	50	60	50	53.33	*
10	Alice	78	85	95	86.00	

Figure 20.8.

Notice that there is an asterisk in the appropriate cells in Column F for students whose average is below 65 percent.

Here is another, more difficult example. You will create a worksheet to calculate the wages of employees who earn hourly wages to include:

- Employees earn straight time for all hours worked to 40 hours.
- Employees earn time and a half for all hours worked over 40 hours.

Create a worksheet from figure 20.9.

First, you need to calculate Regular Hours worked in cell B8. Regular Hours are the hours for which an employee did not earn any overtime wages—that is, the number of hours the employee worked, but in no case more than 40 hours.

This is a little more difficult than it at first seems. If an employee worked more than 40 hours, he or she would have worked 40 Regular Hours. But if the employee worked fewer than 40 hours, the number of Regular Hours would be equal to the actual number of Hours Worked. An =IF( ) function can accomplish this in cell B8.

```
=IF(B5>40,40,B5)
```

	A	B
1	**Salary Calculator**	
2		
3	**Employee:**	William Jones
4	**Week Ending:**	7-Jan
5	**Hours Worked:**	50
6	**Hourly Wage:**	10.00
7		
8	**Regular Hours:**	
9	**Regular Wage:**	
10	**Overtime Hours:**	
11	**Overtime Wage:**	
12		
13	**Total Wage:**	
14		

Figure 20.9.

This =IF( ) function assumes that the employee worked more than 40 hours. If this is the case, the employee's regular hours are 40 (remember, Regular Hours cannot exceed 40). But if the employee worked fewer than 40 hours, he or she would get credit only for the actual number of hours worked.

Next, you need a formula in cell B9 to calculate Regular Wage, that is, the wages for working the first 40 hours. This formula is fairly straightforward—multiply Regular Hours worked by the Hourly Wage.

```
=B8*B6
```

Now calculate the number of Overtime Hours worked in cell B10. This is also a little complicated. If an employee worked more than 40 hours, the number of Overtime Hours worked is the total number of Hours Worked minus 40. But if an employee did not work more than 40 hours, he or she earned no Overtime Hours. The formula in cell B10 is:

```
=IF(B5>40,B5-40,0)
```

You now have to calculate Overtime Wages. Since you know the number of Overtime Hours, Overtime Wages are Overtime Hours multiplied by Hourly Wage multiplied by 1.5 (time and a half is equivalent to regular wages multiplied by 1.5). The formula in cell B11 is:

=B10*B6*1.5

The last formula is the easiest. To calculate Total Wage you simply add Regular Wage and Overtime Wage. The formula in cell B13 is:

=B9+B11

Now, let's see if it works.

	A	B
1	Salary Calculator	
2		
3	Employee:	William Jones
4	Week Ending:	7-Jan
5	Hours Worked:	50
6	Hourly Wage:	10.00
7		
8	Regular Hours:	40
9	Regular Wage:	400.00
10	Overtime Hours:	10
11	Overtime Wage:	150.00
12		
13	Total Wage:	550.00

Figure 20.10.

Employee William Jones worked 50 hours, 40 Regular Hours, and 10 Overtime Hours. Jones earned $400 in regular wages plus $150 in overtime hours, a total of $550.

Let's try another example. Suppose that the following week, Jones only worked 37 hours (Fig. 20.11).

This time, there are no overtime hours, so the number of Hours Worked is 37, and the Total Wage is $370.

This is *not* an easy worksheet. But this is the first time you have tried it. Try it again. And then, create a few worksheets that include an =IF( ) function, and you will quickly become proficient at it.

	A	B
1	Salary Calculator	
2		
3	Employee:	William Jones
4	Week Ending:	7-Jan
5	Hours Worked:	37
6	Hourly Wage:	10.00
7		
8	Regular Hours:	37
9	Regular Wage:	370.00
10	Overtime Hours:	0
11	Overtime Wage:	-
12		
13	Total Wage:	370.00
14		

Figure 20.11.

THE =AND( ) FUNCTION

The =AND( ) function allows you to evaluate two statements simultaneously. It is commonly used along with =IF( ). The =AND( ) function requires that two statements be true. It takes the form:

=AND(statement1,statement2)

The following example should make clear how =AND works. Type the following in cell A5:

=IF(AND(A1=5,B1=5),"YES","NO")

This function will direct Excel to enter YES in cell A5 only if the number 5 appears in both cell A1 and cell B1. Obviously, if the number 5 is not entered in cells A1 and B1, Excel will enter NO in cell A5. And if there is a 5 in only cell A1 or cell B1, Excel will still enter NO in cell A5.

THE =OR( ) FUNCTION

The =OR( ) function works like the =AND( ) function with one major exception. With =OR( ), the entire =IF( ) statement is true if *either part* of the =OR( ) statement is true. It takes the form:

=OR(statement1,statement2)

Enter the following formula in cell A7:

=IF(OR(A1=5,B1=5),"YES","NO")

In this case, Excel will return YES if the number 5 appears in either cell A1, or cell B1, or in both.

EXERCISE 20

1. List the most common logical operators, and describe what each means.
2. Explain how to use the =IF( ) function to enter a text message in a cell.
3. Explain how to use the =IF( ) function to perform a calculation in a cell.
4. Explain how to use =AND( ).
5. Explain how to use =OR( ).
6. Create a worksheet from figure 20.12. Write a formula in cell F4 to calculate the first student's average, and copy the formula to

	A	B	C	D	E	F
1	Adjusted Exam Averages					
2						
3	First	Last	Exam 1	Exam 2	Exam 3	Average
4	James	Adams	95	85	90	90
5	Denise	Baker	100	110	110	100
6	William	Carlos	85	95	85	88
7						
8						

Figure 20.12.

B5:B6. However, since the student's average cannot be greater than 100 percent, use an =IF( ) statement to convert averages that are greater than 100 percent to 100 percent.

7. Describe a worksheet in which you could use an =IF( ) function to enter text into a cell.
8. Describe a worksheet in which you could use an =IF( ) function to enter a formula into a cell.
9. Create one of the worksheets.

21

CELL ADDRESSES AND THE =VLOOKUP( ) FUNCTION

This chapter will cover two topics, the first of which, cell addresses, is useful to know on its own. But it is necessary to understand the different kinds of cell addresses before you can understand the second topic, the =VLOOKUP( ) function.

You have seen how Excel formulas automatically adjust themselves when you copy them. That is, if you enter the formula =A1+A2 in cell A3, and then copy the formula to cell B3, the formula in cell B3 will be =B1+B2. This is precisely what you want, perhaps 95 percent of the time. But sometimes you will write a formula in a cell that you do not want to be adjusted when you copy it. In the first part of this chapter you will learn why you sometimes do not want formulas to be adjusted when you copy them and how to accomplish that.

The second topic is the lookup function. The *lookup function* allows you to create a table of data in a worksheet. You can then have Excel automatically access data from that table whenever you need it. For example, suppose you had a mail order business and you had to charge the appropriate sales tax to customers in different states. You could create a table that contained the sales tax amounts for each state. Then, when you entered the name of the state into a cell in your worksheet, Excel would automatically look up the appropriate sales tax for you. It all probably sounds much more complicated than it is.

KINDS OF CELL ADDRESSES

You have been using cell addresses since you began using Excel. As you have learned, the address of a cell is simply the letter of the column that it is in, followed by the number of the row that it is in. But that is only one kind of cell address. Actually, there are three different kinds of Excel cell addresses:

1. Relative cell addresses,
2. Absolute cell addresses,
3. Mixed cell addresses.

Relative Cell Addresses

Relative cell addresses are the cell addresses you have already learned about and have been using in formulas, such as: A1, B12, CX99. They are called *relative cell addresses* because they change when you copy them from one cell to another. In other words, they are relative to the cells in which they are located.

In the example above, you entered =A1+A2 in cell A3. Because A1 and A2 are relative cell addresses, when you copied the formula that contains those cell addresses, the formula changed to =B1+B2. You generally want your formulas to adjust when you copy them. So relative cell addresses are the kind of cell addresses you use most of the time.

Absolute Cell Addresses

Occasionally, you will write a formula you will not want to change when you copy it to another cell. In these cases, you will use absolute cell addresses in your formula. *Absolute cell addresses* remain the same when they are copied.

If you want to type an absolute cell address, simply type a dollar sign ($) in front of each element of the cell address you do not want to change. For example, A1 would be a relative cell address, but $A$1 would be the absolute address of that same cell. Try it. Enter the following formula in cell D3:

=$D$1+$D$2

Now copy the formula to cell E3. Click on cell E3 to select it. Now look at the formula bar at the top of your worksheet to see the cell content. The formula has not been adjusted. It is still:

=$D$1+$D$2

This must all be sounding very theoretical. To see why you might want to use an absolute cell address in a formula, we will create a worksheet. Assume that students can earn extra credit by answering supplemental questions on an exam, but that on some exams supplemental questions earn more extra credit than on others. In this worksheet, you will enter the number of points that each extra credit question earns, and the worksheet will calculate the total number of extra credit points that the student earned.

As a starting point, assume that you award 2 points for each extra credit question answered correctly, and that you want to create a worksheet to calculate how many extra credit points to award to students. Create a worksheet from the example in figure 21.1 to accomplish this task.

	A	B
1	Extra Credit Calculator	
2		
3	Points Per Question	2
4		
5	Questions	Points
6	1	2
7	2	
8	3	
9	4	
10	5	

Figure 21.1.

Now write a formula in cell B6 to calculate the number of extra credit points earned, at 2 points per question, for each extra question answered correctly.

=B3*A6

This formula produces the calculation you need.

	A	B
1	Extra Credit Calculator	
2		
3	Points Per Question	2
4		
5	Questions	Points
6	1	2
7	2	4
8	3	6
9	4	8
10	5	10

Figure 21.2.

But a problem occurs when you copy the formula to B7:B8. The reference to cell A6 is automatically adjusted for its new location, A7 in cell B7, and A8 in cell B8. This is precisely what you want. But when you copy the formula, the reference to cell B3 will also be adjusted. This is not what you want—you do not want B3 to change. You want the reference to cell B3 to remain B3, even when the formula is copied.

Retype the formula in cell B6 so that B3 is entered as an absolute cell address. In that way it will not change when you copy the formula.

=A6*$B$3

In this formula, A6 will adjust for its new location when you copy it, but $B$3 will always remain $B$3. Copy the formula in cell B6 to the range of cells B7:B8. Note that you have achieved the result that you want.

The formula in cell B7 is: =A7*$B$3.
The formula in cell B8 is: =A8*$B$3.

	A	B
1	Extra Credit Calculator	
2		
3	Points per Question	2
4		
5	Question	Points
6	1	2
7	2	4
8	3	6
9	4	7
10	5	10

Figure 21.3.

The formula in cell B9 is: =A9*$B$3.
The formula in cell B10 is: =A10*$B$3.

Mixed Cell Addresses

There is a third type of cell address called a mixed cell address. Mixed cell addresses are much less commonly used than relative or absolute cell addresses. But since you might occasionally encounter a mixed cell address, you should be familiar with the concept.

In a *mixed cell address*, part of the cell address will change when it is copied, but part of it will not. As you might expect, you create a mixed cell address by typing a dollar sign ($) in front of the part of the cell address you do not want to change. The following examples should make this concept clear.

- A1—*relative cell address*—if copied to another cell, the cell address will change.
- $A$1—*absolute cell address*—the cell address will not change if copied to another cell.
- $A1—*mixed cell address*—if copied, the letter A will not change, but the number 1 will change depending on its location.
- A$1—*mixed cell address*—if copied, the letter A will change depending on its location, but the number 1 will not change.

A SIMPLE WAY TO WRITE ABSOLUTE AND MIXED CELL ADDRESSES

The concept of absolute and mixed cell addresses is fairly straightforward. But in practice, typing all the dollar signs can become a little tedious. Fortunately, Excel provides a way to simplify things.

1. Click on cell G3 to select it.
2. Type =G1.
3. Press the [F4] key at the top of your keyboard. Pressing [F4] changes a cell address from relative to absolute. The entry in cell G3 is now =$G$1.
4. Type +G2.
5. Again, press the [F4] key. G2 is changed to $G$2.
6. Press [Enter].

You can also use the [F4] key to write mixed cell addresses. Each time you press [F4] you will cycle from one kind of address to another: Relative—Absolute—Mixed—Mixed.

THE =VLOOKUP( ) FUNCTIONS

Now that you have learned how to write formulas with absolute cell addresses, you are ready to learn how to use the =VLOOKUP( ) function to create a table in your worksheet. Then, when you need data from the table, Excel will automatically find the data and insert it into the cell you specify.

Actually, there are two lookup functions in Excel, one for tables in a vertical format, =VLOOKUP( ), and another for tables in a horizontal format, =HLOOKUP( ). The discussion here will deal with vertical lookup tables because most Excel tables are in a vertical format. However, once you understand how to use the vertical lookup function, you will also be able to use the horizontal lookup function.

Begin by creating a worksheet from figure 21.4.

When this worksheet is completed, you will enter a student's name in Column B, and that student's letter grades. For each grade, Excel will

	A	B	C	D	E	F	G
1	Calculate GPA From Letter Grades					Lookup Table	
2						A	4
3	Student	Smith				B	3
4						C	2
5	Grade 1	A				D	1
6	Grade 2	B				F	0
7	Grade 3	C					
8	Grade 4	B					
9	Grade 5	D					
10							
11		GPA	=AVERAGE(C5:C9)				
12							

Figure 21.4.

look up the appropriate grade point equivalent in the lookup table and will enter it in Column C. The formula you have already entered in cell C11 will then calculate the student's grade point average.

Notes:

1. Generally, the lookup table is located farther from the worksheet and is not visible on the screen. We have located it here in the range F2:G6 to make it easy to see while you learn how to use the lookup function.
2. The heading Lookup Table is not part of the lookup table and is not necessary. We have included it here for descriptive purposes only. The range of this lookup table is F2:G6.
3. This is a vertical lookup table because the letter grades and grade point equivalents are located in vertical or column format in the lookup table. In a horizontal lookup table, the letter grades and grade point equivalents would be located in horizontal or row format.

HOW THE LOOKUP FUNCTIONS WORKS

The format for the vertical lookup function is:

=VLOOKUP(cell,range-of-lookup-table,column-offset)

The format for the horizontal lookup function is:

=HLOOKUP(cell,range-of-lookup-table,column-offset)

In both cases:

- **cell** is the cell that the lookup function is looking at
- **range** is the range of the lookup table
- **column offset** is the number (usually 2) of the column (to the right in a vertical lookup table, down in a horizontal lookup table) where the data to be found are located in the lookup table

While this may appear confusing, it will become clearer as you build the lookup function into your worksheet.

WRITING A LOOKUP FUNCTION

Your first lookup function will appear in cell C5. The function will look at cell B5 to determine what the student's first grade is. Then, it will look at the lookup table to determine the grade point equivalent of that grade. Finally, it will insert the appropriate grade point equivalent from the second column in the lookup table, in cell C5.

Enter the following function in cell C5:

=VLOOKUP(B5,$F$2:$G$6,2)

Here is an analysis of the lookup function that you have written:

1. The function is located in cell C5 because that is where you want the grade point equivalent for the student's first grade to be entered.
2. You used =VLOOKUP( ) because your lookup table is in a vertical format.
3. Cell B5 is the cell that the lookup function will look at to find the student's first grade.
4. F2:G6 is the range of the lookup table. You have used absolute cell addresses ($F$2:$G$6) because you will be copying the lookup function to the cells below it. Since the lookup table will always be

in the same place, you do not want those cell addresses to change when you copy them.

5. Column 2 is the offset in the lookup table. The commission rate is in Column 2 of the lookup table.

COMPLETE THE WORKSHEET

Now complete the worksheet.

1. Copy the lookup function in cell C5 to the range of cells C6:C9.

	A	B	C	D	E	F	G
1	Calculate GPA From Letter Grades					Lookup Table	
2						A	4
3	Student	Smith				B	3
4						C	2
5	Grade 1	A	4			D	1
6	Grade 2	B	3			F	0
7	Grade 3	C	2				
8	Grade 4	B	3				
9	Grade 5	D	1				
10							
11		GPA	2.6				
12							

Figure 21.5.

EXERCISE 21

1. What is a relative cell address?
2. What is an absolute cell address?
3. What is a mixed cell address?
4. Which of these types of addresses is used most frequently?
5. Explain how to type an absolute cell address.
6. Explain how to convert a relative cell address to an absolute cell address.

7. Describe a worksheet in which you would need to use an absolute cell address. Explain why an absolute cell address would be necessary.
8. Explain what the lookup function does.
9. Why are there two lookup functions?
10. Which lookup function is used most often?
11. Explain the elements of the lookup function.
12. Explain why the range in a lookup table is always expressed using absolute cell addresses.
13. Describe two worksheets in which you could use a lookup function.
14. Create one of the worksheets.

22

DATES AND TIMES IN WORKSHEETS

This chapter explains how to enter dates and times into Excel worksheets. Although it is an easy process, if you understand how dates and times work using them can be a powerful addition to your worksheet skills. You can ask Excel to perform calculations based on dates. How many days, for example, are there between two dates? Or what will the date be, exactly forty-five days from today? And if you use dates in a database, you will see how you can sort a database by date.

EXCEL AND DATES

Type 12/25/2000 into a cell in Excel, and Excel will display exactly what you have typed. Although the process seems very simple, a great deal has gone on behind the scenes. Excel uses a mathematical system of dates in which the first day Excel can recognize is January 1, 1900.

In Excel's system of dates:

1. January 1, 1900, is day number 1,
2. January 2, 1900, is day number 2,
3. January 3, 1900, is day number 3, and so on.

Here is what happened behind the scenes when you typed 12/25/2000.

1. Excel began by converting the date to a number based on this system, in this case, the number, 36885.
2. Next, Excel formatted the number for date format.
3. Finally, Excel displayed the formatted date as 12/25/2000, or 12/25/00, depending on how Excel is set up on your computer.

Why did Excel go through this complicated procedure? You will be able to answer this question when you have learned a little more about Excel's system of dates.

Note: You could have typed 12/25/00, rather than 12/25/2000, without creating any problems. But because in some cases Excel might confuse 1900 with 2000, you will avoid potential problems if you get into the habit of typing years as four-digit numbers.

Date Formats

Excel understands a number of date formats. These are the some of the most popular formats that Excel recognizes:

- mm/dd/yyyy—12/26/2000
- dd-mmm-yy—26-DEC-2000
- dd-mmm—26-DEC (Excel knows the year, but does not display it.)
- mmm-yy—DEC-00 (Excel knows the day, but does not display it.)
- mm/dd/yy h:mm—12/26/2000 6:30 (Excel displays the date and time.)

If you enter a date using a format that is not one of Excel's standard date formats, Excel will attempt to display the date in one of the formats it does understand. For example, Excel does not have a date format mm-dd-yyyy (hyphens separating the month, day, and year). So if you type 12-25-2000 into a cell, Excel will display it as 12/25/2000, the most similar format it knows. Similarly, type Dec 25, 2000 into a cell, and Excel will display it as 25-DEC-2000.

Using Dates in Calculations

Because dates in Excel are really numbers, Excel can easily perform calculations based on dates. Create the following worksheet:

1. A1 Enter the date on which Christmas will fall this year: 12/25/200X.
2. A2 Enter today's date.
3. A3 =A1-A2

The formula in cell A3 will automatically calculate the number of shopping days until Christmas.

Note: If you see a date entered in cell A3, it will be necessary for you to remove the date formatting so the result is displayed as a number.

1. Click on cell A3 to select it.
2. Select Format, Cells from the menu.
3. Select General format (General format is no format at all—you could also use one of the Number formats to achieve the same result).
4. Click OK.

Now, enter the following formula in cell B2:

=A2+180

The formula in cell B2 will automatically calculate exactly 180 days from today's date. Again, it might be necessary to format cell B2 appropriately, in this case, using a date format.

TIMES IN EXCEL

Although times are not nearly as useful in Excel worksheets as dates, there may be occasions when you will want to enter times into a worksheet. Times in Excel are a little more complicated than dates. Excel's system of times converts times to the percentage of the day that has elapsed. Excel sees midnight as 0.00, and noon as 0.50. Other than this, the process is quite similar to that for dates.

Excel provides several built-in time formats:

- h:mm AM/PM
- h:mm:ss AM/PM
- h:mm
- h:mm:ss
- m/d/yy h:mm
- mm:ss
- mm:ss.0
- [h]:mm:ss

Today's Date—Dynamic

You will probably enter the current date into Excel worksheets more frequently than any other date. Fortunately, Excel makes this easy.

=TODAY() enters today's date into a cell.
=NOW() enters today's date and the current time into a cell.

Note that you must include the parentheses, even though there is no argument following the function name. Note also that both of these functions always display the current date or the current date and time.

Important:

If you enter =TODAY() into a cell, the function will always display today's date. If you then save the worksheet and open it tomorrow, it will display tomorrow's date.

Remember that =NOW() provides the date and time, and that times are represented by decimals. If you are doing a calculation based on dates, it is usually preferable to use =TODAY() rather than =NOW(). The =NOW() function may introduce unwanted decimals into calculations based on dates.

Today's Date—Static

If you want to enter the date or time in a cell, and you want it to remain as the date or time you entered, Excel also provides an easy way to do that:

- Press [Ctrl] [;] to enter the current date into a cell.
- Press [Ctrl] [:] to enter the current time into a cell.

DATE AND TIME SERIES

You can enter a series of dates (or times) into an Excel worksheet automatically.

1. Type the first date in your series in the first cell to contain the series. In this case, type today's date in cell A1, and press [Enter].
2. Drag your mouse pointer across the range A1:A10 to select it.
3. Select Edit, Fill, Series from the menu.
4. Since you highlighted cells in a column, the Series section should indicate Columns.
5. Since the entry in your first cell is a date, the Type section should indicate Date. If it does not, select Date.
6. For Date Unit select:
   a. Day—to list every day in the series.
   b. Weekday—to list only weekdays.
   c. Month—to list the same date each month.
   d. Year—to list the same date each year.
7. The step value is 1. This will select every date in the series. If you want dates at one-week intervals, such as every Wednesday, simply change the step value to 7.
8. If you want to stop at a particular date, enter it in the Stop Value section. However, it is not necessary to enter a stop value. Excel will automatically stop when it reaches the end of the range of cells you have selected.
9. Click OK, and Excel will enter the series of dates you requested.

Sorting by Date

If you have created a database that includes dates, you can sort on the date field in either ascending or descending order because dates are, in essence, numbers with the earliest dates having the lowest numbers.

	A	B	C
1	**Birthdates**		
2			
3	**First**	**Last**	**Birthdate**
4	Jane	Adams	4/4/1970
5	Adam	Baker	3/3/1972
6	Barbara	Chin	6/6/1972
7	Edward	Davis	8/8/1971
8	Denise	Eaton	1/1/1970
9	Charles	Fredericks	7/7/1970
10	Edith	Gomez	5/5/1971
11	Mary	Hunt	2/2/1971
12			
13			
14	**Unsorted Data**		
15			

Figure 22.1.

	A	B	C
1	**Birthdates**		
2			
3	**First**	**Last**	**Birthdate**
4	Denise	Eaton	1/1/1970
5	Jane	Adams	4/4/1970
6	Charles	Fredericks	7/7/1970
7	Mary	Hunt	2/2/1971
8	Edith	Gomez	5/5/1971
9	Edward	Davis	8/8/1971
10	Adam	Baker	3/3/1972
11	Barbara	Chin	6/6/1972
12			
13			
14	**Sorted By Birthdate**		
15			

Figure 22.2.

EXERCISE 22

1. What is the first date that Excel can "understand"?
2. Explain the process that occurs when you enter a date into a cell.
3. What will happen if you enter a date into a cell in a format that is not one of Excel's standard date formats?
4. Explain how to write a formula to calculate the number of days between two dates.
5. Explain how to write a formula that will calculate the date exactly thirty days from the current date.
6. How would you enter the current date into a cell, if you always want the cell to display the current date?
7. Explain the difference between =TODAY() and [Ctrl] [;].
8. Explain how to enter a series of dates into a range of cells.
9. Create a worksheet from figure 22.3.

	A	B	C	D	E	F
1	Varsity Athletic Team Schedule					
2						
3	Team	Coach	Opponent	Date	Start	Location
4	Football	Smith	West	1/8/2003	3:00 PM	Home
5	Volleyball	Jensen	York	1/8/2003	4:00 PM	Away
6						

Figure 22.3.

10. Add several additional events to the worksheet.
11. Sort the database by Location (Home or Away), and within location, by Date.
12. Create a worksheet that includes dates, and calculations based on those dates.

23

ADVANCED FUNCTIONS: PART I

You have learned how to use the most common as well as some advanced Excel functions. Many very specialized Excel functions are used by accountants, engineers, statisticians, and for practitioners in a wide variety of other fields. Of course, there is no need to learn how to use functions you will never use. But this chapter presents some advanced functions that might very well be useful in some of your worksheets.

BASIC EXCEL FUNCTIONS

You already know how to use the most common Excel functions, so we'll just review them briefly here:

- **=SUM(range)** adds the numbers in a range of cells.
- **=AVERAGE(range)** finds the average of the numbers in a range of cells.
- **=MAX(range)** finds the highest number in a range of cells.
- **=MIN(range)** finds the lowest number in a range of cells.
- **=COUNT(range)** counts the number of cells in a range containing number entries.

- =COUNTA(range) counts the number of cells in a range containing number and text entries.

In addition, you have learned several advanced Excel functions in previous chapters:

- =TODAY( ) enters the current date into a cell.
- =NOW( ) enters the current date and time into a cell.
- =IF(xx,xx,xx) the conditional function, evaluates the truth of a statement and performs an action based on the truth of that statement.
- =VLOOKUP(xx,xx,xx) locates data in a vertical lookup table.
- =HLOOKUP(xx,xx,xx) locates data in a horizontal lookup table.

BASIC CONSIDERATIONS

Remember that there are a number of criteria that all Excel functions must meet:

1. They must begin with an equals sign (=).
2. They cannot contain any spaces, except if the spaces occur within quotation marks.
3. All functions must contain beginning and ending parentheses. This is true even if nothing is enclosed within the parentheses, as in the case of =TODAY() and =NOW().
4. The information that appears within parentheses is called an *argument*.
5. Some functions, such as =IF( ), contain more than one argument. In these cases, the arguments are separated by commas (,).
6. It is sometimes useful to include one function within another, in a process called *nesting*.

STATISTICAL FUNCTIONS

Actually, the =SUM( ), =AVERAGE( ), =MIN( ), =MAX( ), =COUNT( ), and =COUNTA( ) functions are referred to as *statistical functions*. There are a few other statistical functions you might find useful.

Median and Average

When most people think of averages, they think of adding all the numbers in a range of cells, and then dividing the sum of the numbers by the number of items. Statisticians call this a *mean*, and it is only one of several kinds of averages (technically called *measures of central tendency*) that statisticians use. The median is another kind of average that is useful for analyzing some kinds of numerical data.

The median arranges all the numbers in a range of cells into numerical order, and then finds the middle item. Create a worksheet from figure 23.1.

	A	B
1	Student Absence	
2		
3	John	2
4	Mary	1
5	Carlos	100
6	David	2
7	Edward	1
8		
9	Average	
10		

Figure 23.1.

Now calculate the average in cell A9:

1. Type: =AVERAGE(B3:B7)

	A	B
1	Student Absence	
2		
3	John	2
4	Mary	1
5	Carlos	100
6	David	2
7	Edward	1
8		
9	Average	21.2
10		

Figure 23.2.

The average or mean number of days that students were absent is 21.2 days. Obviously, the average student absence is not 21.2 days. The fact that one student was absent 100 days results in an average that is not appropriate for this data.

Remember, the median arranges all the numbers in a range of cells into numerical order, and then finds the middle item. In this case, the median would be a more useful average than the mean. Calculate the median staff salary in cell A10:

1. Type: =MEDIAN(B3:B7)

	A	B
1	Student Absence	
2		
3	John	2
4	Mary	1
5	Carlos	100
6	David	2
7	Edward	1
8		
9	Mean	21.2
10	Median	2

Figure 23.3.

The median number of days absent is 2, which in this case is a more reasonable measure of average student absence.

Standard Deviation and Variance

If you are involved in performing sophisticated statistical analyses, the *standard deviation* and *variance* are measures that are used to describe how far an individual item is from the mean. Since Excel has functions for both standard deviation and variance, all you need to do is list your data in a column or row and apply the appropriate function: =STDEV(range) or =VAR(range).

DATE FUNCTIONS

You have already learned about the most common date functions, =TODAY() and =NOW(). Another date function you might find useful occasionally is: =DATE(yyyy,mm,dd). You can use =DATE (yyyy,mm,dd) to enter any date into a cell. For example, if you enter =DATE(2000,12,25) into a cell, Excel will display the date, 12/25/2000.

You might wonder why anyone would ever need this function, since it is so easy to enter dates by simply typing the date as 12/25/2000. The answer is that you might come across a worksheet in which months, days, and years are entered in separate columns. In these cases, you can use =DATE(yyyy,mm,dd) to convert the dates to standard Excel dates.

	A	B	C	D
1	MM	DD	YYYY	Date
2	12	25	2000	12/25/2000
3				
4				
5			=DATE(C2,A2,B2)	
6				

Figure 23.4.

FINANCIAL FUNCTIONS

Excel contains many built-in financial functions. Unless you are an accountant, =PMT( ), =FV( ), and =NA( ) are probably the only functions you will likely use.

Loan Payments

The loan function enables you to calculate all kinds of loan payments. While this function is very useful in a variety of personal situations, it can also be useful in deciding whether to finance major school and school district projects. To calculate loan payments, you will need to know the:

1. Principal of the loan
2. Interest rate
3. Terms of the loan
4. Number of payments per year

The loan function has the form: =PMT(rate,term,principal). This function seems to be fairly straight forward, but as a practical matter its use is complicated by the fact that the rate and term must be converted into the unit of time that corresponds to the number of payments per year. In other words, if you make 12 payments per year, you must divide the interest rate by 12 to calculate the monthly interest rate, and you must also multiply the term in years by 12 to calculate the term of the loan in months: =PMT(rate/payments-per-year,term*payments-per-year,principal). It probably sounds very complicated. Create a worksheet from figure 23.5 and you will see that it is easier than it sounds.

	A	B
1	Loan Calculator	
2		
3	Principal	100,000.00
4	Interest	8.20%
5	Term in Years	10
6	Payments per Year	12
7		
8	Payments	($1,223.87)
9		
10		
11	=PMT(B4/B6,B5*B6,B3)	
12		

Figure 23.5.

Of course, you can substitute any numbers for the principal, interest, and terms. The function works equally well for home mortgages, car loans, and bank loans. Note how the interest rate and terms have been converted to monthly rates, because the loan is being paid off in monthly installments.

Since the annual interest rate is 8.2 percent, the monthly interest rate is calculated 8.2%/12. The term in months of a ten-year loan is calculated 10*12.

Note also that Excel displays the payment as a negative number. The rationale is that it represents the amount of money to be paid. If that doesn't make sense to you, in the next chapter you will learn another Excel function that allows you to convert a negative number to a positive number.

Future Value

The future value function enables you to calculate the future value of equal payments or investments, and as such, is very useful in calculations regarding employee retirement plans. For example, if an employee invests $100 each month into a retirement account, plans to work for ten more years, and expects his or her investment to appreciate at a rate of 13 percent a year, the future value function will determine what the employee's investment will be worth when he or she is ready to retire. The format of the future value function is: =FV(rate,term,payment).

To see how the future value function works, create a worksheet from figure 23.6.

	A	B
1	Future Value Calculator	
2		
3	Principal	100.00
4	Term in Years	10
5	Interest	13%
6	Payments Per Year	12
7		
8	Future Value	($24,403.69)
9		
10		
11		
12		

=FV(B5/B6,B4*B6,B3)

Figure 23.6.

Note that like =PMT( ), =FV( ) requires you to convert the interest and terms to the unit of time that corresponds to the number of payments you will be making each year. Note also that =FV( ) can take into account a lump sum payment at the beginning of the term: =FV(rate,term,payment,initial-payment).

Not Available

Sometimes you will create a worksheet in which you will not want your formulas to calculate until all data have been received. In those cases, use =NA(), the not available function, in cells in which data are not yet available. The cell will display #NA, and any cells that contain calculations that depend on the cells with missing data will also indicate #NA.

	A	B	C
1	Average Student Exam Scores		
2			
3	John	75	
4	Mary	65	
5	Carlos	85	
6	David	#N/A	
7	Edward	75	
8			
9	Mean	#N/A	
10			

Figure 23.7.

EXERCISE 23

1. Describe the basic Excel functions you have learned, and how to use each.
2. Discuss the criteria that all Excel functions must meet.
3. Describe what the =MEDIAN( ) function does, a situation in which you might use it rather than =AVERAGE( ), and how to use it.
4. Describe a worksheet in which you might want to use =DATE(yyyy,mm,dd).

5. What is the =PMT( ) function used for?
6. Describe how to use =PMT( ) in a worksheet.
7. What does the =FV( ) function do?
8. Explain how you would use =FV( ) in a worksheet.
9. Why might you use =NA() in a worksheet?
10. Create a worksheet that uses =PMT( ) or =FV( ).

24

ADVANCED FUNCTIONS: PART 2

In the previous chapter you learned a number of advanced Excel functions. This chapter will present even more advanced functions. Although you will most likely never use all of these functions, there will undoubtedly be times when one or another will be very useful in some of your worksheets.

MATHEMATICAL FUNCTIONS

You have already learned a number of mathematical functions such as =SUM( ) and =COUNT( ). You might also find the following mathematical functions useful in some of your advanced worksheets.

Absolute Value

The *absolute value* of a number is the positive value of that number. For example, the absolute value of both 5 and −5 is 5. The Excel function is =ABS(xx) (Fig. 24.1).

Both function statements return 5, the positive value of the numbers they refer to. You can use the =ABS( ) function together with the

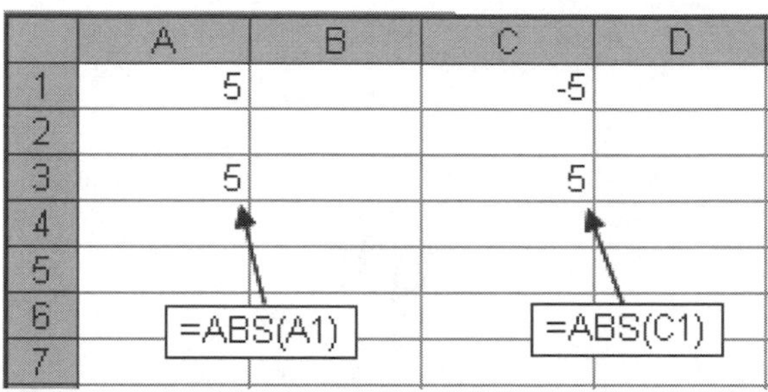

	A	B	C	D
1	5		-5	
2				
3	5		5	
4				
5				
6	=ABS(A1)		=ABS(C1)	
7				

Figure 24.1.

=PMT( ) function to convert the negative value that =PMT( ) function returns to a positive value. The function would then be expressed =ABS(PMT(rate,interest,principal)). Note that in this statement, there are two beginning and two ending parentheses because each function contains one pair of parentheses.

Integer

The *integer* of a number is the number without any decimal places. The number is not rounded off. Any numbers after the decimal place are simply dropped. The integer of both 5.1 and 5.9 is 5. The Excel function is =INT(xx).

	A	B	C	D
1	5.1		5.9	
2				
3	5		5	
4				
5				
6	=INT(A1)		=INT(C1)	
7				

Figure 24.2.

Integers can be very useful. For example, in a factory that produces widgets a worksheet may indicate that 9.9 widgets have been completed by the end of the day. However, since only completed Widgets can be shipped, only 9 widgets have been completed.

Modulus

The *modulus* of a number is the remainder when one number is divided by another. Note that the modulus is not the result of the division. It is the remainder only. In figure 24.3, if you divide 5 by 2, the result is 2 with a remainder of 1. The Excel function used is =MOD(xx,xx). Note that the =MOD( ) function uses a comma to separate the cells that it refers to.

	A	B
1	5	
2	2	
3	1	
4		
5		
6	=MOD(A1,A2	
7		

Figure 24.3.

Random Numbers

Random numbers are necessary for certain quality control operations and also for some statistical calculations. Excel can easily generate one random number, or as many random numbers as you require. The format for the random number function is: =RAND().

Enter =RAND() into a cell, and Excel will produce a random number between 0 and 1 in that cell. Copy the =RAND() function from one cell to a range of cells, and you can have as many random numbers as you need.

	A	B	C	D
1	0.808714			
2	0.185158			
3	0.648419			
4	0.329475			
5	0.980888		=RAND()	
6	0.508868			
7	0.804328			
8	0.521189			
9				

Figure 24.4.

Note that each time you make a change to your worksheet, the random numbers change. A function is essentially a formula, and Excel recalculates the formula whenever you make a change to your worksheet.

If you prefer to generate random numbers between 1 and 10 rather than decimals, you can move the decimal point one place to the right by multiplying by 10,using the function =RAND()*10.

	A	B	C	D
1	3.298664			
2	7.643665			
3	0.545898			
4	3.372766			
5	6.046719		=RAND()*10	
6	6.943531			
7	4.532141			
8	2.270765			
9				

Figure 24.5.

Finally, if you want only integer (whole number) random numbers, multiply by 10 and include the integer function =INT(RAND()*10).

	A	B	C	D	E
1	1				
2	8				
3	0				
4	8				
5	2		=INT(RAND()*10)		
6	5				
7	4				
8	3				

Figure 24.6.

Round

The =*ROUND function* rounds a number to the number of digits you specify. The format of the =ROUND function is: =ROUND(number,number-of-decimal-places).

Remember:

1. When you format a cell, you are changing only the cell display, not the cell content (the actual number). In other words, if you have the number 1.445 in a cell and you format the cell for two decimal places, you will see 1.45 in the cell. But the cell content will remain 1.445, and Excel will use 1.445 in calculations that reference that cell.
2. But if you enter =ROUND(1.445,2) in a cell, Excel will round the number to two decimal places, will display 1.45, and will use 1.45 in calculations that reference that cell. In other words, the =ROUND( ) function actually changes the cell content.

Most commonly, you will use a cell reference or a formula, rather than a number, with the =ROUND( ) function.

	A	B	C	D	E
1	1		1		
2	2		2		
3	3		3		
4	5		5		
5	7		7		
6	11		11		
7					
8	4.833333		4.83		
9					
10					
11	=AVERAGE(A1.A6)				
12					
13			=ROUND(AVERAGE(A1.A6),2)		
14					

Figure 24.7.

TEXT FUNCTIONS

Most Excel functions apply to numbers. The following functions, however, apply specifically to text entries.

Concatenate

The =*CONCATENATE(xx) function* allows you to join or add text elements. Its form is: =CONCATENATE(cell1,cell2). The example in figure 24.8 demonstrates how concatenate is used.

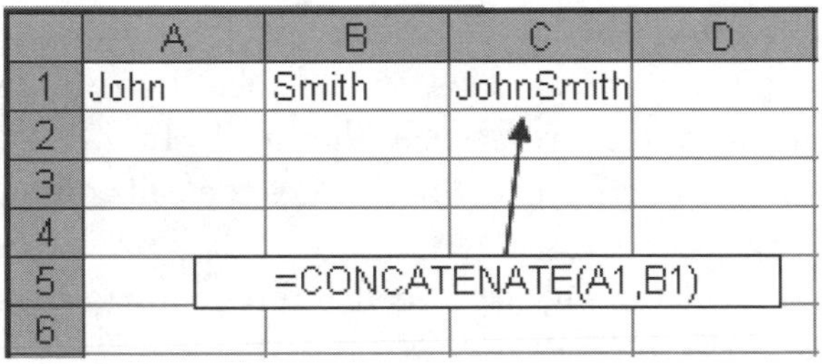

	A	B	C	D
1	John	Smith	JohnSmith	
2				
3				
4				
5		=CONCATENATE(A1,B1)		
6				

Figure 24.8.

You can include a space between the two items, if you wish, by including " " between the cell references.

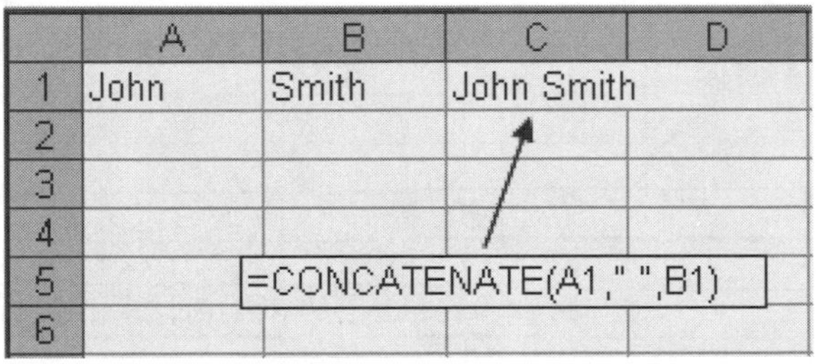

	A	B	C	D
1	John	Smith	John Smith	
2				
3				
4				
5		=CONCATENATE(A1," ",B1)		
6				

Figure 24.9.

Dollar

The *dollar function* allows you to enter a dollar amount in a text entry. The format of this function is: =DOLLAR(number,number-of-decimal-places). The worksheet on figure 24.10 indicates how =DOLLAR( ) is used.

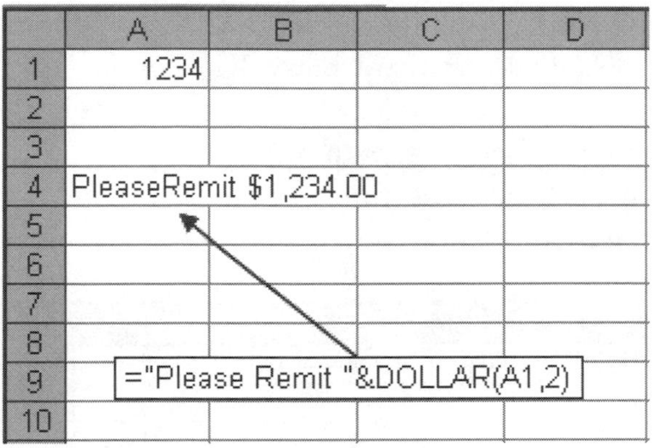

	A	B	C	D
1	1234			
2				
3				
4	PleaseRemit $1,234.00			
5				
6				
7				
8				
9	="Please Remit "&DOLLAR(A1,2)			
10				

Figure 24.10.

Left, Right, and Mid

These functions allow you to display a few selected characters from the text entry in a cell. The =*LEFT( ) function*, for example, allows you to display the leftmost number of characters you specify. It has the form: =LEFT(text,number-of-leftmost-characters).

Suppose, for example, that all parts in an organization's inventory are represented by a six-character part number. Suppose also that the first two digits of the part number indicate the warehouse location of that part. You could use the =LEFT( ) function to return only the code representing the warehouse location.

	A	B	C
1	Part No.		Location
2	ABCDEF		AB
3			
4			
5			
6		=LEFT(A2,2)	
7			

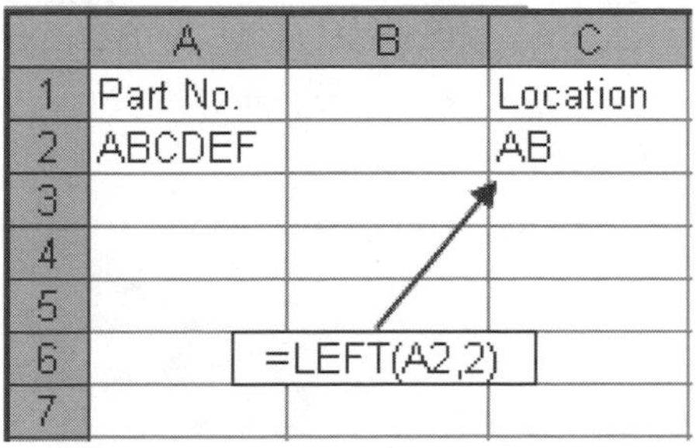

Figure 24.11.

Similarly, the =*RIGHT( ) function* will return the rightmost number of characters of a text entry that you specify. The format for =RIGHT( ) is: =RIGHT(text,number-of-rightmost-characters).

Finally, the =*MID( ) function* will return a specified number of characters from the middle of a text entry. The format for =MID( ) is: =MID(text,number-of-characters-from-the-left-where-the-specified-text-begins,number-of-characters-to-display).

To see how each of these functions works, create the worksheet shown in figure 24.12.

	A	B	C	D	E
1	ABCDEF	AB	← =LEFT(A1,2)		
2					
3	ABCDEF	DEF	← =RIGHT(A3,3)		
4					
5	ABCDEF	CD	← =MID(A5,3,2)		
6					

Figure 24.12.

Lower Case, Upper Case, and Proper Case

These functions convert text to lower case, upper case, or proper case (the first character only of each word is converted to upper case), respectively: =LOWER(text); =UPPER(text); =PROPER(text).

	A	B	C	D	E
1	ABRAHAM LINCOLN	abraham lincoln	← =LOWER(A1)		
2					
3	abraham lincoln	ABRAHAM LINCOLN	← =UPPER(A3)		
4					
5	abraham lincoln	Abraham Lincoln	← =PROPER(A5)		
6					

Figure 24.13.

Trim

When data are imported into an Excel worksheet from a database, it is not uncommon, in the conversion process, for extra spaces to be inserted. The =*TRIM( ) function* removes all spaces between words but one.

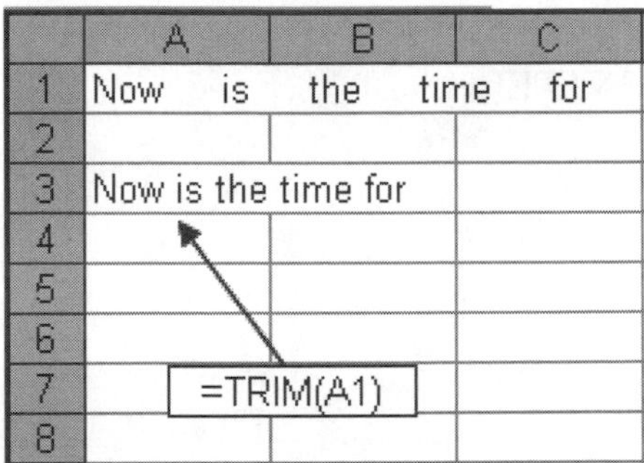

Figure 24.14.

OTHER FUNCTIONS

There are many additional Excel functions, but most are very specialized and have only limited applicability. If your work requires specific kinds of calculations, there is a good chance that Excel has functions to meet at least some of your needs. You can find them in the Excel Help facility.

1. Select Help, Microsoft Excel Help from the Excel menu.
2. Type Excel Functions, and then click on the Search button.
3. Click on, Examples of commonly used formulas.
4. Select the type of function you are looking for.

EXERCISE 24

1. Describe how to use each of the following functions, and give an example of how you might use each:

   =ABS( )
   =INT( )
   =MOD( )
   =RAND( )

=ROUND( )
=CONCATENATE( )
=DOLLAR( )
=LEFT( )
=RIGHT( )
=MID( )
=LOWER( )
=UPPER( )
=PROPER( )
=TRIM( )

2. Create a worksheet that employs some of the functions you have learned in this chapter.

25

LINKING WORKSHEETS

Many people keep their worksheets relatively small, because it is easier to work with smaller worksheets. And if you need to find a mistake, it is easier to do on a smaller worksheet than on a big one.

But if you keep your worksheets small, you might want to combine data from different worksheets—for example, you might keep January student grades in one worksheet, February student grades in another, and so on. In this case, you may want to have one worksheet that keeps track of student grades for the year, which gets its data from the other worksheets. This is fairly easy to do if you create several related worksheets within one Excel workbook.

This chapter explains several simple worksheets, and then one worksheet that collects data from the others. Of course, the process also works with more complicated worksheets.

CREATE A WORKSHEET

Begin by creating the worksheet shown in figure 25.1.

	A	B	C
1	Students Passing State Exams		
2	Grade 6		
3			
4	Passed		
5	Failed		
6	Total	=B4+B5	

Figure 25.1.

NOW CREATE A SECOND WORKSHEET

Although it is not critical, it is easiest to link similar worksheets. In this case, you will create almost identical worksheets by copying the first worksheet and pasting it into the second worksheet.

1. Drag across the range of cells A1:B6.
2. Select Edit, Copy from the menu.
3. At the bottom of your worksheet, click on the tab for Sheet 2.
4. Be certain that cell A1 in Sheet 2 is selected.
5. Select Edit, Paste from the menu.
6. Change the entry in cell A2 to Grade 5.

	A	B	C
1	Students Passing State Exams		
2	Grade 5		
3			
4	Passed		
5	Failed		
6	Total	=B4+B5	

Figure 25.2.

NEXT CREATE A THIRD WORKSHEET

In the same way, create a third worksheet that contains data for the month of March.

1. Drag across the range of cells A1:B6.
2. Select Edit, Copy from the menu.
3. Click on the tab for Sheet 3.
4. Be certain that cell A1 is selected.
5. Select Edit, Paste from the menu.
6. Change the entry in cell A2 to Grade 6.

	A	B	C
1	Students Passing State Exams		
2	Total		
3			
4	Passed		
5	Failed		
6	Total	=B4+B5	

Figure 25.3.

FINALLY CREATE A FOURTH WORKSHEET

You will now create a worksheet that will calculate your total Sales, Costs, and Profits. But first, if your workbook has only three worksheets, you will need to add another.

1. From the menu, select Insert, Worksheet. A fourth worksheet will be created in your workbook.

Note: It is likely that the worksheet you have just created is not in the correct order. Note here, Sheet 4 appears between Sheet 2 and Sheet 3.

Figure 25.4.

You can easily move Sheet 4 to its correct location.

1. Point to Sheet 4.
2. Hold down the left mouse button.

3. Drag Sheet 4 to the right, just beyond Sheet 3. Note the arrow that indicates where Sheet 4 will be moved to.

Figure 25.5.

4. Release the mouse button, and Sheet 4 should be located correctly.

Figure 25.6.

You can now create the worksheet that will calculate your totals.

1. Drag across the range of cells A1:B6 in Sheet 3.
2. Select Edit, Copy from the menu.
3. Click on the tab for Sheet 4.
4. Be certain that cell A1 is selected.
5. Select Edit, Paste from the menu.
6. Change the entry in cell A2 to Total.

	A	B	C
1	Students Passing State Exams		
2	Grade 4		
3			
4	Passed		
5	Failed		
6	Total	=B4+B5	

Figure 25.7.

NAME THE WORKSHEETS

Although you can certainly leave the worksheets labeled Sheet 1, Sheet 2, Sheet 3, and Sheet 4, working with the worksheets will be easier if you assign appropriate names to them.

1. Double click on the Sheet 1 tab, just below your worksheet. Sheet 1 will be highlighted.
2. Type a new name for the worksheet. In this case, name the worksheet Grade 4.

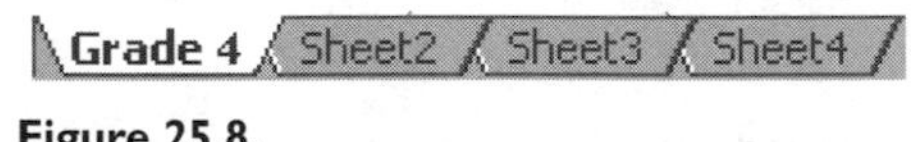

Figure 25.8.

3. You have changed the name of Sheet 1 to Grade 4.
4. In the same way, change the name of Sheet 2 to Grade 5.
5. Next, change the name of Sheet 3 to Grade 6.
6. Finally, change the name of Sheet 4 to Total.

Figure 25.9.

WRITE A LINKING FORMULA

You will now write a linking formula in cell B4 of the Total worksheet. This formula will total the number of students passing in Grade 4, Grade 5, and Grade 6. You will write the formula using the pointing technique, rather than by actually typing the formula.

1. Be certain that the Total worksheet is displayed on your screen.
2. Click on cell B4, the first cell that will contain a linked formula.
3. Type an equals sign (=) to indicate to Excel that you are writing a formula.
4. Click on the Grade 4 tab.
5. Click on cell B4.
6. Type a plus (+).
7. Click on the Grade 5 tab.
8. Click on cell B4.
9. Type a plus (+).
10. Click on the Grade 6 tab.

11. Click on cell B4.
12. Press [Enter].
13. The formula you have created in cell B4 of the Total Sales worksheet is:

    =Grade 4!B4+Grade 5!B4+Grade 6!B4.

Of course, you could have written the formula by typing it directly into cell B4 of the Total worksheet, but doing so would have been much more complicated than creating the formula using the pointing technique. Most people find it easier, particularly when they are learning to write linking formulas, to do it by pointing.

COMPLETING THE WORKSHEET

You can copy the formula in cell B4 of your Total Sales worksheet to cell B5. But, it will be good practice to create the formula the way you created the formula in cell B4.

Note: In some older versions of Excel you cannot copy linking formulas—you must create each separately.

1. Be certain that the Total worksheet is displayed on your screen.
2. Click on cell B5, the cell that will contain your second linked formula.
3. Type an equals sign (=) to indicate to Excel that you are writing a formula.
4. Click on the Grade 4 tab.
5. Click on cell B5.
6. Type a plus (+).
7. Click on the Grade 5 tab.
8. Click on cell B5.
9. Type a plus (+).
10. Click on the Grade 6 tab.
11. Click on cell B5.
12. Press [Enter].

13. The formula in cell B5 of the Total Sales worksheet is:

    =Grade4!B5+Grade5!B5+Grade6!B5.

It is not necessary to write a linked formula in cell B6 of the Total Sales worksheet, since a simple subtraction formula will do:

=B4-B5

After you have written the formula in cell B6, save the worksheet.

Now enter some numerical data into cells B4 and B5 in the January, February, and March worksheets, and notice how your data are reflected on the Total Sales worksheet.

EXERCISE 25

1. Explain how you can simplify the creation of multiple worksheets within a workbook when formulas in the worksheets will be linked.
2. Explain the process of writing a linking formula.
3. Create several similar worksheets, and then create a worksheet that contains one or more linking formulas.

	A	B	C
1	Students Passing State Exams		
2	Grade 4		
3			
4	Passed	20	
5	Failed	5	
6	Total	25	
7			

	A	B	C
1	Students Passing State Exams		
2	Grade 5		
3			
4	Passed	18	
5	Failed	8	
6	Total	26	
7			

	A	B	C
1	Students Passing State Exams		
2	Grade 6		
3			
4	Passed	16	
5	Failed	11	
6	Total	27	
7			

	A	B	C
1	Students Passing State Exams		
2	Total		
3			
4	Passed	54	
5	Failed	24	
6	Total	78	
7			

Figure 25.10.

26

GRAPHICS: PART I

For some time now you have been creating very impressive looking worksheets. But there will be times when adding graphic elements to a worksheet will make your worksheet even better. You can draw lines, boxes, circles, and all kinds of graphic elements in a worksheet. You can even insert text in a "text box," and have an arrow point from that box to a cell in your worksheet. This chapter explains how to include a number of graphic elements in your worksheets.

THE DRAWING TOOLBAR

The first step in adding graphics to an Excel worksheet is to display the Drawing toolbar. There are three ways to do this:
A. Displaying the Drawing toolbar from the menu.

1. Select View, Toolbars, Drawing from the menu.
2. Click on Drawing. A checkmark will appear to the left of Drawing.
3. Click OK.

B. Displaying the Drawing toolbar from any other toolbar.

1. Point to a blank space on any existing toolbar.
2. Click the right mouse button.
3. Click on Drawing.

C. Displaying the Drawing toolbar from the Standard toolbar.

1. Click on the Drawing toolbar button on the standard toolbar.

Figure 26.1.

MOVING A TOOLBAR

The Excel toolbars you are familiar with are probably located at the top of your screen. However, you can locate any toolbar in several different locations.

- To move a toolbar, point to the faint vertical line at the left side of the toolbar, and drag it to a new location.
- If you move a toolbar to the right or left edge of the screen, it will adapt to a vertical format.
- If you move a toolbar to the top or bottom of the screen, it will adapt to a horizontal format.
- Toolbars may also float in the work area. This is probably the least popular location for a toolbar, because it obscures some of your work area.
- Many people find it convenient to locate the Standard and Formatting toolbars at the top of their screen, and the Drawing toolbar at the bottom.

THE DRAWING TOOLS

As with all Excel toolbars, you can tell what a button or tool does by pointing the cursor to it. Excel will display the tool's function. In figure 26.2, the mouse pointer is positioned on the Rectangle tool, and a box has opened just below the mouse pointer containing the word, Rectangle.

Figure 26.2.

AUTOSHAPES

The *AutoShapes button* allows you to choose from a number of graphics, and to include those graphics in a worksheet in a size and orientation that you choose.

Figure 26.3.

1. Click on the AutoShapes button.
2. Select a category.
3. Select a specific graphic.
4. Point to where you want the graphic to begin in your worksheet.
5. Hold down the left mouse button and drag it until the size of the graphic is appropriate for your needs.
6. Release the mouse button.
7. If you want to modify an AutoShape, click an area you want to modify to select it, and use the sizing handles that surround it to make your changes.
8. If you want to move an AutoShape, point to it, hold down the left mouse button, and drag it to a new location.

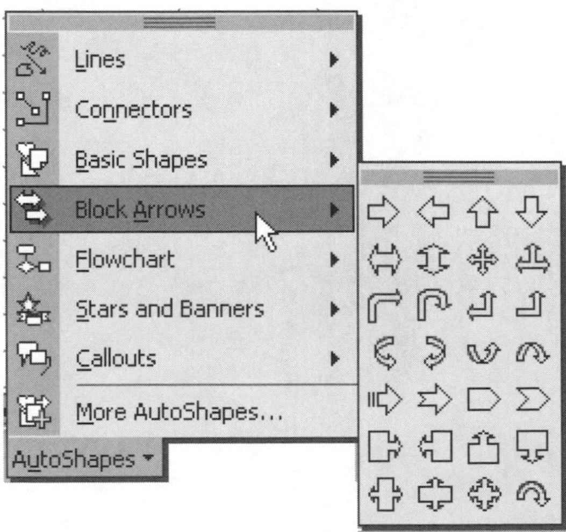

Figure 26.4.

The Line Tool

The *Line tool* enables you to draw straight lines in your worksheet.

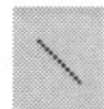

Figure 26.5.

1. Click on the Line tool to select it.
2. Point to where you want a line to begin.
3. Hold down the left mouse button, and drag the pointer to where you want the line to end. Then release the mouse pointer.

You can draw a line at any angle. However, if you want to draw a line at exactly 0, 15, 30, 45, 60, 75, or 90 degrees, hold down the [Shift] key while you draw the line.

The Arrow Tool

The *Arrow tool* works the way that the Line tool works, but as you can imagine, it enables you to create arrows rather than lines.

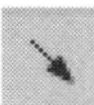

Figure 26.6.

1. Point to where you want the arrow to end—that is, the end opposite where you want the arrowhead to appear.
2. Hold down the left mouse button, and drag to where you want the arrowhead to point.
3. Release the mouse button.

If the arrow does not point exactly where you want it to point, click on it to select it, and drag either of the sizing handles to reposition the beginning or the end of the arrow. You can also move the arrow by selecting it, and then dragging it to a new location.

The Rectangle Tool

The *Rectangle tool* enables you to draw rectangles and squares.

Figure 26.7.

1. Select the Rectangle tool.
2. Point to where you want one corner of the rectangle to appear.
3. Hold down the left mouse button.
4. Drag the pointer to where you want the opposite corner of the rectangle to appear.
5. Release the mouse button.

If you want to draw a square, hold down the [Shift] key as you describe your rectangle.

The Ellipse Tool

The *Ellipse tool* enables you to draw ellipses and circles.

Figure 26.8.

1. Select the Ellipse tool.
2. Point to where you want the ellipse to begin.
3. Hold down the left mouse button.
4. Drag the pointer to describe an ellipse.
5. Release the mouse button.

If you want to draw a circle, hold down the [Shift] key as you describe the ellipse.

The Text Box Tool

The *Text Box tool* allows you to draw a box, and include text within the box. You can use it, for example, to draw attention to some data in your worksheet.

Figure 26.9.

1. Click on the Text Box tool.
2. Point to where you want the text box to begin.
3. Hold down the mouse button and describe the text box.
4. Release the mouse button.
5. Type the text in your text box.

You can format the text in a text box. Drag the mouse pointer across the text, and use the Format, Cells menu as you would with any other text.

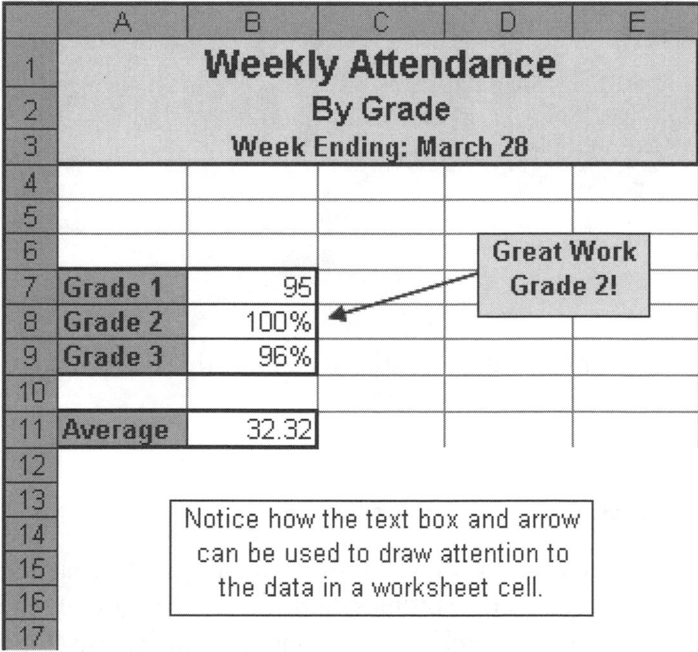

Figure 26.10.

Word Art

With *Word Art* you can create fancy titles. Word Art has fairly limited use in most business worksheets, but in schools and some organizations, Word Art may be just what you need to draw attention to your worksheet.

Figure 26.11.

1. Click on the Word Art button.
2. Choose a Word Art design and click OK.
3. Type your text.
4. Click OK, and voila! Your text is transformed into a fancy title.

Figure 26.12.

Click on a Word Art object, and you can use the Word Art toolbar to modify it.

Fill Color, Line Color, and Font Color

As their names suggest, these buttons enable you to change the fill color of an object, the color of lines, and the color of text. Experiment with them, and you will quickly see how easy they are to use (Figs. 26.13 and 26.14).

Line, Dash, and Arrow Styles

With these buttons, you can change the style of lines, dashes, and arrows. As with the fill buttons, their use should be fairly obvious (Fig. 26.15).

Figure 26.13.

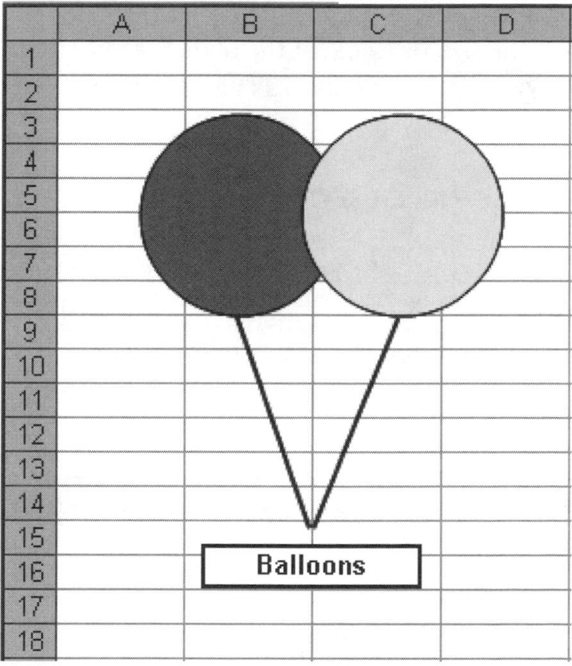

Figure 26.14.

Figure 26.15.

MODIFYING A GRAPHIC OBJECT

It is easy to modify the size of any graphic object.

1. Position the mouse pointer directly on the object, or if the object is enclosed, such as a rectangle or an ellipse, inside the object. Click the left mouse button, and sizing handles will appear around the object.
2. To change the size or shape of the object, point to one of the handles and drag inward or outward (Fig. 16.16).

MOVING A GRAPHIC OBJECT

1. Point to any graphic object. Your pointer will change to a four-sided arrow.
2. Hold down the left mouse button and drag the object to a new location.

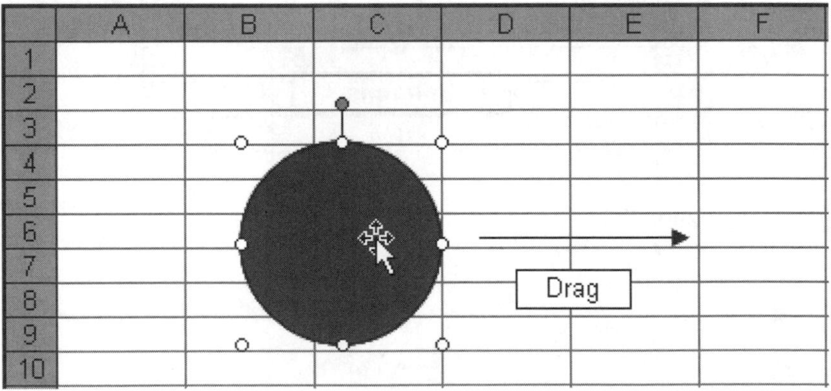

Figure 26.16.

To allow the object to move only horizontally or vertically, hold down the [Shift] key while you drag it. To clone or copy the object, hold down the [Control] key while you drag it.

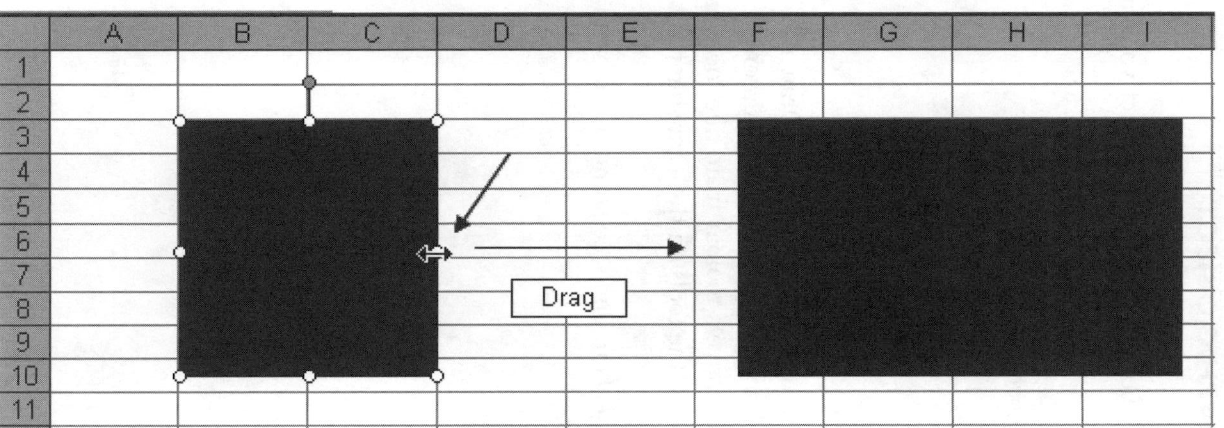

Figure 26.17.

REMOVING A GRAPHIC OBJECT

If you decide you do not want a graphic object you have created, it is easy to remove it.

1. Click on the object to select it.
2. Press the [Delete] key on your keyboard.

EXERCISE 26

1. Describe the three ways to display the Drawing toolbar.
2. Where can toolbars be located on your screen?
3. Describe how to move a toolbar from one location to another.
4. Explain how to use the tools on the Drawing toolbar that you have learned about.
5. Use graphic objects to enhance some of the worksheets you have previously created.

27

GRAPHICS: PART 2

In the previous chapter you learned how to include graphic objects in your worksheets. Since graphic objects can add so much impact to your worksheets, this chapter will continue with even more about adding graphic objects to Excel worksheets.

MORE GRAPHICS TOOLS AND SHORTCUTS

Select Objects (Arrow)

The *Select Objects tool*, which looks like an arrow, allows you to select a graphic object, or several graphic objects you have created. Of course you can select one graphic object by simply clicking on it. But if you select a second graphic object, the first will no longer be selected. With the Select Objects tool, you can select multiple graphic objects at one time. This enables you, for example, to move several objects at one time.

Figure 27.1.

1. Create two or more graphic objects.
2. Click on the Select Objects tool.
3. Position the pointer above and to the left of the leftmost graphic object.
4. Hold down the left mouse button and drag right and down until all the graphic objects are enclosed.
5. When you release the mouse button, all the graphic objects you have enclosed will be selected. You will see sizing handles around each (Figs. 27.2 and 27.3).

The Select Objects tool remains "on" until you have turned it off. So when you have finished using the Select Objects tool, click on it again to turn it "off."

You can also select multiple drawing objects in another way.

1. Click on the first object to select it.
2. Hold down the [Shift] key and click on the second drawing object.
3. Select additional drawing objects, if necessary, in the same way.

Moving and Resizing Multiple Drawing Objects

When you have selected two or more drawing objects, you can move or resize them together.

1. Select two or more graphic objects using either of the techniques described above. The sizing handles around each object will indicate that it is selected.
2. Point within any one of the graphic objects, and drag it to another location. All the selected drawing objects will move together to the new location.
3. Point to any sizing handle and resize the object. All of the selected objects will be resized together.

Bring to Front and Send to Back

Sometimes you will have two or more overlapping graphic objects, and you will want to move the forward one to the rear, or the rearward one to the front.

Figure 27.2.

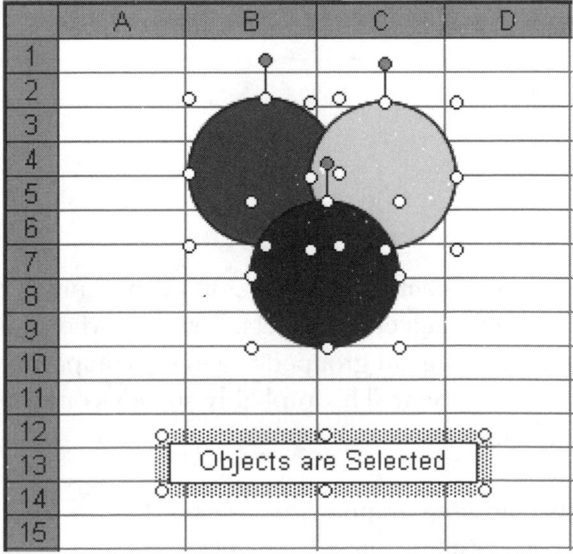

Figure 27.3.

1. Draw one rectangle, and then draw an overlapping rectangle. Use the Fill Color button to apply different colors to each. The colors will enable you to easily see which rectangle is in the foreground.
2. Click on the rear rectangle to select it.
3. Click on the Draw button, select Order, and then select Bring to Front. Notice that the relative positions of the rectangles have changed.

The *Send to Back option* works in the same way, but as you would expect, it moves an object from the foreground to the background.

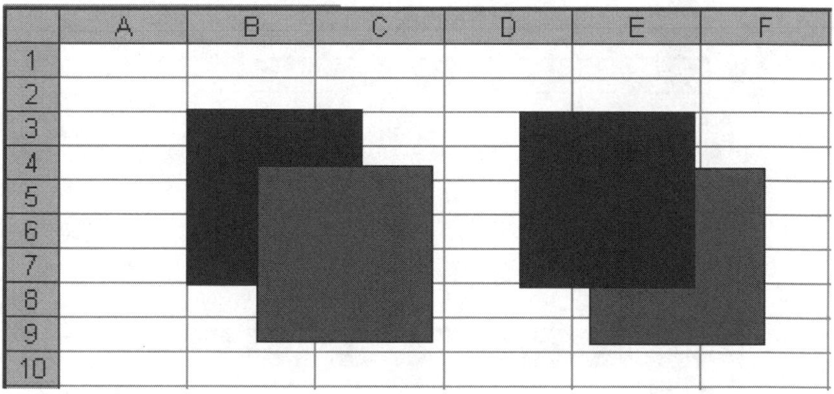

Figure 27.4.

Group Objects

The *Draw button* also allows you to group two or more graphics into a single object. Unlike selecting objects, however, when you group two or more objects they remain grouped together, semipermanently, until you actively ungroup them. This probably sounds confusing, but once you do it, it will make sense.

1. Create two or more graphic objects.
2. Click on one graphic object to select it.

3. Hold down the [Shift] key and click on another graphic object to select the two simultaneously (you could also select multiple graphic objects by using the Drawing Selection tool).
4. Now click on the Draw button, and select Group. Note that only one set of handles surrounds both graphic objects. You have combined two or more graphic objects into one. You can manipulate the graphic objects as if they were one object.
5. Move the grouped drawing objects together, as a group, or resize them and they will increase or decrease in the same proportion to each other.

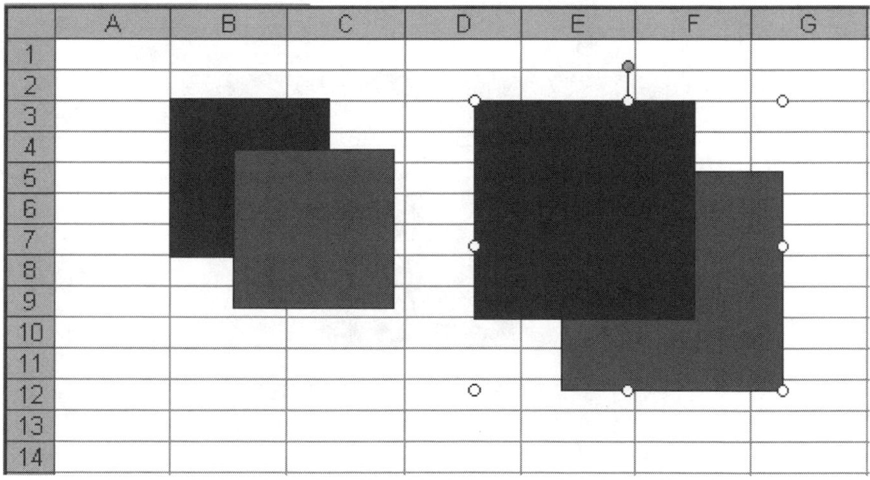

Figure 27.5.

Ungrouping Graphic Objects

When you group graphic objects, they will remain grouped until you specifically ungroup them. Try it. Click anywhere outside the objects you have grouped to deselect them. Now click on one of the graphic objects, and you will see that they are still grouped.

1. To ungroup graphic objects, begin by clicking on the combined graphic objects to select them.
2. Click on the Draw button on the Drawing toolbar.
3. Select Ungroup.

Shadow Tool

The *Shadow tool* allows you to apply a shadow effect to a graphic object.

Figure 27.6.

1. Click on a graphic object.
2. Click on the Shadow tool.
3. Select a type of shadow effect.

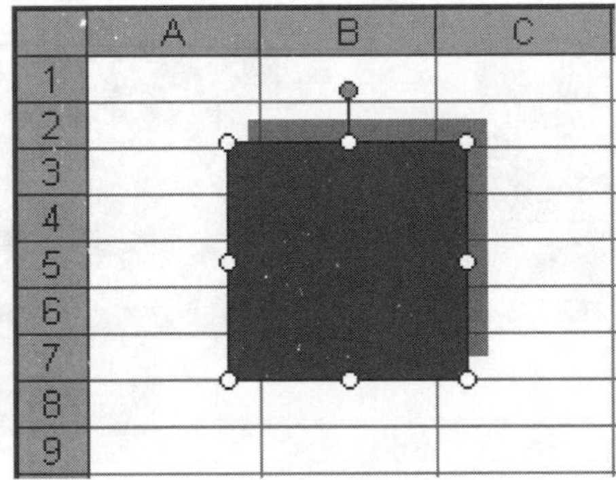

Figure 27.7.

3D Button

The *3D button* works almost exactly as the Shadow button does. But rather than a shadow, it applies a 3D effect to your graphic object.

Figure 27.8.

1. Click on a graphic object to select it.
2. Click on 3D button.
3. Select a 3D effect.

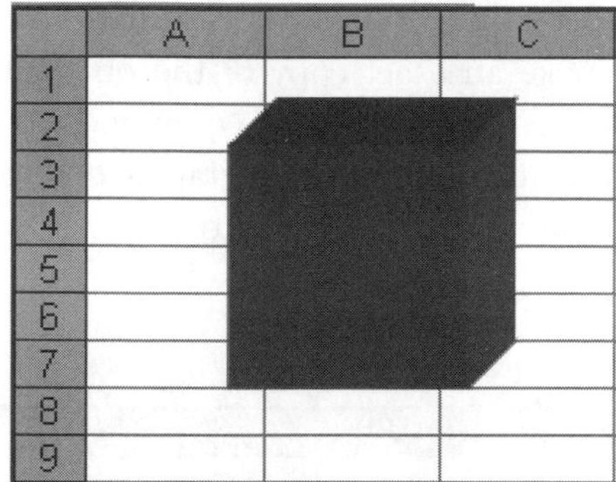

Figure 27.9.

Cutting, Copying, and Pasting Graphic Objects

You can use the Cut, Copy, and Paste commands to make exact copies of graphic objects. The process is identical to cutting and pasting or copying and pasting cell contents.

1. Select the graphic object.
2. Select Edit, Cut or Edit, Copy from the menu.
3. Select the cell where you want to paste the graphic object.
4. Select Edit, Paste from the menu.
5. When you paste a graphic object, it almost never ends up exactly where you want it to be. If this is the case, simply click on the graphic object to select it, and drag it to a new location.

A FEW ADDITIONAL THINGS YOU SHOULD KNOW ABOUT GRAPHIC OBJECTS

1. You can format a graphic object by pointing to it and clicking the right mouse button, and then selecting Format, AutoShape from the options that appear.
2. If you hold down the [Shift] key while you move a graphic object, you can move the object at only a 0 degree or 90 degree angle (horizontally or vertically).

3. Holding down the [Ctrl] key while you move a graphic object allows you to make an exact copy of the object. The result is the same as using the Copy and Paste commands.
4. It is sometimes difficult to position graphic objects precisely—they appear to jump slightly as you create or move them. You can create and move graphic objects precisely by holding down the [Alt] key as you create or move them.

	A	B	C	D	E
1–4	Varsity Teams				
7–8			Fall, 2003		
11		TEAM		COACH	
14		Baseball		Jones	
15		Basketball		Smith	
16		Bowling		Walker	
17		Football		Adams	
18		Volleyball		Jensen	

Figure 27.10.

EXERCISE 27

1. Describe the two ways to select multiple drawing objects at one time.
2. Explain two reasons you might want to select multiple drawing objects at one time.

3. Explain how Bring to Front and Send to Back work.
4. Explain why you might want to group drawing objects together.
5. Describe how to group drawing objects together.
6. Describe how to ungroup drawing objects you have previously grouped.
7. Describe what the Shadow and 3D buttons do, and describe how to use them. Why might you want to create a shadow or 3D effect?
8. Explain how to format a drawing object.
9. Describe how to copy and paste drawing objects, and how to cut and paste drawing objects.
10. Describe what will happen if you hold down the [Shift] key while you move a drawing object.
11. Describe what will happen if you hold down the [Ctrl] key while you move a drawing object.
12. Describe why you might hold down the [Alt] key while you move a drawing object.
13. Create the worksheet shown in figure 27.11. Use graphic effects to enhance the appearance of the worksheet.

	A	B	C	D	E	F	G
1	School Bus Schedule						
2							
3	Route	Stop 1	Stop 2	Stop 3	Stop 4	Stop 5	Arrival
4	1	8:00 AM	8:10 AM	8:20 AM	8:30 AM	8:40 AM	8:50 AM
5	2	7:55 AM	8:05 AM	8:15 AM	8:25 AM	8:35 AM	8:45 AM
6	3	8:05 AM	8:15 AM	8:25 AM	8:35 AM	8:45 AM	8:55 AM
7	4	8:10 AM	8:20 AM	8:30 AM	8:40 AM	8:50 AM	9:00 AM

Figure 27.11.

28

WORKSHEET PROTECTION

When most people think about worksheet protection, they think about protecting a worksheet from prying eyes. Although this is certainly a protection issue, worksheet protection usually does not refer to preventing other people from viewing your worksheets. Rather, protection usually means allowing other people to use a worksheet you have created, but not to change parts of it, or in some cases, any of it. This chapter explains both kinds of worksheet protection.

THE RISKY WAY OF KEEPING OTHER PEOPLE FROM SEEING YOUR WORKSHEET

Many people are concerned about preventing other people from having access to worksheets they have created. There are two ways to keep other people from seeing a worksheet you have created. Both work, but one is riskier than the other.

The risky way to keep other people from seeing a worksheet you have created involves password protecting it. When you *password protect* a worksheet, someone who uses your computer will see the worksheet listed when they select File, Open from the menu. But unless they know the password you have assigned to that worksheet, they will not be able to open the worksheet. The following steps will enable you to password protect a worksheet you have created.

1. Select File, Save As from the menu.
2. Assign a file name to your worksheet.
3. Now select Tools, General Options from the Save As menu.
4. If you assign a "Password to Open," a user will have to know the password in order to open the worksheet.
5. If you assign a "Password to Modify," a user will be able to open your worksheet without knowing the password, but in "Read Only" mode. That is, the user will not be able to make any changes to the worksheet.
6. Click OK.
7. You will be asked to retype your password. This ensures that you if you mistyped the password, your document will not be inadvertently saved with a password you do not know.
8. Click Save.

Your document has now been saved with the file name and password you have indicated.

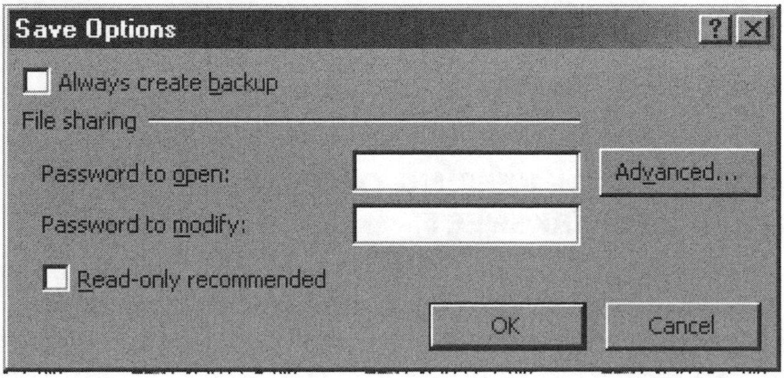

Figure 28.1.

To open a worksheet that has been password protected, follow the standard method for opening any worksheet. However, when you select a password-protected worksheet, you will be asked to enter the password.

Note that passwords may contain up to fifteen characters, including letters, numbers, and symbols. They are case sensitive. That is, uppercase characters are considered to be different from lowercase characters. MRSMITH is not the same as MrSmith. That sounds pretty straightforward. Why, you may ask, is it risky?

1. If you choose a password that is easy to remember, say your husband's, wife's, child's, dog's, or cat's name, it is relatively easy for anyone who knows even a little about you to discover it.
2. The only way to be sure that your password is secure is to choose a password that is difficult to remember, and then, to change it fairly often.
3. But if you choose a password that is difficult to remember, and you change it periodically, you run the risk of forgetting it. And if you forget your password, *you will be unable to open your workbook—ever!*

PROTECTING A WORKSHEET FROM UNAUTHORIZED CHANGES

There is a variation to password-protecting worksheets that should be mentioned here. *Write protecting* a worksheet makes it possible for other people to see your worksheet, but not to change it unless they know the password you have assigned to it (in computer terminology, "they can read the worksheet, but they cannot write to it"). Excel makes it easy to write protect a worksheet. As in the previous section, the risk is that you will forget the password you assigned, or that someone else will discover your password.

1. Select File, Save As from the menu.
2. Assign a file name to your worksheet.
3. Select Tools, General Options.
4. Type a password in the Password to Modify box.
5. Select Read Only Recommended.
6. Click OK.
7. Retype the password.
8. Click OK to accept your choice and close the Password dialog box.
9. Click OK again to save your worksheet and close the Save As dialog box.

Read Only Recommended allows other people to open your document. They can make changes to the document. But if they want to save their changes, they can do so only by assigning another file name. They cannot change your worksheet and save it with the name you have assigned. In any event, your version of the worksheet will remain unchanged. Again, Read Only Recommended involves assigning a password to your worksheet. As such, it involves the same risks as other methods that require passwords.

THE SAFEST WAY OF PREVENTING OTHER PEOPLE FROM SEEING YOUR WORKSHEET

The safest way to keep other people from seeing one of your worksheets is really quite simple:

1. Do not save the worksheet on your computer's hard disk!
2. Save your worksheet on a diskette instead, and always take the diskette with you!

If you have not saved the worksheet on your computer's hard disk, obviously no one can see it. "But," you will say, "that's inconvenient." It certainly can be. In the final analysis, it all depends on just how secure you want your data to be.

WORKSHEET PROTECTION

Now that you know how to password protect a worksheet, you will learn about the other kind of worksheet protection. Sometimes you will want to allow other people to look at a worksheet you have created, and even to use the worksheet. But you will want to restrict their ability to change some parts of the worksheet. For example, you may want to allow other people to enter data into a worksheet, but not to change cells that contain formulas.

In other words, it is not that you want to prevent other people from using your worksheet. You only want to keep them from changing, perhaps inadvertently, parts of the worksheet that they should not change.

1. With your worksheet on the screen, select Tools, Protection from the menu.
2. Indicate whether you want to protect a sheet (Protect Worksheet) or the entire workbook (Protect Workbook).
3. The dialog box that you will see will depend on whether you are protecting the worksheet or the entire workbook. In either case, leave the default selections.
4. If you wish to assign a password, type it and click OK. You will be asked to retype the password to confirm that you have spelled it correctly. If you choose to assign a password, note that as in previous sections, passwords are case sensitive (upper case and lower case characters are seen as different). Again, keep in mind the cautions regarding passwords.
5. Click OK.

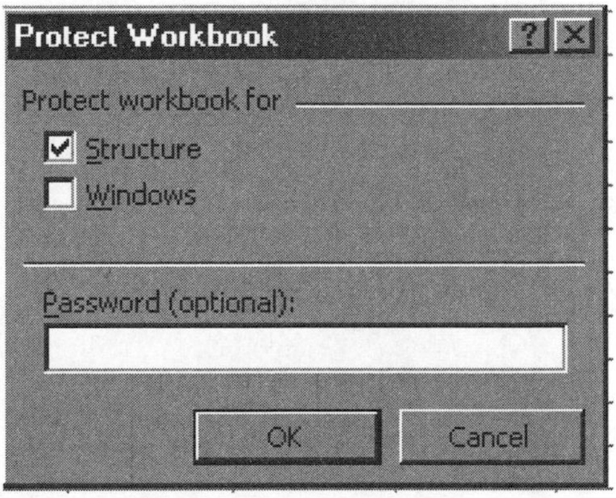

Figure 28.2.

Now try to type an entry into a cell. You will be advised that the cell or chart that you are trying to change is protected and therefore read-only (Fig. 28.3).

Microsoft Excel
The cell or chart you are trying to change is protected and therefore read-only.
To modify a protected cell or chart, first remove protection using the Unprotect Sheet command (Tools menu, Protection submenu). You may be prompted for a password.
OK

Figure 28.3.

1. Click OK to return to the worksheet.

UNPROTECTING A WORKSHEET

You unprotect a worksheet in the same way you protected it.

1. With your worksheet on the screen, select Tools, Protection from the menu.
2. Select Unprotect Worksheet from the Protection dialog box.
3. If you assigned a password, you will be asked to enter it.
4. Click OK.

Your worksheet is now unprotected.

PROTECTING PART OF A WORKSHEET

Now you have learned how to protect everything in the worksheet. Most often, you will want to leave certain cells, or ranges of cells, unprotected so that users can change only the data in those cells. This involves a two-step process:

1. First, you must unprotect the cells or ranges of cells that you do not want protected.
2. Then, you must protect the entire worksheet or workbook.

An example should make the process very clear. Begin by creating a worksheet from figure 28.4. Copy the formulas as indicated by the arrows.

	A	B	C	D	E	F	G	H
1	Library Books Borrowed							
2								
3		Mon	Tue	Wed	Thu	Fri	Total	
4	Fiction						=SUM(B4:F4)	
5	Non-fiction							
6	Biography							
7	Total	=SUM(B4:B6)						
8								

Figure 28.4.

In this case, you will want to protect your formulas in the ranges of cells B7:F7, and also G4:G7. But you will want to leave cells B4:F6 unprotected, so that the user can enter data into them, and then change those data as necessary.

1. Drag across the cells you want to remain unprotected, in this case, cells B4:F6.
2. Select Format, Cells, Protection from the menu.
3. Click on the check box next to Locked to deselect it.
4. Click OK.

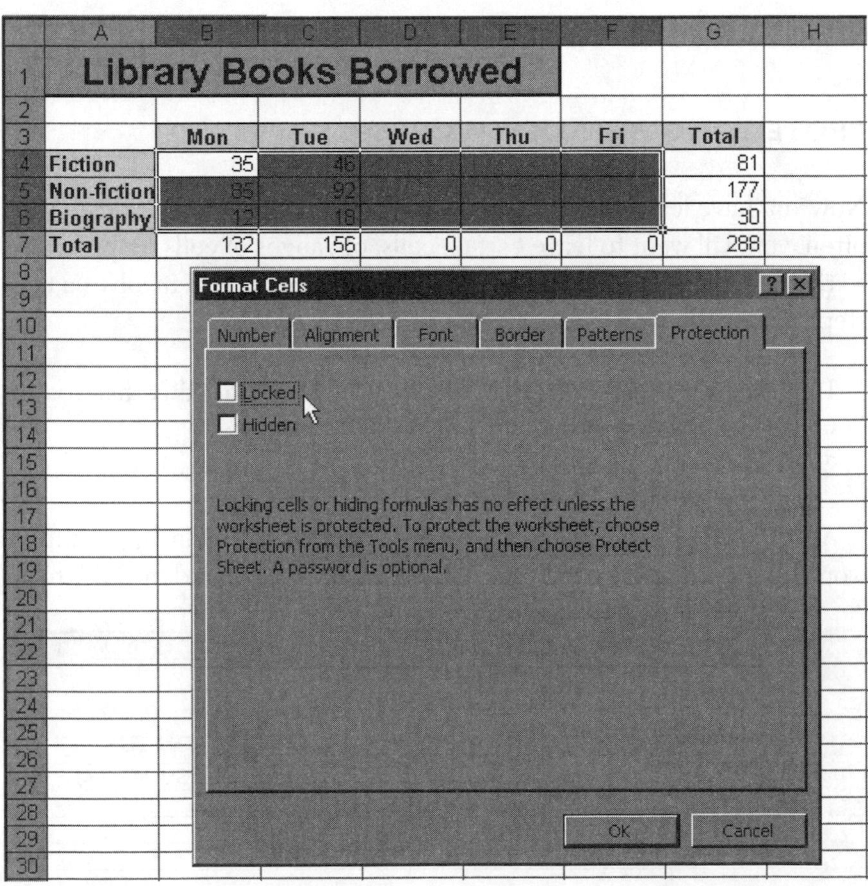

Figure 28.5.

5. Now, select Tools, Protection, Protect Sheet from the menu, and click OK.
6. You want to allow users to select (that is change) only the cells you have unlocked. To accomplish this, click on Select Unlocked Cells to select it (that is, to checkmark it).

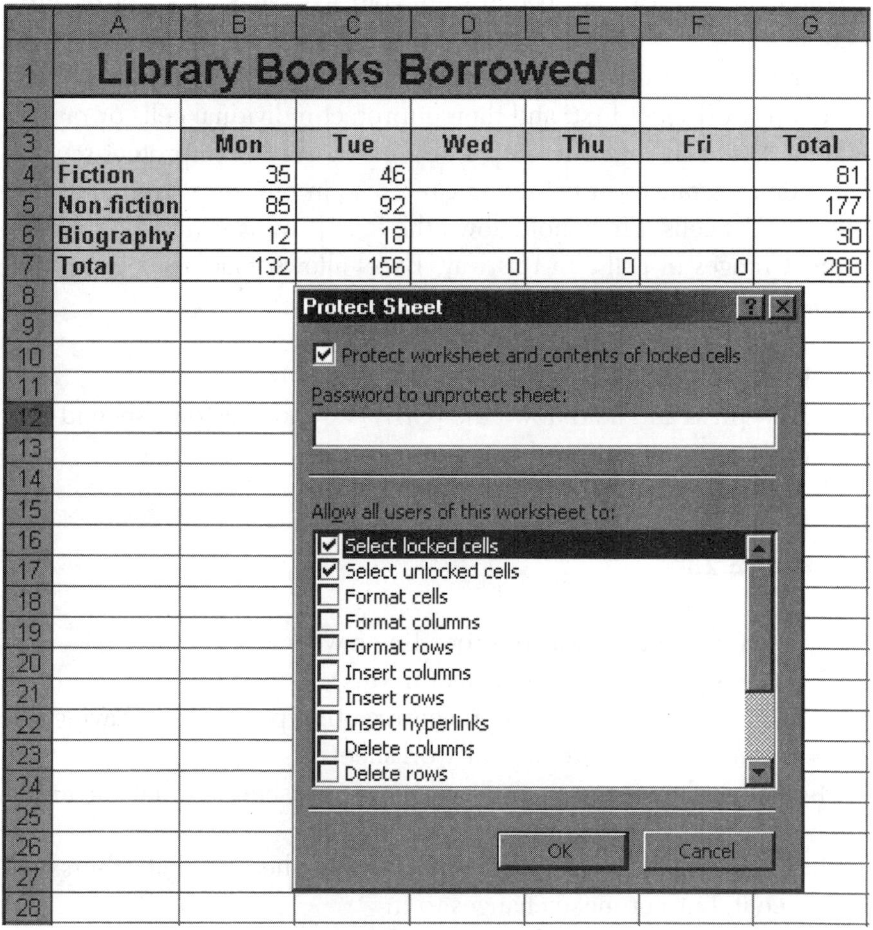

	A	B	C	D	E	F	G
1	Library Books Borrowed						
2							
3		Mon	Tue	Wed	Thu	Fri	Total
4	Fiction	35	46				81
5	Non-fiction	85	92				177
6	Biography	12	18				30
7	Total	132	156	0	0	0	288

Protect Sheet

Protect worksheet and contents of locked cells

Password to unprotect sheet:

Allow all users of this worksheet to:

Select locked cells
Select unlocked cells
Format cells
Format columns
Format rows
Insert columns
Insert rows
Insert hyperlinks
Delete columns
Delete rows

OK Cancel

Figure 28.6.

The user of this worksheet now only has access to the cells you have unprotected.

Remember: Protecting parts of a worksheet is a two-step process.

1. First, unprotect the cells or ranges of cells you do not want protected by selecting the cells or ranges and using the Format, Cells menu.
2. Then, protect the entire worksheet using the Tools, Protection menu.

Until you perform the second step, your worksheet will not be protected.

Note that the process must be done in this order. You cannot protect the entire worksheet first, and then unprotect individual cells or ranges of cells. Note also that if in Step 1 above you want to unprotect several discontinuous ranges of cells, you can do so in one step. Highlight the first range of cells. Then, hold down the [Ctrl] key as you highlight subsequent ranges of cells. In this way, Excel allows you to select several discontinuous ranges at one time. Try it:

1. Click on a cell or drag across a range of cells.
2. Now press and hold down the [Ctrl] key and click on a second cell or drag across a second range of cells.

EXERCISE 28

1. What is the risky way of protecting a worksheet?
2. Why is protecting a worksheet in this way risky?
3. What is the safest way of preventing other people from having access to one or more of your worksheets?
4. Explain how to password protect a worksheet so that unauthorized people will not have access to it.
5. Explain how to password protect a worksheet so that others can see it, but not make changes to it.
6. Explain why you might want to allow someone to change the entries in some cells in your worksheet, but not others.
7. What happens when you protect some cells in a worksheet and someone tries to type an entry into one of the protected cells?
8. Explain how to protect some cells in a worksheet from changes, while allowing changes to be made to other cells.

9. Explain how to unprotect a worksheet you have protected.
10. What are the two steps involved in protecting part of a worksheet?
11. Explain how to select several discontinuous cells or ranges of cells at one time.
12. Create a worksheet from figure 28.7 and apply what you have learned in this chapter.

	A	B	C	D	E	F	G	H	I	J
1	**Teacher Schedule**									
2	**Academic Year: 2002-2003**									
3										
4										
5			**Period**							
6	**Teacher**	**Department**	**1**	**2**	**3**	**4**	**5**	**6**	**7**	**8**
7	**Jones**	**English**	Remedial	English 09	Duty	English 10H	Lunch	Engl 09	Prep	Engl 10H
8	**Walker**	**English**	Engl 10	English 10	Prep	Duty	Engl 10	Lunch	Engl 11H	Engl 11H
9										
10										
11										
12										

Figure 28.7.

29

MACROS

A *macro* is a program you write to simplify using an Excel worksheet. Don't be concerned if you have never written a computer program, or if you have tried but weren't successful. Excel has a *macro recorder* that makes it easy for you to write macros.

Actually, you can learn a lot about Excel macros, and it is possible to write very sophisticated macros. This chapter only introduces you to the subject, and you will write only fairly simple macros.

EXCEL MACROS

Macros are particularly useful for frequently performed operations and can easily automate operations in your worksheets. Macros are also useful if you create worksheets other people are going to use, especially if they do not know as much about Excel as you do.

However, there is a downside to using Excel macros. Some people have created computer viruses that are transmitted through macros in Microsoft Excel worksheets. As a result, many people, and even some organizations, avoid worksheets that contain macros.

CREATE A WORKSHEET

To see how the procedure works, begin by creating a worksheet from figure 29.1, which will calculate a student's high school average:

	A	B
1	Average Calculator	
2		
3		
4	Student	Mary Jones
5	Course 1	85
6	Course 2	90
7	Course 3	75
8	Course 4	80
9	Course 5	85
10	Course 6	90
11		
12	Average	=AVERAGE(B5:B10)
13		

Figure 29.1.

START THE MACRO RECORDER

You are now ready to write your first macro. Assume that the person who will be using this worksheet knows virtually nothing about Excel. All that they know how to do is enter data into cells. You want to write a macro to simplify printing the worksheet.

1. Select Tools, Macro, Record New Macro . . . from the menu.
2. The default Macro Name is Macro1. Do not change it.
3. In the Ctrl+ box, press [p]. You could select any letter, but the letter p seems appropriate for a print macro.
4. Click OK.
5. You have started the macro recorder. It will record each of your keystrokes and mouse clicks, so be careful not to press any keys you do not want to be part of your macro. In fact, do not do any-

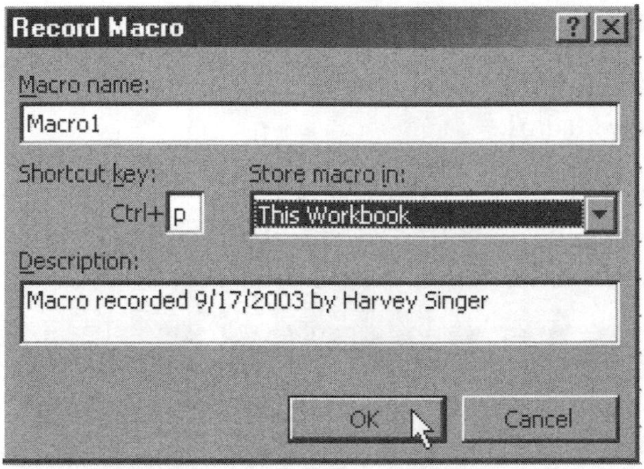

Figure 29.2.

thing you do not want to be part of your macro. Note that a Macro Stop button is floating on your worksheet, probably near the upper right corner.

Figure 29.3.

6. Now, perform the operation you want the macro to perform.
   a. Select File, Print from the menu.
   b. Change the Number of Copies to 2.
   c. Click OK.
7. You have finished the procedure you want the macro to perform, so turn the macro recorder off by clicking on the Stop button.

RUN THE MACRO

Since you included a shortcut key with your macro, there are two ways to run your macro: the standard way and the shortcut key way.

Standard Method

1. Select Tools, Macro from the menu.
2. Click on Macro1.
3. Click on the Run button.

The macro you have written has directed Excel to print two copies of your worksheet, just as if you had selected File, Print, 2 Copies, OK.

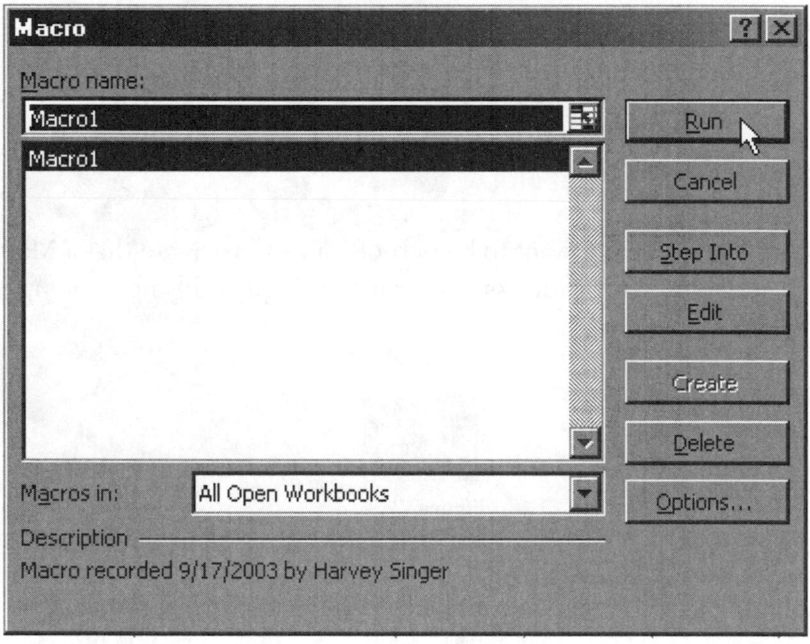

Figure 29.4.

Shortcut Key Method

Since you created a shortcut key, you can also run this macro from the keyboard.

1. Simply hold down the [Ctrl] key and press [p].

CREATE A MACRO BUTTON

You can also create a macro button to make it even easier to run your macro and to make your worksheet look even more professional.

1. From the drawing toolbar, click on the Text Box button.
2. Draw a rectangle about the size of the button you would like. Type the word Print in the text box.
3. Right click on one of the sizing handles that surround your button. A shortcut menu will appear (Fig. 29.5).
4. Select Assign Macro from the shortcut button.
5. Remember that your macro was named Macro1. Click on Macro1 to select it.
6. Click OK (Fig. 29.6).

Now, whenever you want to print two copies of your worksheet, simply click on the Print macro button and your macro will perform the task.

WRITE ANOTHER MACRO

The macro you have written is not a very important macro. There is already a Print button on the Excel Standard toolbar. Nevertheless, you have learned how to write a macro, and you have written your first macro.

You will now sharpen your macro skills by writing another, slightly more ambitious macro. But before you do that, it will be helpful to remember that writing a macro involves several distinct steps:

1. Start the macro recorder (and establish a shortcut key if you want one).
2. Type the keystrokes you want the macro to perform.
3. Stop the macro recorder.
4. Optionally, you may want to create a macro button to run your macro.

Your second macro will erase the data in the worksheet, and also position the cursor in the first data entry cell, cell B4.

1. Select Tools, Macro, Record Macro . . . from the menu.
2. The default Macro Name for your second macro is Macro2. Do not change it.
3. In the Ctrl+ box, press [e] (for erase).

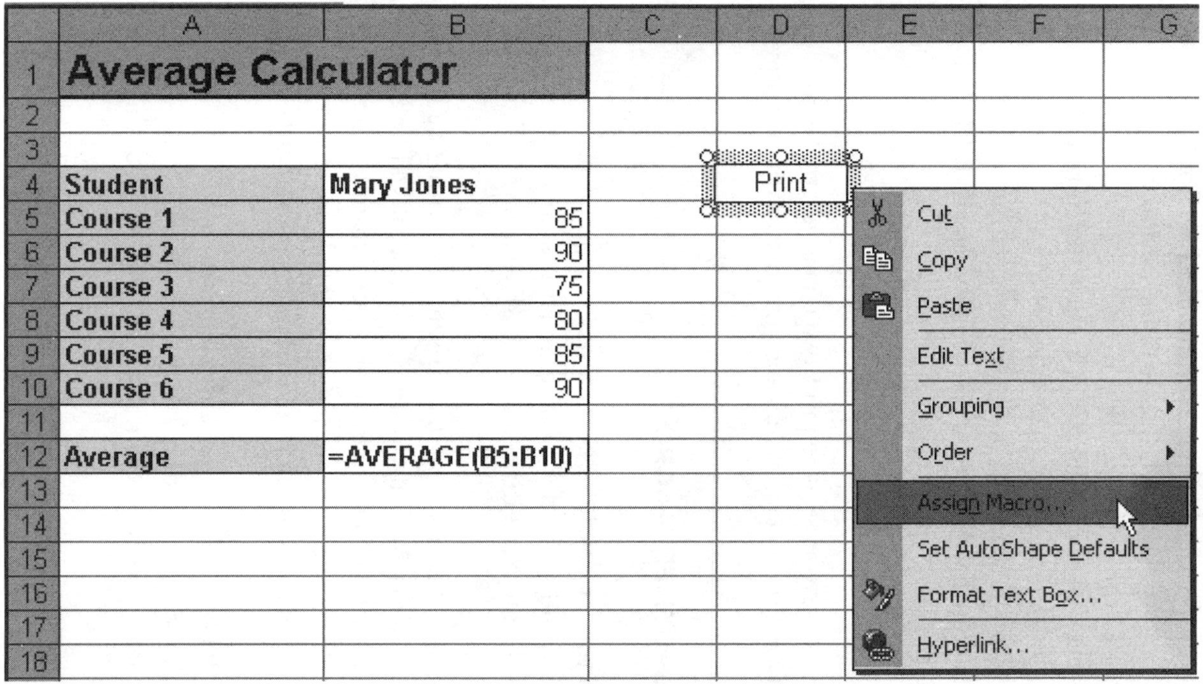
A
B
C
D
E
F
G
Average Calculator
Student
Mary Jones
Course 1
85
Course 2
90
Course 3
75
Course 4
80
Course 5
85
Course 6
90
Average
=AVERAGE(B5:B10)
Print
Cut
Copy
Paste
Edit Text
Grouping
Order
Assign Macro...
Set AutoShape Defaults
Format Text Box...
Hyperlink...

Figure 29.5.

	A	B	C	D
1	Average Calculator			
2				
3				
4	Student	Mary Jones		Print
5	Course 1	85		
6	Course 2	90		
7	Course 3	75		
8	Course 4	80		
9	Course 5	85		
10	Course 6	90		
11				
12	Average	84.17		
13				

Figure 29.6.

4. Click OK.
5. You have started the macro recorder. The macro recorder starts only after OK has been clicked in step 3.
6. Now, perform the operations you want the macro to perform.
   a. Point to the center of cell B4. Hold down the left mouse button, and drag across cells B4:B10.
   b. Press the [Delete] key, or select Edit, Clear, Contents from the menu.
   c. Click on cell B4 to reposition the cursor in that cell.
7. You have finished the procedure you want the macro to perform, so turn the macro recorder off by clicking on the Stop button.

RUN THE MACRO

Since you included a shortcut key with your macro, there are two ways to run this macro, the standard way, and the shortcut key way. You can run the macro in either way, as described above.

When you run this macro, notice that the data in your worksheet will be cleared, and the first cell in which you will enter data, cell B3, will be the active cell. You will be ready to enter new data into your worksheet.

CREATE A MACRO BUTTON

You can also create a macro button to make it even easier to run your macro, and to make your worksheet look even more professional.

1. Click on the text box button on the drawing toolbar.
2. Draw a rectangle about the size of the button that you would like to create. Type the word, Reset, in the text box.
3. Right click on one of the sizing handles that surround your button. A shortcut menu will appear (Fig. 29.7).
4. Select Assign Macro from the shortcut button.
5. Remember that this macro was named Macro2. Click on Macro2 to select it.
6. Click OK.

Now, whenever you want to erase the data in your worksheet and reposition the cursor in cell B4, simply point to the Reset button you have created and click on it.

	A	B	C	D
1	Average Calculator			
2				
3				
4	Student	Edward Jones		Print
5	Course 1	90		
6	Course 2	85		
7	Course 3	90		Reset
8	Course 4	85		
9	Course 5	90		
10	Course 6	85		
11				
12	Average	87.50		
13				

Figure 29.8.

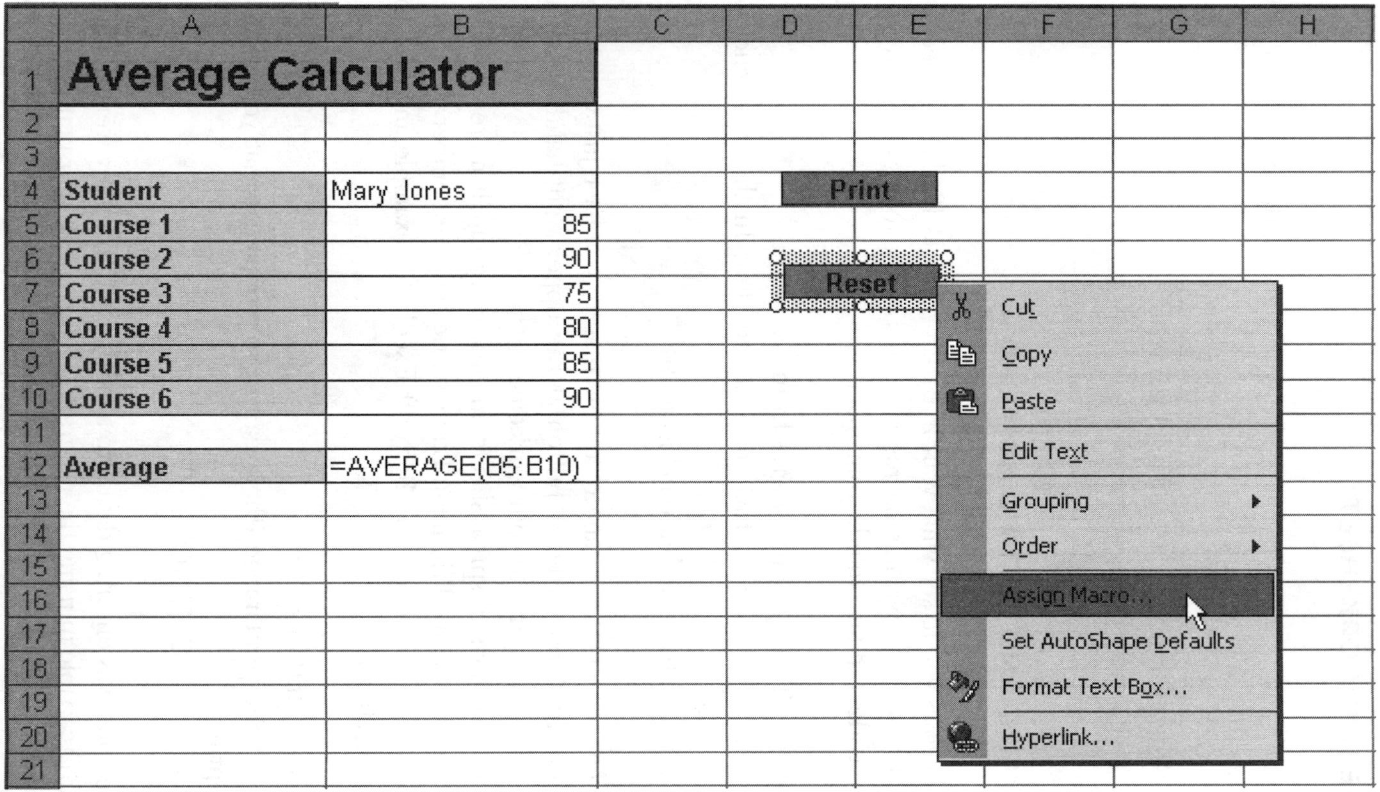

Average Calculator

	A	B
4	Student	Mary Jones
5	Course 1	85
6	Course 2	90
7	Course 3	75
8	Course 4	80
9	Course 5	85
10	Course 6	90
12	Average	=AVERAGE(B5:B10)

Print

Reset

Cut
Copy
Paste
Edit Text
Grouping
Order
Assign Macro...
Set AutoShape Defaults
Format Text Box...
Hyperlink...

Figure 29.7.

SAVE THE WORKSHEET

Complete the process by saving the worksheet and along with it, the macros you have written.

1. Select File, Save As . . . from the menu.
2. Assign a file name, and click OK.

VIEWING AND EDITING A MACRO

Excel allows you to see what your macro code looks like. If you become really proficient in writing macros, you will be able to not only view your macro code, but also to edit your macros.

1. Select Tools, Macro, Macros from the menu.
2. Click on the macro that you want to view. In this case, click on Macro2.
3. Click on the Edit button (Fig. 29.9).

Of course, you don't want to edit the macros you have just written. So click on the Close Window button at the upper right-hand corner of your screen to return to your worksheet.

In the old days of spreadsheets, macros were much more important than they are today. Printing a Lotus worksheet (remember that Lotus 1-2-3 was the forerunner of Microsoft Excel), for example, involved the following steps:

1. Type [/] [P] [P] [R].
2. Set the print range (the area of the worksheet that you want to print).
3. Type [A] [G] [P] [Q].

If someone was entering data into a worksheet, and they were not particularly capable in using the program, macros were indispensable.

Today, programs like Excel are much more sophisticated, and so much easier for a novice to use that writing macros is far less important.

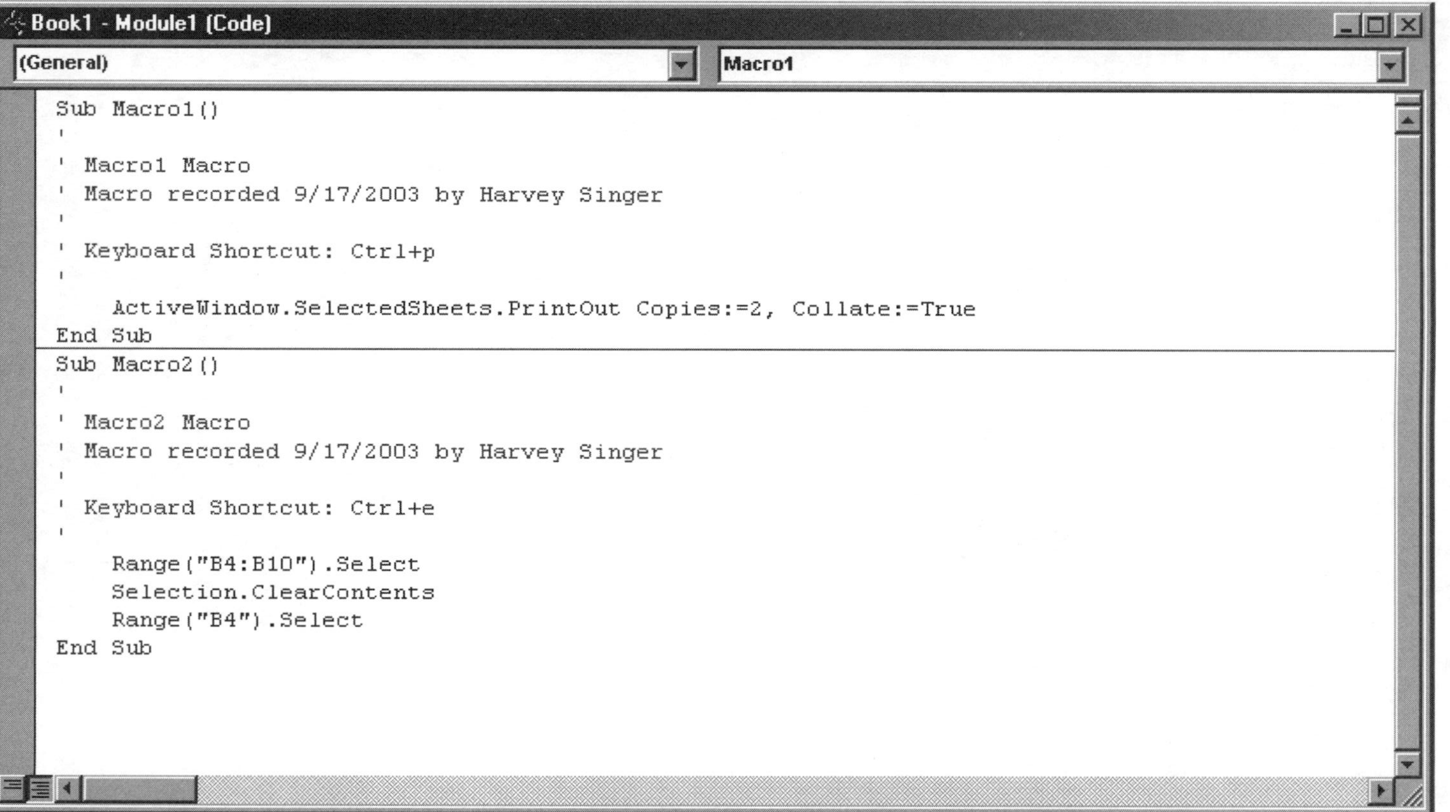
Book1 - Module1 (Code)
(General)
Macro1
Sub Macro1()
'
' Macro1 Macro
' Macro recorded 9/17/2003 by Harvey Singer
'
' Keyboard Shortcut: Ctrl+p
'
ActiveWindow.SelectedSheets.PrintOut Copies:=2, Collate:=True
End Sub
Sub Macro2()
'
' Macro2 Macro
' Macro recorded 9/17/2003 by Harvey Singer
'
' Keyboard Shortcut: Ctrl+e
'
Range("B4:B10").Select
Selection.ClearContents
Range("B4").Select
End Sub

Figure 29.9.

But as we have mentioned earlier, macros are still useful if a spreadsheet novice is going to be entering data into one of your worksheets. And macros can also give your worksheets a really slick appearance.

EXERCISE 29

1. What is a macro?
2. Explain why you might want to write a macro.
3. Describe the steps in the process of writing a macro.
4. Why will you want to create a shortcut key for most of your macros?
5. Describe the standard and shortcut key methods of running a macro.
6. Explain how to create a button to run a macro.
7. Create a worksheet, and create two macros for the worksheet.

APPENDIX A

IMPORTANT MENU COMMANDS AND OPERATIONS

Basic Menu Commands

Microsoft Excel

© H. Singer, 1996, 2003

	Menu	*Keyboard*	*Toolbar*
Clear a Cell	Edit, Clear All	[Delete]	
Undo	Edit, Undo	[Ctrl] [Z]	
Save a Worksheet (first time)	File Save As... Type a file name Save	[Ctrl] [S] Type a file name Save	
Save a Worksheet (subsequent)	File, Save	[Ctrl] [S]	
Close a Worksheet	File, Close		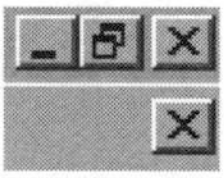
Open a Worksheet	File, Open Click on file name Open	[Ctrl] [O] Click on file name Open	
Print a Worksheet	File, Print Print	[Ctrl] [P] Print	
Start a New Worksheet	File, New, New, Blank Workbook	[Ctrl] [N]	
Exit from Excel	File, Exit	[Alt] [F4]	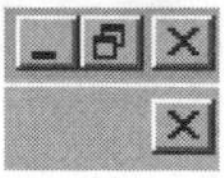

Copy, Cut and Paste

Microsoft Excel

© H. Singer, 1996, 2003

Copy and Paste	*Menu*	*Keyboard*	*Toolbar*
Standard Method	Select source cell	Select source cell	Select source cell
	Edit, Copy	[Ctrl] [C]	
	Select destination cell	Select destination cell	Select destination cell
	Edit, Paste	[Ctrl] [V]	
Fill Method	Select source cell thru destination cell		
	Edit, Fill Right, Left, Up, Down		
Drag Method	Click on source cell Point to box in lower right corner of cell		
	Drag thru destination cells		

Cut and Paste	*Menu*	*Keyboard*	*Toolbar*
Standard Method	Select source cell		
	Select source cell	Select source cell	
	Edit Cut	[Ctrl] [X]	
	Select destination cell	Select destination cell	Select destination cell
	Edit, Paste	[Ctrl] [V]	
Drag and Drop	Click on source cell		
	Click on edge of source cell		
	Drag to destination cell		

Basic Formulas

Microsoft Excel

© H. Singer, 1996, 2003

FORMULAS:

Basic Concepts:

All formulas must begin with an equals sign (=).

Wherever possible, use cell addresses rather than numbers in formulas:

=A1+A2, rather than =3+4

Operation	*Sign*	*Example*
Addition	+	=A1+A2
Subtraction	-	=A1-A2
Multiplication	*	=A1*A2
Division	/	=A1/A2
Percent	* %	=A1*25%

Reminders:

A formula may include a series of cells or numbers:

=A1+A2+A3+A4+A5

Remember the order of precedence:

1. Parentheses
2. Multiplication and Division
3. Addition and Subtraction

You may never divide a number by zero (0).

Basic Functions

Microsoft Excel

FUNCTIONS:

Basic Concepts:

All formulas must begin with an equals sign (=).

Wherever possible, use cell addresses rather than numbers in formulas:

=A1+A2, rather than =3+4

Operation	*Function*	*Example*
Addition	=SUM(range)	=SUM(A1:A10)
Average	=AVERAGE(range)	=AVERAGE(A1:A10)
Highest	=MAX(range)	=MAX(A1:A10)
Lowest	=MIN(range)	=MIN(A1:A10)
Cells in a Range Containing Numbers	=COUNT(range)	=COUNT(A1:A10)
Cells in a Range Containing Any Entries	=COUNTA(range)	=COUNTA(A1:A10)

Reminders:

Do not include the cell that contains a function in the range. This would produce a *circular reference*.

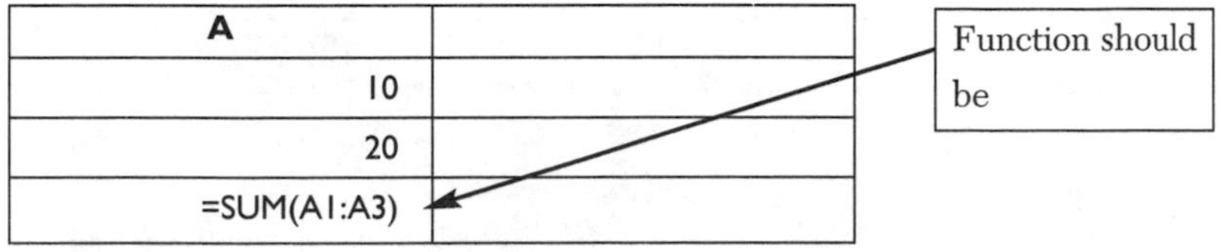

Number Formatting

Microsoft Excel

Number formatting is accomplished most easily from the toolbar:

Toolbar Button	*Format*	*Example*
$	Currency – dollar sign, commas set off thousands	$1,234.56
%	Percent zero decimal places	12%
,	Comma – like Currency but without dollar sign	1,234.56
+.0 .00	Increase decimal places	
.00 +.0	Decrease decimal places	

Number formatting can also be accomplished from the Format, Cells, Number menu.

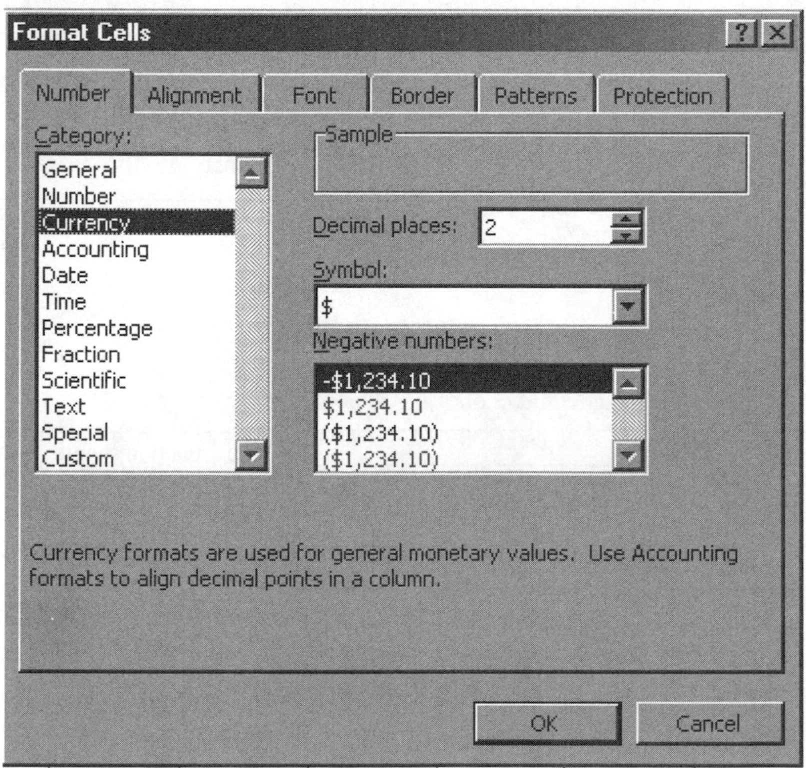

APPENDIX B

Teacher	Enrollment	Students Scoring Above Grade Level			
		Number Reading	Number Math	Percent Reading	Percent Math
Adams	25	18	16	72.0	64.0
Baker	27	19	20	70.4	74.1
Chin	29	24	23	82.8	79.3
Davis	26	24	25	92.3	96.2

Total	107	85	84
Average	26.8	21.3	21.0
Highest	29	24	25
Lowest	25	18	16

North Street Elementary
Student Achievement By Teacher
Third Grade

Student			Admissions			Discharges		
Date	First	Last	Grade	From	To H. R.	Grade	To	From H. R.
9/15/03	Mary	Jones	10	North H.S.	106			
9/16/03	William	Alvarez	11	South H.S.	203			
9/16/03	Derek	Williams				12	Work	307
9/22/03	Margaret	Edwards				12	GED	

Excelsior High School
Admissions and Discharges
Month, Year: September 2003

Examination	Score					Total	Percent				
	1	2	3	4	5		1	2	3	4	5
Art History	0	0	4	5	5	14	-	-	28.6	35.7	35.7
Biology						0					
Calculus AB						0					
Calculus CD						0					
Chemistry						0					
Computer Science A						0					
Computer Science AB						0					
Economics Macro						0					
Economics Micro						0					
English Language and Comp						0					
Total	0	0	4	5	5	14	-	-	28.6	35.7	35.7

Excelsior High School
Advanced Placement Examination Scores
2002–2003

Course	Students			
	2000-2001	2001-2002	2002-2003	2003-2004
Biology	12	14	18	15
Calculus	14	15	22	27
Chemistry	8	14	15	17
Economics	20	24	28	27
English	32	35	35	39
Physics	8	6	9	10
Total	94	108	127	135

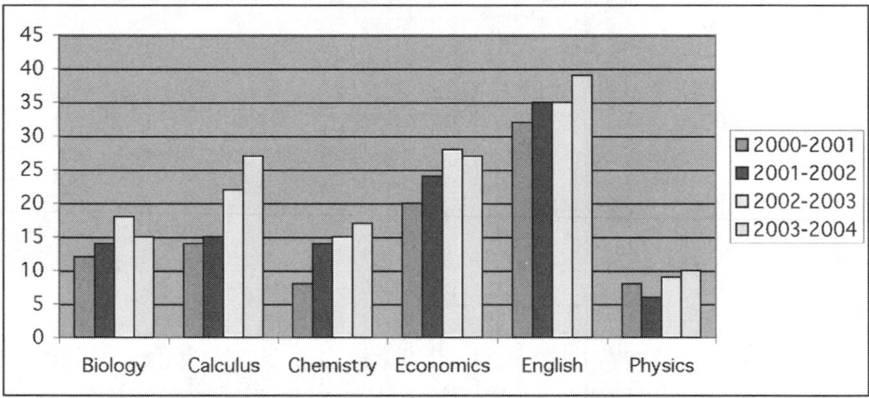

Excelsior High School
AP Course Analysis

	Jun, 2001		Jun, 2002		Jun, 2003	
Type of Institution	Number	Percent	Number	Percent	Number	Percent
4 Year State College	253	42.2	289	44.5	274	38.9
4 Year Private College	167	23.4	147	22.6	152	25.7
2 Year Community College	218	34.5	249	38.3	224	33.5
2 Year Private College	12	2.8	14	2.2	18	1.8
Total	650		699		668	

Excelsior High School
College Acceptances

INSTRUCTIONS
To enter a date, type the number of the month, a slash, and the number of the date.
To enter the current date, press [Ctrl] + [;].
To sort by Last Name, click on any student's last name, and then press A↓Z
To sort by College/University, click on any College/University name, and then press A↓Z

Last Name	First Name	College/University	Early Decision	Application Sent	Transcript Sent	Acceptance Rsvd
Fredericks	Barbara	SUNY Stony Brook		5-Nov	7-Nov	
Fredericks	Barbara	SUNY Oneonta		5-Nov	7-Nov	
Baker	Deena	Yale	X	12-Oct	14-Oct	15-Dec
Baker	Deena	Princeton		12-Oct	14-Oct	
Chin	Edward	University of Virginia	X	15-Oct	18-Oct	
Chin	Edward	SUNY Binghampton		17-Oct	18-Oct	
Adams	John	SUNY Buffalo		2-Dec	6-Dec	
Adams	John	SUNY Binghampton		2-Dec	6-Dec	
Adams	John	SUNY Fredonia		4-Dec	6-Dec	
Davis	Marissa	School of Visual Arts		20-Nov	25-Nov	22-Dec
Eaton	William	Nassau Community College		5-Dec	9-Dec	
Eaton	William	SUNY Purchase		5-Dec	9-Dec	

Excelsior High School
College Placement Tracker
Academic Year: 2003–2004

Department	Number of Students	Number Passing	Percent Passing
English	1,783	1,475	82.7
Social Studies	1,803	1,468	81.4
Mathematics			#DIV/0!
Science			#DIV/0!
Foreign Language			#DIV/0!
Technology			#DIV/0!
Business Ed			#DIV/0!
Music			#DIV/0!
Art			#DIV/0!
Physical Ed			#DIV/0!
Total	3,586	2,943	82.1
Average	1,793	1,472	

Excelsior High School
Comparative Department Achievement
By Department
June 2003

Department:	English

Teacher	Course			State Exam		
	Students	No. Passing	% Passing	No. Taking	No. Passing	% Passing
Monroe	130	120	92.3	125	118	94.4
Olsen	129	101	78.3	128	112	87.5
Peterson	130	114	87.7	132	82	62.1
Quinones	127	122	96.1	123	107	87.0
Rubin	118	117	99.2	121	119	98.3
Samuels	112	105	93.8	119	101	84.9

Excelsior High School
Comparative Department Achievement
By Teacher
June 2003

Total Graduates Per Program	2000	2001	2002
College Preparation	249	320	386
College Technical Prep	124	118	108
Career Preparation	74	82	88
Total	447	520	582

Percent Graduates Per Program	2000	2001	2002
College Preparation	55.7	61.5	66.3
College Technical Prep	27.7	22.7	18.6
Career Preparation	16.6	15.8	15.1
Total	100.0	100.0	100.0

Excelsior High School
Diplomas Granted
By Type

Number of Students Dropping Out

	Starting Enrollment	Dropout Number	Dropout Percent
Grade 9	749	10	1.3
Grade 10	687	14	2.0
Grade 11	662	32	4.8
Grade 12	726	26	3.6
Total	**2824**	**82**	**2.9**

Reasons Students Left School

Reason	Number	Percent
Do not like	14	17.1
Failing	33	40.2
Job related	21	25.6
Pregnant	5	6.1
Other	9	11.0

Excelsior High School
Drop Out Analysis
Academic Year: 2002–2003

Academic Year: **2003-2004**

Statistics	
Total Left:	3

						Prevention Initiatives			
Date	First	Last	Grade	Interviewed By	Destination	Counselor	Social Worker	Parent Conf.	Special Svcs.
10/22/03	William	Jennings	12	J Walker	GED Program	M Dominguez	J Sharf	M Dominguez	Declined
10/27/03	Mary	Jackson	12	M Tierney	Work	M Dominguez	T Ryan	T Ryan	Yes
10/29/03	Carlos	Ortiz	12	J Walker	US Army	T Wolff	J Sharf	J Sharf	Yes

Excelsior High School
Student Drop Outs
Academic Year: 2003–2004

Second Language:	5
Speak English on G.L.	4
Read English on G.L.	3
Write English on G.L.	2

Last	First	Grade	Ethnic Background	2nd Lang At Home	Speak Engl Grade Level	Read Engl Grade Level	Write Engl Grade Level
Herrera	Maria	3	Puerto Rico	Spanish	X	X	
Guy	Pierre	2	Haiti	French	X		
Ortiz	Julio	5	Cuba	Spanish			
Donofrio	Antonio	2	Italy	Italian	X	X	X
Ortega	Carlos	4	Cuba	Spanish	X		

North Side Elementary School
Need for ESL and Bilingual Services
School Year: 2003–2004

Students - Number

Category	Grades			
	1 - 5	6 - 8	9 - 12	Total
White	440	218	235	893
Hispanic	350	168	174	692
African American	90	49	58	197
Filipino	30	16	22	68
Asian or Pacific Islander	90	41	52	183
American Indian/Alaskan Native	20	9	12	41
Multiple	10	4	6	20
No Response	10	5	6	21
Total	1,040	510	565	2,115

Students - Percent

Category	Grades		
	1 - 5	6 - 8	9 - 12
White	42.3	42.7	41.6
Hispanic	33.7	32.9	30.8
African American	8.7	9.6	10.3
Filipino	2.9	3.1	3.9
Asian or Pacific Islander	8.7	8.0	9.2
American Indian/Alaskan Native	1.9	1.8	2.1
Multiple	1.0	0.8	1.1
No Response	1.0	1.0	1.1
Total	100.0	100.0	100.0

Northwest District School
Racial and Ethnic Distribution of Student Population
September 2003

Students in Attendance	1	2	3	4	5	6	7	8	9	10	11	12	13	14	15	16	17	18	19	20	21	22	23	24	25	26	27	28	29	30	31
Washington Elem	500	500	500	500	500	500	500	500																							
Adams Elem	550	550	550	550	552	552	552	552																							
Jefferson Elem	575	575	573	573	573	573	573	573																							
Madison Elem	600	600	600	600	600	602	602	602																							

Students Absent	1	2	3	4	5	6	7	8	9	10	11	12	13	14	15	16	17	18	19	20	21	22	23	24	25	26	27	28	29	30	31
Washington Elem	12	14	13	11	9	12	14	15																							
Adams Elem	13	14	14	15	15	12	11	10																							
Jefferson Elem	14	16	18	20	22	22	24	25																							
Madison Elem	15	14	14	13	13	12	12	11																							

Percent Absent	1	2	3	4	5	6	7	8	9	10	11	12	13	14	15	16	17	18	19	20	21	22	23	24	25	26	27	28	29	30	31
Washington Elem	2.4	2.8	2.6	2.2	1.8	2.4	2.8	3.0																							
Adams Elem	2.4	2.5	2.5	2.7	2.7	2.2	2.0	1.8																							
Jefferson Elem	2.4	2.8	3.1	3.5	3.8	3.8	4.2	4.4																							
Madison Elem	2.5	2.3	2.3	2.2	2.2	2.0	2.0	1.8																							

Analysis	Avg Present	Avg Absent	% Absent
Washington Elem	500	13	2.5
Adams Elem	551	13	2.4
Jefferson Elem	574	20	3.5
Madison Elem	601	13	2.2

Western School District
Evaluation of Attendance Initiatives
Analysis: January 2003

	Feeder School				Analysis			
	North Middle	South Middle	East Middle	West Middle	Total	Average	Highest	Lowest
North High	200	220	180	175	775	193.8	220	175
South High	175	218	162	135	690	172.5	218	135
Technology Magnet	160	148	215	245	768	192.0	245	148
Arts Magnet	150	182	145	166	643	160.8	182	145
Business Careers Magnet	225	118	242	317	902	225.5	317	118
Total	910	886	944	1038	3778			
Average	182.0	177.2	188.8	207.6	755.6			
Highest	225	220	242	317	902			
Lowest	150	118	145	135	643			

Northwest School District
Feeder School Patterns
September 2002

Students Receiving Free Lunch

First	Last	Grade	Recertify
Mary	Mohoney	1	1/1/04
Danielle	Nielson	2	1/1/05
Carmen	Olivera	1	6/1/05
David	Parson	3	1/1/05
John	Quincey	2	1/1/04
Todd	Rosen	4	6/1/05
Carol	Samuels	2	1/1/04
Nina	Tierney	6	1/1/04
Clifford	Unidas	3	6/1/05

SORTING INSTRUCTIONS

To sort by Last Name, Grade, or Recertification Date:
1. Click on any item in the Last, Grade, or Recertify column.
2. Click on the sort button on the toolbar. A↓Z

North Avenue Elementary
Students Receiving Free Lunch
2003–2004

Organization	Boys	Girls	Total	Pct Boys	Pct Girls
Debate	12	14	26	46.2	53.8
Drama	15	28	43	34.9	65.1
Student Newspaper	16	14	30	53.3	46.7
Yearbook	17	28	45	37.8	62.2
Homecoming	13	24	37	35.1	64.9
Student Government	18	17	35	51.4	48.6
Football	52	0	52	100.0	-
Basketball-Boys	32	0	32	100.0	-
Basketball-Girls	0	29	29	-	100.0
Field Hockey	0	48	48	-	100.0
Wrestling	18	0	18	100.0	-
Swimming	22	18	40	55.0	45.0
Volley Ball	5	28	33	15.2	84.8
Gymnastics	14	22	22	63.6	100.0

Analysis - All Activities	
Total Boys	234
Total Girls	270
Total All	504
Pct Boys	46.4
Pct Girls	53.6

Excelsior High School
Gender Integration in Activities
10/01/03

Students Graduated	2000	2001	2002
Students in Grade 12	425	456	475
Number Graduated	403	445	474
Percent Graduated	94.8	97.6	99.8

Graduates' Plans - Number of Students	2000	2001	2002
College	283	322	360
Work	118	122	101
Military	8	4	4
Undecided	16	8	10

Graduates' Plans - Percent of Students	2000	2001	2002
College	66.6	70.6	75.8
Work	27.8	26.8	21.3
Military	1.9	0.9	0.8
Undecided	3.8	1.8	2.1

Excelsior High School
Graduates' Plans

	House 1	House 2	House 3
Administrator	Wilson	Walker	Levinson
Clerical Staff	Reston	Baker	Orem
Counselor	Fenmore	Treat	Unitas
Faculty			
English	Adams	Gomez	Quit
Social St	Davis	Isaacs	Reseda
Math	Chin	Franklin	Monte
Science	Edwards	Kramer	Samuels
Shared Faculty			
Art	Winston	Winston	Nolte
Music	Davis	Davis	Perez
Technology	Eaton	Herrera	Herrera
Business Ed	Edwards	Jones	Jones

Northwest Middle School
House Plan Organization
2003–2004 Academic Year

Guidance Service	9/1	9/2	9/3	9/4	9/5	9/6	9/7	9/8	9/9	9/10	9/11	9/12	9/13	9/14	9/15
College Advisement	1	2													
Work Advisement	3	4													
Schedule Advisement	5	6													
Schedule Change	7	8													
Problem in Class	2	3													
Problem with Student	4	5													
Problem at Home	0	1													
Other	3	4													
Total	25	33	0	0	0	0	0	0	0	0	0	0	0	0	0

Guidance Service	9/16	9/17	9/18	9/19	9/20	9/21	9/22	9/23	9/24	9/25	9/26	9/27	9/28	9/29	9/30
College Advisement															
Work Advisement															
Schedule Advisement															
Schedule Change															
Problem in Class															
Problem with Student															
Problem at Home															
Other															
Total	0	0	0	0	0	0	0	0	0	0	0	0	0	0	0

Analysis

Guidance Service	Total
College Advisement	3
Work Advisement	7
Schedule Advisement	11
Schedule Change	15
Problem in Class	5
Problem with Student	9
Problem at Home	1
Other	7
Total	58

Excelsior High School
Utilization of and Need for Guidance Services
September 2003

House 1

Objective	Sep	Oct	Nov	Dec	Jan	Feb	Mar	Apr	May	Jun	Total
Minor Infractions	12	9	11	6							38
Major Infractions	0	2	0	1							3
Absence	145	135	137	128							545
Failure Notices	45	35	35	25							140

House 2

Objective	Sep	Oct	Nov	Dec	Jan	Feb	Mar	Apr	May	Jun	Total
Minor Infractions											0
Major Infractions											0
Absence											0
Failure Notices											0

House 3

Objective	Sep	Oct	Nov	Dec	Jan	Feb	Mar	Apr	May	Jun	Total
Minor Infractions											0
Major Infractions											0
Absence											0
Failure Notices											0

Northwest Middle School
House Objectives
Analysis and Evaluation
School Year: 2003–2004

Teacher:	Mrs. J. Smith
Class:	Remedial Reading 101
Term:	Spring, 2002

First	Last	Diagnostic Examination					
		Jan	Feb	Mar	Apr	May	Jun
William	Adams	6.2	6.4	7.1	7.3		
Denise	Baker	7	7	6.9	7.2		
Edward	Chin	5.4	5.9	6.2	6.8		
Myra	Davis	6.8	7	7.2	7.4		
Thomas	Eaton	5.5	6.8	6.7	7.1		
Barbara	Franklin	4	4.6	5.2	5.4		

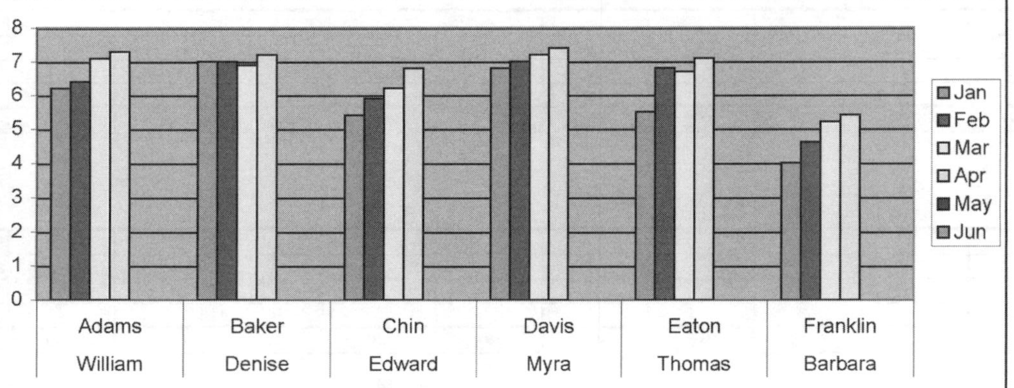

Excelsior High School
Reading Progress

	Students Jun, 2003	5 Percent Increase	10 Percent Increase
English	576	605	634
French	132	139	145
Spanish	276	290	304
Global Studies	618	649	680
U. S. History	589	618	648
Math Course 1	622	653	684
Math Course 2	601	631	661
Math Course 3	428	449	471
Earth Science	608	638	669
Biology	576	605	634
Chemistry	245	257	270
Physics	112	118	123
Total	5,383	5,652	5,921

Excelsior High School
Regents Examinations: Initiative to Increase Participation

Exam	Students Taking Exam	Students Pasing Exam	Percent Passing Exam	Percent Passing Plus 5 Percent	Percent Passing Plus 10 Percent
English	576	502	87	92	97
French	132	122	92	97	100
Spanish	276	223	81	86	91
Global Studies	618	496	80	85	90
U. S. History	589	512	87	92	97
Math Course 1	622	452	73	78	83
Math Course 2	601	463	77	82	87
Math Course 3	428	392	92	97	100
Earth Science	608	425	70	75	80
Biology	576	485	84	89	94
Chemistry	245	221	90	95	100
Physics	112	107	96	100	100
Total	5,383	4,400	82	87	92

Excelsior High School
Regents Examinations: Initiative to Increase Students Passing
June 2003

	Percent Of Students Passing Exam					Statistics		
Exam	1999	2000	2001	2002	2003	Average	Highest	Lowest
English	79	82	80	83		81.0	83	79
World History	68	72	75	71		71.5	75	68
American History	75	71	78	68		73.0	78	68
Math 9						#DIV/0!	0	0
Math 10						#DIV/0!	0	0
Math 11						#DIV/0!	0	0
Earth Science						#DIV/0!	0	0
Biology						#DIV/0!	0	0
Chemistry						#DIV/0!	0	0
Physics						#DIV/0!	0	0
Spanish 3						#DIV/0!	0	0
French 3						#DIV/0!	0	0
Italian 3						#DIV/0!	0	0

Average	74.0	75.0	77.7	74.0	#DIV/0!
Highest	79	82	80	83	0
Lowest	68	71	75	68	0

Excelsior High School
School Statewide/Regents Examination Results
Percent of Students Passing By Year

	Number Of Students					Total
Class	Below 65	66-75	76-85	86-95	Over 95	Students
English 101	3	4	7	12	1	27
English 102	3	6	11	8	0	28
English 103	1	2	7	14	4	28
English 104	4	1	10	9	1	25
English 105	2	4	12	7	0	25

Average	2.6	3.4	9.4	10.0	1.2
Highest	4	6	12	14	4
Lowest	1	1	7	7	0

Excelsior High School
English Statewide/Regents Examination Results By Class
Percent of Students Passing By Year
Academic Year 2002

Total Registrations:	6
Total Discharges:	5

Registrations

Date	Stud No	First	Last	Grade
9/8/03	43336	Mary	Jones	3
9/8/03	43337	Carlos	Rivera	4
9/8/03	43338	Tina	Donato	5
9/8/03	43339	David	Adams	3
9/8/03	43340	Marty	Abel	2
9/9/03	43341	Edith	Eng	1
	43342			
	43343			
	43344			
	43345			
	43346			
	43347			
	43348			
	43349			
	43350			
	43351			
	43352			
	43353			
	43354			
	43355			
	43356			
	43357			
	43358			

Discharges

Date	Stud No	First	Last	Grade	Disposition
9/8/03	32740	David	Williams	1	Moved
9/8/03	28917	Maria	Arroyo	3	Moved
9/8/03	42206	William	Rowan	5	Transferred to Wing Street School
9/9/03	22179	Elise	Browne	2	Moved
9/9/03	30414	Michael	Davis	4	Moved

Excelsior Elementary School
Registrations and Discharges
September 2003
Page 1

First	Last	Birthdate	Parent First	Parent Last	Address	City	ST	Zip	Telephone	Emergency
Tina	Adams	1/2/97	Anthony	Adams	111 First Street	New York	NY	10001	999-8888	987-6543
Mary	Baker	2/3/97	Gina	Baker	222 Second Ave	New York	NY	10002	888-7777	876-5432
Edward	Chin	3/4/97	Thomas	Chin	333 Third Road	New York	NY	10003	777-6666	765-4321
William	Davis	4/5/97	Esther	Williams	444 Fourth Street	New York	NY	10001	666-5555	654-3210
Eve	Eaton	5/6/97	William	Eaton	555 Fifth Ave	New York	NY	10002	555-4444	543-2109
Thomas	Franklin	6/7/97	David	Franklin	666 Sixth Lane	New York	NY	10001	444-3333	432-1098
Maria	Gomez	7/8/97	Carlos	Gomez	777 Seventh Street	New York	NY	10001	333-2222	321-0987

Student Register
Class 101

First	Last	Verbal	Math	Combined
Thomas	Adams	550	520	1070
Edith	Baker	570	540	1110
Edward	Chin	590	500	1090
Mary	Davis	610	560	1170

Analysis			
	Average	Highest	Lowest
Verbal	580	610	550
Math	530	560	500
Combined	1110	1170	1070

Excelsior High School
SAT Scores and Analysis
March 2002

	Percent Passing					Statistics		
Subject	1999	2000	2001	2002	2003	Average	Highest	Lowest
English 9	79	82	86	85		83.0	86	79
English 10	82	84	81	86		83.3	86	81
English 11						#DIV/0!	0	0
English 12						#DIV/0!	0	0

Average	80.5	83.0	83.5	85.5	#DIV/0!
Highest	82	84	86	86	0
Lowest	79	82	81	85	0

Excelsior High School
School Achievement By Subject
Subject: English

On Friday of each week, several designated school personnel will rate school tone for the week on a scale of 1 (poorest) to 10 (best). These scores will be tabulated and evaluated on a monthly and half-yearly basis.

	Week Ending																	Statistics		
Rater	9/5	9/12	9/19	9/26	10/3	10/10	10/17	10/24	10/31	11/7	11/14	11/21	11/28	12/5	12/12	12/19	12/26	Average	Highest	Lowest
Principal	7	8																7.5	8	7
Assistant Principal	8	8																8.0	8	8
Guidance Counselor	8	7																7.5	8	7
Team Leader Grade 1	7	8																7.5	8	7
Team Leader Grade 2	8	8																8.0	8	8
Team Leader Grade 3	7	7																7.0	7	7
Team Leader Grade 4	6	8																7.0	8	6
Team Leader Grade 5	8	7																7.5	8	7
Average	7.4	7.6	#####	#####	#####	#####	#####	#####	#####	#####	#####	#####	#####	#####	#####	#####	#####	7.5	7.9	7.1
Highest	8	8	0	0	0	0	0	0	0	0	0	0	0	0	0	0	0	8	8	8
Lowest	6	7	0	0	0	0	0	0	0	0	0	0	0	0	0	0	0	7	7	6

Northwest Elementary School

School Tone

Date	Day	Grade 1		Grade 2		Grade 3		Grade 4		Grade 1	Grade 2	Grade 3	Grade 4
		Pres	Total	Present	Total	Pres	Total	Pres	Total	Pct Pres	Pct Pres	Pct Pres	Pct Pres
6-Sep	Mon	22	28	28	29	26	26	27	27	78.6	96.6	100.0	100.0
8-Sep	Tue	24	28	29	29	26	26	25	27	85.7	100.0	100.0	92.6
9-Sep	Wed	25	28	29	29	26	26	26	26	89.3	100.0	100.0	100.0
10-Sep	Thu	25	28	27	30	25	26	27	26	89.3	90.0	96.2	103.8
11-Sep	Fri												
12-Sep	Mon												
15-Sep	Tue												
16-Sep	Wed												
17-Sep	Thu												
18-Sep	Fri												
19-Sep	Mon												
22-Sep	Tue												
23-Sep	Wed												
24-Sep	Thu												
25-Sep	Fri												
26-Sep	Mon												
29-Sep	Tue												
30-Sep	Wed												

Excelsior High School
Student Attendance
September 2003

	Sep	Oct	Nov	Dec	Total
In-School Suspensions					
1 day	14	18			32
2 days	12	14			26
3 days	8	7			15
Total In-School Suspensions	34	39	0	0	73
Total Out-Of-School Suspensions	5	7			12
Total Suspensions	39	46	0	0	85

Excelsior High School
School Suspensions
2002–2003 Academic Year

Date	Day	Sick	Personal	Professional	Total
9/8/03	Mon	0	0	0	0
9/9/03	Tue	1	0	0	1
9/10/03	Wed	0	0	0	0
9/11/03	Thu	0	0	0	0
9/12/03	Fri	1	1	2	4
9/15/03	Mon	2	0	2	4
9/16/03	Tue	2	2	0	4
9/17/03	Wed	3	1	0	4
9/18/03	Thu				0
9/19/03	Fri				0
9/22/03	Mon	Holiday	Holiday	Holiday	Holiday
9/23/03	Tue				0
9/24/03	Wed				0
9/25/03	Thu				0
9/26/03	Fri				0
9/29/03	Mon				0
9/30/03	Tue				0
	Total Absence	**9**	**4**	**4**	**17**
	Average	**1.1**	**0.5**	**0.5**	**1.1**
	Highest	**3**	**2**	**2**	**4**
	Lowest	**0**	**0**	**0**	**0**

Wilson Middle School
Teacher Attendance
September 2003

ABOUT THE AUTHOR

Harvey Singer has been a public school teacher, counselor, administrator, and business trainer. He has taught computer science classes at Suffolk Community College, Dowling College, and Broward Community College, and has served as an administrator at Suffolk Community College and Dowling College.